MEMOIRS FROM

THE BEIJING FILM ACADEMY

■

ASIA-PACIFIC:

CULTURE, POLITICS, AND SOCIETY

Editors: Rey Chow, H. D. Harootunian,

and Masao Miyoshi

MEMOIRS FROM

THE BEIJING FILM ACADEMY

The Genesis of China's Fifth Generation

■

NI ZHEN

Translated by Chris Berry

DUKE UNIVERSITY PRESS

Durham & London 2002

© 2002 Duke University Press

All rights reserved

Printed in the United States of America on

acid-free paper ∞ Designed by Amy Ruth Buchanan.

Typeset in Carter & Cone Galliard by Tseng Information

Systems Inc. Library of Congress Cataloging-in-Publication

Data appear on the last printed page of this book.

© 1995 original edition by National Publishers of

Japan (Cinema Skhole) and Ni Zhen

© 2002 English translation by

Duke University Press

CONTENTS

■

TRANSLATOR'S INTRODUCTION

■

When my former colleague at the magazine *China Screen,* Zhang Dan, invited me to lunch with our mutual friend Professor Ni Zhen of the Beijing Film Academy, I accepted with alacrity. Professor Ni is erudite, cultured, and something of a gourmet, so I expected both interesting conversation and good food. Little did I know I would also be asked to consider translating this book. I was aware of the honor Professor Ni was bestowing on me, but worried if I had the time. When I read the manuscript, however, such concerns evaporated: I knew at once that this was a most unusual and exciting work. Therefore, my first thanks are to Zhang Dan for arranging lunch and to Professor Ni for giving me the opportunity to translate this fascinating book.

The appeal of *Memoirs from the Beijing Film Academy* for me lies in its unusual and accessible style and in its scholarly significance: it is both a good read and a contribution to knowledge and debate. No one could dispute that the emergence of the "Fifth Generation" of Chinese filmmakers in the mid-1980s was the breakthrough that brought Chinese cinema to the attention of the world. As the English critic Tony Rayns writes, "It's tempting to put an exact date to the birth of the 'New Chinese Cinema': 12 April

1985. That was the evening when *Yellow Earth* played to a packed house in the Hong Kong Film Festival in the presence of its two main creators, director Chen Kaige and cinematographer Zhang Yimou. The screening was received with something like collective rapture, and the post-film discussion stretched long past its time limit."[1]

Given this crucial role, the absence of a monograph in either Chinese or English devoted specifically to the Fifth Generation is striking. I am happy to say that *Memoirs from the Beijing Film Academy* fills that gap. In the process it gathers together a large amount of vital information about the early days of the Fifth Generation and also rectifies many misunderstandings about them. As Professor Ni points out in the preface he wrote specially for this edition, the prominence attained by Chen Kaige and Zhang Yimou through successes such as *Farewell, My Concubine* and *Raise the Red Lantern* has obscured the fact that the Fifth Generation includes many other equally distinctive filmmakers, each with his or her own style and interests.

The reasons for the absence of a monograph on the Fifth Generation in China itself are readily inferred from Professor Ni's postscript, which was also written specially for this edition. There, he frankly lays out the critical fate of the Fifth Generation in post-Tiananmen China, where the rhetoric of postcolonial theory has been appropriated to accuse these filmmakers of pandering to the Western colonial desire for the exotic. In this way, he makes it clear that this book is intended as a critical intervention in that debate and a reminder of the ideals and concern for China that have motivated the Fifth Generation from their earliest days.

Memoirs from the Beijing Film Academy also reminds us that critical discourse cannot be divorced from the operations of power that either suppress or facilitate its production and distribution. For all the loosening of government control in the People's Republic, we cannot lose sight of the fact that none of the local uses of postcolonial and postmodern theory in China today would be possible if they offended the regime. However, although these contemporary critical currents may suit the regime, they are the products of today's intellectuals. Therefore, we also need to ask why so many of today's generation in China feel a need to denigrate and dismiss the more radical culture of the 1980s, which culminated in the 1989 Democracy Movement. Is it really simply that they are callous, materialistic, and unmoved by all those lives lost on or maybe—as the Chinese government insists—"only" near Tiananmen Square? Or are they angry with

From left: New Zealand scholar Paul Clark; head of Xi'an Film Studio and director of *Old Well*, Wu Tianming; the translator of this volume, Chris Berry; and Zhang Yimou, in Beijing in 1986. Photo courtesy of the author.

their predecessors because ultimately they failed to produce lasting political and cultural reform to match China's economic transformation? Or is it that the regime's determination to keep political reform off the agenda means that dismissing the 1980s is crucial to maintaining social cohesion in the People's Republic today? At present, we can only speculate about this, for the frank discussion of the topic remains off-limits within the People's Republic itself.

In addition to its contribution to knowledge and debates about recent Chinese cinema and society, the narrative style of *Memoirs from the Beijing Film Academy* is striking and unusual. In the first chapter, Professor Ni remarks that the story of the Fifth Generation is "like a legend." And indeed, he tells the story as though it were an episode about a band of Robin Hood-style heroes from *The Water Margin* or a similar Chinese martial arts classic. This strategy is an interesting one. First, it communicates the appeal of the Fifth Generation phenomenon for its many supporters, and it makes the book a joy to read. Second, it highlights the way in which all history narrativizes factual data, as well as the role that this process plays in deciding what and who gets the spotlight. For example, as one of the Duke University Press readers pointed out, there is no doubt that the legend of the Fifth Generation is a male one. The female members of the group, although not ignored, get relatively less attention. It is also a highly patriotic narrative.

The unique style in which this volume is written—blurring the boundaries of conventional academic analysis, biography, and storytelling—is a strong part of its appeal. When we consider the author's background, however, this style is not a surprise. Professor Ni is not only one of China's leading film scholars, he is also one of the teachers of the Fifth Generation and a leading screenwriter responsible for some of their most noteworthy films. In his work as a professor at the Beijing Film Academy since 1980, Ni Zhen came to know the Fifth Generation as students and friends long before they ever made films, giving him access to the personal histories and frank comments given here. As the chief editor of the Academy's journal, he has also written numerous scholarly articles, some of which have previously appeared in English. Moreover, Professor Ni is the author of a number of the most important contemporary monographs on Chinese cinema, including *The Exploratory Screen* and *Reform and the Chinese Cinema*.[2] This scholarly effort accounts for the rigorous research and detail of the volume. Finally, Professor Ni's storytelling skills are attested to by his numerous film and television screenplays, including the Fifth Generation classics *Blush,* directed by Li Shaohong, and *Raise the Red Lantern,* directed by Zhang Yimou, which was nominated for an Academy Award for Best Foreign Language Film.

Professor Ni has also brought his scholarly eye for detail here to the production of the English edition. To help the reader less familiar with China and the world of Chinese cinema, he has not only produced a new preface and postscript, but also worked with me to provide the necessary citations for quotations and references that the educated Chinese reader would take for granted. We have also inserted the dates of all films mentioned in the main text on their first appearance, except where the date is clear from the immediate context. In addition, I am particularly grateful to Professor Ni for taking time out from his hectic schedule to answer my numerous questions about the text itself. Much of this additional work occurred during a trip funded by the International Researcher Exchange Program of the Australian Research Council. It was also during this period of work together that we decided to add the elements mentioned above.

I also want to thank Duke University Press editor Reynolds Smith for his good humor, patience, and persistence. Thanks also to Cui Jian for answering my "stupid foreigner" questions as I translated the manuscript. My old friend and colleague from China Film Corporation, Shan Dongbing, who has always been generous with his time and knowledge, helped me again by tracing numerous English export titles of films and reading my translation against the original. I am forever in his debt. Cui Junyan also checked the translation against the original. I relied on that most dedicated fan of Hollywood classics, Chen Mei, to help me trace back the original English titles from the Chinese, and on Aiko Yoshioka, Dr. Raj Pandey, Seio Nakajima, and Professor Chong Suwon to help me trace Japanese names and film titles. Sally Ingleton helped with film production terminology, and Dr. Bill Routt with references to Soviet cinema. To all of them, I am very grateful. Last, and maybe most important of all, Freda Freiberg gave generously of her time to read the final manuscript and make numerous astute suggestions regarding correct and felicitous use of English; with gratitude, I incorporated nearly all of them. Any remaining problems and errors are, of course, my own.

Chris Berry

PREFACE TO THE ENGLISH EDITION

■

When they came to Beijing in March 1994, my Japanese friends Kimata Junji and Seki Masami urged me to write a book about the early days of the Fifth Generation. They requested an account of their youthful experiences before entering the Beijing Film Academy and during the movement to send educated youths up into the mountains and down to the countryside, their student days at the Academy, and the production of their first films. As I understood it, they wanted me to write a kind of prehistory of Fifth Generation cinema.

They stipulated accurate historical materials and lively writing with an emphasis on fact over commentary, so that readers could trace the emergence of the Fifth Generation for themselves. Because I began teaching at the Beijing Film Academy in the early 1980s, I became both mentor and friend to the Fifth Generation. When *One and Eight* and *Yellow Earth* appeared, I also wrote quite a few reviews to draw attention to them. That is why Kimata Junji and Seki Masami felt I would be suited to the task they proposed. And this is how the first edition of this book came to be published in Japanese in Nagoya, Japan.

In the early 1980s, Zhang Yimou, Chen Kaige, Tian Zhuangzhuang, Li

Shaohong and the other members of the Fifth Generation were still only students, but their outlines were becoming visible on the horizon. Events from their student days in a flotilla of buildings landlocked by the fields of Zhuxin Village outside Beijing came readily and vividly to my mind. However, they had taken separate creative paths over the last decade, and so I felt I should interview each of these directors, cinematographers, sound designers, and production designers that I used to be so close to. With their agreement, between March and May 1994 I took advantage of gaps in their busy shooting schedules to seek them out one by one and conduct detailed interviews with them.

What a wonderful and happy time that was! We went over familiar and moving stories, delving deep into their memories for past events. We remembered bitter and almost unbelievable incidents from the Cultural Revolution period. And we reviewed the many slings and arrows Fifth Generation cinema had endured as it emerged. While we talked, I experienced the mixture of distance and understanding that characterizes the special relationship between two generations. I heard many stories from their youths that were unique yet also had much in common with other tales from the upheavals of the Cultural Revolution. Together, they constituted the prehistory of a film art movement that this book supplies, as well as a collective biography of the Fifth Generation filmmakers. From these empirical materials, I not only gained a deeper understanding of the artistic tendencies of early Fifth Generation cinema, but I also formed the structure of my argument, which reveals itself between the lines of this text.

Whenever anyone mentions China's Fifth Generation cinema today, the focus of attention is sure to be on Chen Kaige and Zhang Yimou. This tendency evolved gradually over the last fifteen years. There is no question that their work together produced the stark look, powerful emotions, national anxiety, and deep reflection that characterize early Fifth Generation cinema. Their collaboration and later split shaped this film art movement decisively. However, the most noteworthy historical facts documented here concern the development of another Fifth Generation filmmaker, Tian Zhuangzhuang. He was very prominent during their college days and around the time of their graduation, and his lyrical artistic style, organizational abilities, and personal charisma indicated that he was destined to lead a group of artists. Yet, ultimately, it was Zhang Yimou, with his assertively expressive film style, extraordinary artistry and energy, abso-

The author, Professor Ni Zhen, teaching in the Academy's Production Design Department in 1981. Photo courtesy of Beijing Film Academy.

lute refusal to accept fate, and meticulous organizational skills, who became the actual figurehead of Fifth Generation cinema. His sudden emergence unexpectedly changed the public face of this art movement from a potential continuation of Fourth Generation lyricism and naturalistic realism to peculiarly Chinese imagery in strong and expressive colors. I feel that uncovering the underlying reasons for this change and the historical origins of this artistic formation are important contributions to history.

■

At the end of May 1994, I began writing the first chapter of this book in high spirits. Because the materials were complete and I was familiar with the cast of characters, I finished the chapter in one stretch over a few days. Sadly, just then my wife Zhao Fengxi discovered during a medical checkup that she had lung cancer and that it was already advanced. This terrible blow had an immediate effect on my writing. I became very distracted. My wife was an associate professor in the Cinematography Department of the Beijing Film Academy. She had a very close student-teacher relationship with Zhang Yimou, Hou Yong, Lü Yue, Gu Changwei, and many others.

She was also a typically tireless and selfless Chinese woman. As she ignored her illness and exercised determined self-control, continually encouraging me and spurring me on, I did my very best between June and early August to focus on completing the remaining three chapters. There are evident disparities between the first chapter and the last three, which are less sophisticated and more hastily written. Furthermore, there are some interview materials that I was unable to include in full, to my deep regret. I will never forget early spring 1995. My wife's illness had become critical. Lü Yue, Hou Yong, and Xiao Feng came to her sickbed to express their concern, and Zhang Yimou called from Tokyo, where he was engaged in postproduction, especially to extend his sympathy. I have detailed these events here because I want to express my profound gratitude to my late wife Zhao Fengxi. I also wish to offer a brief explanation of the weaknesses and inadequacies of this book.

■

Quite a number of overseas scholars expressed an interest in translating this book for publication in English. My friend Chris Berry was one of them. He worked in Beijing between 1985 and 1988, during which time he was the English-language consultant for China Film Corporation's *China Screen,* the sole periodical on Chinese film in foreign languages at that time. This experience has been an enormous aid to him in the translation of this book, for he himself witnessed the burgeoning of Fifth Generation cinema. To ensure accurate and expressive translation, he came especially to Beijing for a month in winter 1999, and together we carefully checked the historical details in the translation manuscript and the precise meaning of Chinese literary allusions and quotations in the text. I have been very impressed by Chris Berry's exhaustive work on the English translation and his meticulous attention to detail. I have taken advantage of the occasion of the English edition to make a few additions to various chapters, sections, and passages, but without altering the framework or scope of the original. Apart from this, the number of photographs has been increased significantly, from the original twenty-two to a final total of eighty-eight.

I would like to express my thanks to all of the Fifth Generation filmmakers discussed in the book. Their generous provision of written materials and photographs, as well as their willingness to be interviewed, has enabled the completion of the book and the strengthening of its contents.

At the same time, I wish to thank Chris Berry for his efforts on all fronts concerning the translation and publication of the English edition, as well as Duke University Press and Reynolds Smith, without whose dedication its publication would have been less swift.

I must also mention my friend, Mr. Shan Dongbing. His assistance in proofreading, carefully checking the English translation against the original Chinese manuscript, and his work in finding source materials for the filmography have involved a lot of effort and have been an enormous help in producing the English edition of this book. Here, I express my gratitude to him.

The directing class of 1982, photographed on entry to the Academy. Front row: second from left, Li Shaohong; sixth, Professor Wang Suihan; seventh, Professor Situ Zhaodun. Second row: second from left, Pan Hua; second from right, Hu Mei; third, Chen Kaige; fifth, Wu Ziniu. Third row: Liu Miaomiao at left, and Peng Xiaolian at right. Back row: second from left, Tian Zhuangzhuang; fourth, Xie Xiaojing; sixth, Pan Yuanliang; second from right, Xia Gang; fourth, Zhang Junzhao. Photo courtesy of Beijing Film Academy.

CHAPTER 1

ADMISSION

■

The term "Fifth Generation cinema" does not sound strange to anyone anymore, but when the first Fifth Generation Chinese films appeared in the mid-eighties no one had ever heard the phrase before. Then one talented young director after another emerged, accompanied by equally outstanding cinematographers and production designers. They attracted attention as a group. When the public discovered that these filmmakers had all graduated from the same college in the same year, they became even more intrigued, not only with the filmmakers themselves but also with their alma mater. In this way the Beijing Film Academy became the object of considerable curiosity, too.

It is difficult to prove who first coined the term "Fifth Generation." However, with the passing of time and increased use in critical and scholarly articles, it seems Fifth Generation cinema has almost become a synonym for Chinese cinema of the 1980s. At least that is how it looks to people who lack detailed knowledge of Chinese film. Indeed, some of them only began to get interested in Chinese film because of the notion of Fifth Generation cinema.

The two earliest films, *One and Eight* (1983) and *Yellow Earth* (1984), communicated powerful national spirit through tragic stories set during bleak but heroic times. The authentic and primordial quality of the characters and settings made Chinese spectators gasp with astonishment. Did our forefathers, our native land, and our original homeland around the Yellow River really look like that? University students adored the films. People in the film world were awestruck. Even their opponents knew the curtain had gone up on an innovative film movement that would rewrite history. The Fifth Generation directors had embarked on a voyage into uncharted waters.

After more than a dozen years of hard work, the Fifth Generation has reached maturity. Their works now have greater character and psychological depth, and the overemphasis on the visual image in their earliest works has been superseded by a smooth and complete command of narrative. They combine well-balanced intelligence with skilled craftsmanship, and their triumphs at numerous international film events in Europe and America have drawn attention to Chinese film and to Asian cinema in general.

In May 1993, Chen Kaige's *Farewell, My Concubine* won the Palme d'Or at Cannes. Chen Kaige has always been drawn to the struggles of individuals with nature and culture, as fate hurls them up and down in the torrent of history. In *Farewell, My Concubine* he also combined film and Beijing opera. The complex lives and loves of his main characters combined with half a century of the twists and turns of Chinese history to leave his audiences with memories to savor for days afterward. Both *Temptress Moon* (1995) and *The Emperor and the Assassin* (1998) can be seen as extensions of this historical discourse.

Zhang Yimou studied cinematography at the Academy and launched his film career as the cinematographer of *One and Eight* and *Yellow Earth*. However, he soon proved his directorial abilities with the beautifully designed *Red Sorghum* (1987). In 1992, he won the Venice Golden Lion award for *The Story of Qiu Ju,* and *To Live* received the Grand Jury Prize at Cannes in 1994. After that, *Shanghai Triad* (1995) and *Keep Cool* (1997) opened up the exploration of different kinds of materials. If Chen Kaige can be said to resemble a deeply thoughtful poet, then Zhang Yimou is even more like an adept professional storyteller. His forte is the weaving of rites and folk customs into legends. European folklorists and anthropologists have

Director Chen Kaige in the 1980s. Photo from the 1985–1986 volume of *China Screen*.

Professor Ni Zhen congratulates Zhang Yimou on winning the Golden Bear award in Berlin for *Red Sorghum* in 1988. Photo courtesy of the author.

even studied his tales as a kind of folk text about the oppression of Chinese women under feudal violence.

These are the reasons why Chen Kaige and Zhang Yimou are perceived as the two outstanding representatives of the Fifth Generation. But in fact the Fifth Generation comprises many filmmakers, each with their own style but with a shared aesthetic direction and sense of history. They include skilled and sharp-eyed cinematographers as well as painstaking and creative production and sound designers totally committed to their art. The Fifth Generation directors could work as a team with these old classmates and collaborators because they shared a tacit understanding, and they needed them as surely as one hand needs the other to clap. Without them they would have achieved only half as much, even if they had worked twice as hard.

Some say the Fifth Generation is more a phenomenon than a school of filmmakers because they have embraced such a variety of styles and themes. For example, the director Tian Zhuangzhuang pursued an on-location realist style for a long time. He detailed the lifestyle of the Inner Mongolian steppe in *On the Hunting Ground* (1984) and told the story of the Tibetan plateau herdsmen in *Horse Thief* (1986). In 1992, he directed *Blue Kite,* a film about the many difficult experiences of an ordinary Beijing household during the fifties and sixties. With stirring emotions and a narrative that is

Director Tian Zhuangzhuang in the 1980s. Photo from the 1985–1986 volume of *China Screen.*

Director Wu Ziniu in the 1980s. Photo from the 1985–1986 volume of *China Screen.*

plain but strong, it is a portrayal that speaks clearly through its silence and is gentle but deeply meaningful.

Wu Ziniu is Tian's direct opposite. His cinematic hallmarks are dramatic intensity, violence, and vigor, and his favorite subjects are war, exile, adventure in remote places, and historical incidents. He dwells obsessively on stories that put people in fiery life-and-death situations or where extremes of despair and difficulty torment them. Some people have described Wu Ziniu as a "bloodthirsty director hell-bent on danger and violence." But going by his representative works *Evening Bell* (1988), *Big Mill* (1990), and *The Last Day of Winter* (1986), it is clear that Wu Ziniu's abiding interests are life's vicissitudes and the struggle between love and violence.

Xia Gang's gently humorous character studies, Zhang Jianya's comic panache and urbane temperament, Yin Li's vivid realist studies of the flirtations and affairs of Beijing city folk, and He Qun's sincere and straightforward social issue films all show the range of the Fifth Generation's artistry. Certainly, their work cannot be reduced to one style.

The women directors of the Fifth Generation are not only independent-minded but also distinctively female. They have faced all sorts of difficulties from production problems to censorship, and they have endured the vagaries of the film market. Li Shaohong's *Bloody Morning* (1992) and *A Man at Forty* (1993) both won attention at the Locarno International Film

Festival in Switzerland. Her film on the lives of prostitutes, *Blush* (1995), won the Silver Bear award at the 1995 Berlin International Film Festival. Other films include Hu Mei's *Army Nurse* (1985) and *Far from War* (1987) and Peng Xiaolian's *Me and My Classmates* (1985) and *Three Women* (1987). All of these works examine in microscopic detail the particular character of women's emotions and psychology, as well as their conflicts with traditional social ideas. The youngest Fifth Generation director and the one with the sharpest talent is Liu Miaomiao. She began directing at age twenty-three and has made six features to date. In 1993, her *Innocent Babbler* won the President of the Italian Senate's Gold Medal at the Venice International Film Festival. Petite and red-cheeked, seen from afar she looks like a middle school student, and her eyes always shine with sincerity and trust. She comes from the Hui Autonomous Region of Ningxia in northwest China, where the Gobi Desert stretches endlessly before the eye. To take the entrance exam for the Beijing Film Academy, she had to travel by bus for two days and nights before she even made it out of her own province and into Shaanxi Province, where the exam site was located in Xi'an.

■

The women students in the directing class of 1982 at the Zhuxin campus gate. Third from left, Hu Mei; sixth, Li Shaohong; seventh, Liu Miaomiao; ninth, Peng Xiaolian. Photo courtesy of Beijing Film Academy.

On 28 February 1993, a group of travel-weary filmmakers gathered at Zhuxin Village, a few miles north of Beijing. These were the Academy's graduates of 1982. Coming back as planned to the old home of the Beijing Film Academy in Zhuxin for a tenth-year reunion, the Fifth Generation were returning to their roots.

Beijing in February: there was a chill in the air and a powerful gale was blowing. But the eighty or more former classmates arrived in high spirits from their various homes to board the bus at the designated spot.

"It's been ten whole years since we said goodbye! Ten years ago we were just immature children and now we're going gray already! Ten years and the class of 1982 has already gone into the annals of Chinese cinema history! Ten years from now we should take another day off and meet again."

The invitation to the reunion had clearly asked people not to bring their children, not to invite the press, and not to come in private cars or taxis. This class reunion was to be a genuine return to the old days.

Two large buses took the old classmates through the city and into the northern suburbs. Ten years earlier, how often had the same sort of buses and the same familiar faces traveled from the Academy in the northern outskirts to view movies at the China Film Archive for their studies! Of course, back then there were even more people and it was even more crowded, and the buses were even older and shabbier. No wonder that as soon as their bus turned onto the road to the suburbs, all the songs from the old days started to ring out again. Long-forgotten tunes of yesteryear like "The Heavens are Full of Stars" and "Back from the Shooting Range" wafted out from the bus, echoing along the road.

In what is now a large lecture theater at the Beijing College of Agriculture, the eighty-odd classmates behaved exactly as they had going to class in their student years. Sitting at desks, each wore a white T-shirt with the slogan, "Ten Years—Don't Ask!" How many successes, awards, difficulties, tribulations, injustices, grievances, farewells, and emotional upheavals were covered by this self-mocking phrase? Only the Fifth Generation themselves really knew.

As all sorts of emotions swirled around, Chen Kaige stood up, walked to the lectern, and began to recite:

Cast your minds back then
To Zhuxin Village

One hundred and fifty-three classmates
Carefree youth
Boundless arrogance
Judging past and present
Determined to succeed
Eager to compete with our predecessors
Ten years have passed
We're called the "Fifth Generation"
We've won a little fame
Now we see each other again
There are gray hairs
But we haven't lost our ideals
When we laugh our faces are still childlike
A love of art
A sincere life
Human nature makes us weep
But we stick to the humane path
Ten more years
Let us continue to lead the way
And never break our word!

By "gentlemen's agreement," no one was allowed to talk about films or their work today. They were only to exchange stories about their joys and sorrows, the vicissitudes of the years, their families and children, and their marriages and divorces. There was also the matter of going overseas. Of the original 153 classmates, fully one third were abroad. Peng Xiaolian was toughing it out in New York, looking for funding for her films. Chen Misha and Sun Li were in California. Deng Wei was in England, busy shooting portraits of celebrities. And there were more.

Someone stood up and read aloud from a letter from Australia: "I've been here eight years now. The class of 1982 is becoming more and more famous, and Westerners speak of it as though telling a legend. I don't dare admit I was a member of that group. I cannot be with you today because my visa did not come through in time. But when you all get together, please don't forget to order one of the best dishes for me."

Like a legend, a legend about Chinese film. But where should the first page begin?

■

Zhuxin Village, Beijing, 1978.

It was the second year after the end of the Cultural Revolution. Beijing Film Academy announced that it would enroll undergraduate students for university level courses in all disciplines for the first time since 1965. The minute this was announced, the news raced across the country and the applications poured in. The Academy had intended to take a total of approximately one hundred students into the five departments—Directing, Acting, Cinematography, Production Design, and Sound—with about fifteen to twenty students in each. But so many people were taking the entrance exam that the quota had to be increased. Almost ten thousand people applied for the Acting Department alone. At the examination site in the city, a dense throng spilled out of the yard and even over the sidewalks outside. Xie Yuan was there, the future star of *King of the Children* (1987) and *I Love You No Matter What.* Zhang Fengyi, who would star in *Rickshaw Boy* (1982) and *Farewell, My Concubine,* also stood in line, along with Shen Danping, who would take the female lead in *The Corner Forgotten by Love* (1981) and the Sino-Japanese coproduction *An Unfinished Chess Game* (1982).

It was a thousand-to-one shot, or at least a several hundred-to-one shot. With such bad odds, why were so many eager young people determined to have a go at it? Surely there were other more practical career options they could try in their efforts to get ahead? In order to answer these questions we must go back to the decade before 1978 and start our story there.

The Cultural Revolution began in 1966. It pitched China into a frenzied and irrational political movement. Like the girl in the fairy story who dances madly when she puts on a pair of enchanted slippers and cannot stop no matter what, the Cultural Revolution turned a nation of one billion people into fanatical lemmings. Over a ten-year period, it destroyed China's educational hopes and dreams. Starting in 1968, middle school graduates from across the country were mobilized and sent to rural areas in the movement to send educated youth "up into the mountains and down to the countryside." In practice, it turned them into an agricultural labor force among the farmers in the countryside and in the production brigades in the borderlands. Between 1968 and 1978 as many as twenty million young people underwent this experience. They were sent north to the provinces of Heilongjiang and Liaoning in the far northeast, to Inner Mongolia, to

Xinjiang in Central Asia, and to the poor provinces of Shaanxi and Shanxi. And they were sent south to Yunnan and Sichuan provinces in the southwest, Jiangxi in the southeast, Guangdong in the south, and to Hainan Island off the southern coast. They joined village and production brigade farms there and toiled at heavy physical labor. When they left the cities, most were seventeen- or eighteen-year-old youths, but the youngest included fourteen-year-old children. When they returned, many were already over thirty, their faces deeply etched with lines and wrinkles.[1]

Deng Xian became a writer after seven years of extraordinary experiences in a construction brigade in Yunnan Province. In 1993 he published a reportage novel called *Dreams of China's Educated Youth*.[2] This book details with unimpeachable research, documentation, and statistics the true history of the educated youth movement and the high price they paid. Many people buried their youth forever in the frozen plains of northern China and in the red earth country of the south. This is why Fifth Generation cinema has gone back to represent these basic origins again and again in films such as *Our Fields* (1983) and *King of the Children*.

When the system of admission to universities and vocational colleges by selection on the basis of merit determined by examination was restored on 20 October 1977, it was like a clap of springtime thunder wakening great hope in the many educated youths still in the countryside. For them, it was an opportunity worth the risk of losing everything. The new regulation finally did away with the "admission by recommendation" system, which was used during the Cultural Revolution, and restored the fair competition of selection on the basis of merit.

The origins of the "admission by recommendation system" can be traced back to the appearance of "a hero who handed in a blank paper" in Liaoning Province in 1973. An educated youth named Zhang Tiesheng from a commune in Xingcheng County of Jinzhou Municipality in Liaoning took a general knowledge exam held by university selectors that summer. He did not answer the questions, but instead wrote an angry letter criticizing the general knowledge examination system on the back of the paper. Mao Zedong's wife Jiang Qing and her associates seized this letter as a bargaining chip in their political struggle. They blew it up out of proportion. They argued that the general knowledge examination must be done away with and the "bourgeois education system" eliminated in order to ensure that the gates of the universities were open to worker, peasant, and soldier students. They sought the implementation of a system based on recommendations from people at the grassroots level of factories and the countryside. This would make attitude to labor and politics the primary determinants of university entry, not academic records. The storm that followed this affair turned right and wrong upside down. Zhang Tiesheng had already been admitted to a university without taking the exam. But he was not the only one who benefited from the new system. All young people with patrons and the ability to curry favor and pull strings were able to obtain all sorts of documents covered with supporting seals and "notes" as evidence and enter a university with ease. Others exhausted themselves burning the midnight oil after a hard day's work, but they had only the faintest hope of gaining admission; it was as though they were in a dark tunnel and would never see light at the end.

For the ten million educated youths still in the countryside, as well as for those in the cities who decided to take the exams, the return of the university and vocational college entrance exam system on 20 October 1977 was not just an entrance exam but also a chance to turn their lives around. And it was not just a decisive moment in the lives of the educated youths, with their callused hands and deeply scarred shoulders, but also in the lives of the Chinese people as a whole. This was a last chance, at such an important time near the turn of the century, to choose between entering the door to learning or going deeper into the valley of ignorance.

Later events proved that students of all disciplines who entered the university system in 1977 and 1978 were rare talents compared with both their predecessors and those who came after them. They had not wasted their time struggling to study by the light of oil lamps in the countryside. Like spring bamboo shoots after the rain, once they gained access to the excellent study conditions of the universities they developed very rapidly indeed. In the early 1980s, they moved quickly to take important positions in all the professions, becoming a fresh labor force that filled the shortages at that time. Older members of the educated classes were both delighted and moved by their exceptional, hardworking, brave, and independent minds, and most of all by their unswerving sense of mission. It gave the older generation hope for a bright future.

■

Zhang Min, first president of Beijing
Film Academy. Photo courtesy of
Beijing Film Academy.

The Beijing Film Academy was established in 1956.[3] Its first president was
Zhang Min, and its vice-presidents were Wu Yinxian and Zhong Jingzhi.
Zhang Min was a key figure in the progressive leftist drama and film movement of the 1930s. He was a distinguished playwright and a translator. Wu
Yinxian was a famous veteran from the worlds of photography and cinematography, and Zhong Jingzhi was a stage production designer and a film
educator. In the years between 1956 and 1966, the Academy developed into
a comprehensive college with established departments of screenwriting, directing, acting, cinematography, production design, and film technology.[4]
But the outbreak of the Cultural Revolution in 1966 disrupted normal education and paralyzed the Academy.

In May 1978 the exams for undergraduate admission to the Beijing
Film Academy formally began. Three exam centers were established for the
whole country. They were in Beijing, Shanghai, and Xi'an. Because there
were so many candidates in Beijing, several exam sites had to be set up for
each discipline. For each department there was a first exam and a follow-
up exam. After most of the candidates had been eliminated, the remainder
with outstanding records in the arts went through a general knowledge
exam, and only those who passed were admitted.

For example, the exam for the Directing Department that year included the following elements. In the initial exam there was an oral test, which usually focused on general knowledge of the arts. Then there was a performance test, which could be a song, or a reading from a short story, or a scene composed by the applicant. This was not to exceed five minutes. Next came an acting test. The scene was set on the spot and performed immediately after a short time for preparation. The performance was not allowed to exceed seven minutes. Finally, there was a written essay. For those who made it through to the follow-up exam there was another oral test, which focused on the applicant's grasp of arts policy, analysis of a work of art, and specialist knowledge of film. Next, candidates were required to compose a story on a set theme, perform a small piece, and write an analysis of a film immediately after viewing it.

The film shown for analysis was *Heroic Sons and Daughters* (1964). Set in 1951 and 1952, it was about the Chinese volunteer army in the Korean War. A divisional political commissar is reunited in the heat of battle with his heroic son and daughter, Wang Cheng and Wang Fang, whom he had lost contact with many years before. After the film was screened, the hundreds of candidates were divided up and taken to classrooms. In deep concentration, they scribbled away. After thirty minutes, one candidate quickly handed in his paper.

"Have you finished?" The teacher asked in surprise.

"Yes."

"Do you want to go over it again?"

"No thanks."

He walked out alone and bought a packet of cheap cigarettes and a few ice pops from the campus kiosk. Then he walked over to the shade of a large tree, sat down quietly, and lit a cigarette. He did not touch the paper-wrapped ice pops.

No one else handed in their paper or walked out. All was silent save for the cicadas buzzing from branch to branch in the summer sun. The light flickered through the trees onto the bare ground. An elderly teacher slowly walked over and bent toward the candidate, asking with concern, "What's the matter? Did the exam go badly?"

"No, no. I'm waiting for my friend Chen Kaige. He still hasn't finished writing."

"It isn't that watching *Heroic Sons and Daughters* has upset you?"

"Oh, no. Thank you, sir."

This student's name was Tian Zhuangzhuang. His father, Tian Fang, played the role of divisional political commissar Wang Wenqing in *Heroic Sons and Daughters*. Tian Fang was a brilliant and highly popular actor of the older generation. However, his health was destroyed during eight years of suffering in the Cultural Revolution. He passed away in 1974, unable to hang on and see the day when Mao's wife Jiang Qing and the Gang of Four were toppled.

Bit by bit the ice pops were melting, turning into chilled fruit juice soaking through the wrappers. But Chen Kaige still had not finished and come out of the exam hall.

Tian Zhuangzhuang and Chen Kaige had known each other since childhood. Their parents worked together in the Beijing Film Studio, and their homes were not far from each other—just a few alleyways apart. Tian Zhuangzhuang's family lived in a courtyard house in Baochan Alley near Huguo Temple in the western district of Beijing. The original Chinese characters for "Baochan" meant "Precious Buddha," but because this name implied religious superstition they had been changed to another pair of characters, also pronounced "Baochan" but meaning "Precious Production." There was a hundred-year-old tree in the entrance to the courtyard, and children loved to play in its shade. Chen Kaige's family also lived by Huguo Temple, not far from Tian's house. The little alleyways there ran all over. They had names like Peace Alley and Hundred Flowers Lane, suggesting the quiet contentment and cultured refinement of those times. Later when Chen Kaige was living in New York, he remembered the quiet and peaceful atmosphere of the little alleys very fondly indeed. Out in the warm spring sunshine, peddlers would carry bamboo baskets full of fluffy bright yellow chicks up and down the streets and alleyways. While the chicks chirped softly but piercingly, the peddlers would walk among the children. Pulling out chicks and putting them in the palms of their hands, they would point to the budding willow branches and say, "Look, their feathers are even softer than the white blossoms." On sultry summer nights, old people looking for a cool spot would sit in twos and threes on stools in the alleyways with children playing around them. The deep scent of tuberoses wafted through the air and from near and far came the cries of peddlers selling snacks. This was truly a tranquil night in old Beijing.

Several families lived in the old courtyard house where Tian Zhuang-

Still from *Immortal in the Flames*.
Tian Zhuangzhuang's mother, Yu
Lan, is on the right. Photo from
China Film Album, 1949–1979
(Beijing: China Film Press,
1983), 190.

Still from *Heroic Sons and Daughters*.
Tian Zhuangzhuang's father, Tian
Fang, is on the right. Photo from
China Film Album, 1949–1979
(Beijing: China Film Press,
1983), 187.

Chen Kaige in the 1960s.
Photo courtesy of
Chen Kaige.

zhuang's home was. The Head of the Beijing Film Studio Tian Fang and his wife Yu Lan lived in the rear courtyard. They were both veteran actors well known to the public. Tian Zhuangzhuang was the second of their three children. Their neighbors in the rear section included veteran director Cui Wei, whose films *Song of Youth* (1959), *Women Generals of the Yang Family* (1960), *Wild Boar Forest* (1962), and *Little Soldier Zhang Ga* (1963) were favorites with Chinese audiences. Cui Wei had an imposing physical presence and was a straightforward man with a strong sense of humor. He was also a much-loved actor, and had the lead roles in *Song Jingshi* (1955), *New Legends of Old Soldiers* (1959), and *Song of the Red Flag* (1960), making him a household name in the 1960s. Two other people lived in the front courtyard. One was the watercolorist and production designer Qin Wei, whose free-flowing and lively landscapes were well known in the 1930s. The other person was the famous Beijing Film Studio screenwriter Hai Mo. He loved books like life itself, but he loved children even more. Young Tian Zhuangzhuang was Hai Mo's best friend. He never even had to leave the courtyard to visit Hai Mo. Zhuangzhuang would knock on his back wall from the wall of the rear courtyard, and Hai Mo would call out from his study, "It's Zhuangzhuang, isn't it? Come on over!" Then, like a cat, Zhuangzhuang would leap over the low wall from a tree, land in the yard with a thud, and go into Hai Mo's study. Sometimes, he would knock on the wall and the voice would come back from the study, "It's Zhuangzhuang, isn't it? Don't come over now, I'm busy. Come again tomorrow." They were very close, but there were limits. Zhuangzhuang was not allowed to flip

Chen Kaige in the 1960s.
Photo courtesy of
Chen Kaige.

through or even touch the books in the library—they had an agreement about that. "Whenever you want to read any book, I'll get it ready for you," Hai Mo said.

Tian Zhuangzhuang and Chen Kaige were both born in 1952, a Dragon year. In 1966, they were both fourteen years old and, like all other Beijing fourteen year olds, out of the blue one summer morning they found themselves caught in a dangerous storm. It was a storm that not only changed their lives then, but the rest of their lives as well. Later, when they took up their positions behind the camera, and film became an important part of their lives, the purgatory that started with that catastrophic summer of 1966 was a theme they kept revisiting.

When the Little Red Guards rushed into that peaceful courtyard house in Baochan Alley, film actors and directors recognized and loved by the public, and neighbors who had only yesterday asked warmly after one another as they came and went, suddenly were labeled "members of the black gang in literature and the arts" and "enemies." The old artists stood respectfully in the yard. In the blazing sun, they were made to stand with their heads bowed as a form of punishment while they watched calligraphy, art, and famous works of literature brought out from their own homes, piled up on the dark bricks in the courtyard, and set on fire. Black smoke slowly rose in swirls, filling the air in the alleyways.

Tian Zhuangzhuang's parents were in the line of people punished by being made to stand with their heads bowed for several long hours. But the predicament of Chen Kaige's father, the director Chen Huaikai, was even worse. As a member of the Nationalist KMT (Guomindang) Party during the Anti-Japanese War (1937–1945), he was accused of even more crimes. Soon after, they were all sent to the "cowshed" [slang for a place of imprisonment] at Beijing Film Studio to undertake supervised labor.

One evening before the incident, Hai Mo in the front courtyard suddenly called Zhuangzhuang over. A few small stools in the room were piled high with literary masterpieces. Hai Mo looked at Zhuangzhuang and slowly said, "I've picked out these books for you. Take your time reading them." Zhuangzhuang said, "I've got to ask my mother. If she says I can, I'll come back for them, OK?"

But that night, a group of Little Red Guards came. Some of them were not so little and just called themselves that. They took Hai Mo into custody, and stuck two strips of paper across his door to seal it. A few days later, Beijing Film Studio was notified to send someone to claim his corpse. They said he had resisted interrogation and committed suicide to avoid punishment for his crimes, and that he had alienated himself from the Party and the people.

In the dark of the night, Tian Zhuangzhuang went to the front courtyard. He stood in front of the door to Hai Mo's wing of the courtyard, which was sealed with the two paper strips, and he stood there for a long time. He looked through the window. Although he could not see clearly, he seemed able to make out the piles of hardback literary works on those stools. He felt that he had behaved wrongly toward Hai Mo. Why had he not taken those books immediately that night?

In 1969, Tian Zhuangzhuang and Chen Kaige both left Beijing to be part of the "up into the mountains and down to the countryside" movement. Tian Zhuangzhuang went to a small village on the Nen River in northeast China, whereas Chen Kaige went to Jinghong County in Xishuangbanna in Yunnan Province.

Chen Kaige's mother, who had been sick for many years, packed his bags without saying a word. Kaige's only worries were for her health and his baby sister. After repeated requests in the cowshed, his father, Chen Huaikai, received special permission to go to Beijing railway station and see his son off on the long journey. As the train full of students gradually picked

Chen Kaige visits the Monument
to the People's Heroes in Tiananmen
Square before going down to Yunnan.
The inscription by Chairman Mao reads,
"The People's Heroes are Immortal."
Photo courtesy of Chen Kaige.

up speed and left the platform, a desolate old man ran after it, slowly but
without stopping, all the way to the end of the platform, where he gazed
at it as it disappeared into the distance. As his father on the platform got
smaller and smaller, Kaige could not help becoming choked with tears.

Kaige hung his head so those around him would not see his eyes. They
were full of self-reproach, grief, and guilt. He could never forget the unfor-
givable wound he had inflicted on his father. During a chaotic and terrifying struggle session one night, surrounded in the courtyard by Little Red
Guards and Rebel Factions yelling slogans about destroying the reaction-
ary force, Chen Huaikai, he had rushed up and shoved his father. He was
shocked senseless by this action, and in the future he would talk about the
event again and again. He was a fourteen-year-old child at the time. Why
had he done it? Was it because he was afraid of death? Yes, but there was
something more terrifying. Having been driven out from but wanting to
rejoin the masses who had collectively taken leave of their senses, he hurt
his own gentle and dutiful father in order to be acknowledged as one of
the group.

Surely we should not try to place the responsibility for history on a few
people's shoulders so that millions may freely absolve themselves.

"I am bitterly and painfully obsessed with examining this period of history," Chen Kaige would say later. "And at the same time, I am examining myself. When the Day of Judgment comes, I shall stand up."

The forests of Xishuangbanna are dense and its mountains endless. In the production and construction brigades of Yunnan alone there were more than one hundred thousand educated youths. They felled trees to open up the land, burnt away the forests covering the mountains, and established fields, transforming the primeval forests into terraced fields patterned on those in the model production brigade of Dazhai. The ax blade knew no discrimination. Ancient trees so large that two people could not reach around them, shrubs, and fine grasses were all put to the ax. Chen Kaige witnessed the ghastly sight of a sixteen-year-old from Shanghai struggling with the utmost difficulty to cut down an immense tree, only to be crushed under it as it fell. The teenager's father traveled all the way to the site and went to the fallen tree without a word, his expression full of silent mourning. Kaige also saw the cruel scene of a forestry worker chased by a swarm of furious bees whose hive he had destroyed when cutting down a tree. They chased the unfortunate educated youth all the way to the river, which he plunged into, submerging himself completely. The minute he came up to breathe, however, they stung him to death. When the forest covering the mountains was being cleared by burning, Kaige saw the awe-inspiring scene of the fires racing up to the skies and the trees dancing as they were turned to ashes:

> The whole mountain was seething. Amid the flames, thousands of big trees left the earth and rose to the sky. Just when it seemed as if they would fly away, they would slowly drift down, collide in mid air, then soar up again, up, up, up. The hot air pressed in on all sides, and my hair suddenly stood on end. I dared not touch it, fearing that it might be brittle enough to break into pieces and disperse into the air. The mountain, which looked as if it were scalded, rang with weird cries, a whole universe in panic.[5]

Chen Kaige drew this description from Ah Cheng's novel *The King of Trees* for his autobiography *Young Chen Kaige*. The instigators of the movement to send educated youth "up into the mountains and down to the countryside" could never have anticipated that scene after scene of the somber destruction of flora and fauna would forge witnesses to history who can never forget what they saw. Humanity has recorded hundreds and thousands of years of life and death, dynastic rises and falls, and prosperity and disaster on bamboo strips, sheepskins, hemp paper, and silk. Now there are more recording materials, including film and audiotape. As the years have passed, Jinghong Production Brigade in Yunnan alone has produced many excellent authors and literary works. They include Ah Cheng's *King of the Children* and *The King of Chess,* Ye Xin's *Wasted Years* and *Bastard,* and Deng Xian's *Dreams of China's Educated Youth* and *Soul of the Nation.*[6] It has also given us the film auteur Chen Kaige.

So many young men and women, only sixteen or seventeen, whose lives were just beginning are buried forever under the red soil on the mountain peaks laid bare by hacking and cutting. And those who returned from the red soil have given their lives over to endlessly remembering and talking about it, for each of them is haunted by living spirits they cannot drive away. That is why the literature of the educated youth will never come to a final halt.

Chen Kaige was one of those who returned.

When he left the examination hall, he found himself alone on the shady road outside the Beijing Film Academy gate in Zhuxin Village. The dense leaves at the tops of the towering poplar trees rustled in the wind, and a fodder field stretched over the horizon, running alongside the field crops from the neighboring village. It was a joyous sea of emerald green. Many years later Chen Kaige spoke about it wistfully, saying, "When I saw those two rows of towering poplars and those wide fields, I was delighted. I figured I'd probably passed the exam this time, because it looked just like where we went down to in the countryside."

For a year before he took the Academy entrance exam, Kaige had been studying hard for the entrance exams to Beijing University's Chinese Literature Department. But he had returned from the exams disappointed. This was a terrible blow for him because literature, not film, was his first love, especially Chinese classical poetry. From the age of seven, his mother taught him to recite poetry every day, to practice Chinese characters, and to read. Even today he writes beautiful calligraphy and can recite more than one hundred Tang and Song dynasty poems, thanks to his mother. The year Chen Kaige went down to the countryside, he was carrying two cardboard cases suspended from a shoulder pole. One was full of clothes and practical things, the other was full of books. He had a copy of Engels's *Ludwig Feuerbach and the Outcome of Classical German Philosophy,* Professor Wang Li's *Study of the Rules and Forms of Classical Poetry,* and a set of *A Dream of Red Mansions.*[7] He also had an eight-volume loose-leaf collection of Chinese classical literature. In his hut deep in the forests of Yunnan, by the lamplight late at night, he read the Confucian classics, the heritage of the Tang and Song dynasties, Han Yu's and Liu Zongyuan's essays, the elegant poetry of Li Po, and the stirring works of Xin Qiji.[8] The *ping-ze* tonal patterns of classical Chinese poetry, the antithetical couplet form, the four-line verse, and the various rules on forms and patterns all flowed through the young man's veins. So did ancient admonitions and maxims, such as the advice that cultivating oneself enables regulation of one's family, and this in turn enables correct government of the state, which leads to tranquility throughout the land, or the saying, "If poor, attend to your own virtue in solitude, but if you advance to dignity, make the whole society virtuous, too."[9] These elements composed the deeply Confucian culture that formed the spiritual foundation and source of Chen Kaige's cinema. It is true that the members of the Fifth Generation are highly competitive. But as far as literature is concerned, they all agree that Chen Kaige is the leader of the pack. He wrote the famous sketch of Zhang Yimou, *Man of the Qin,* after the Qin dynasty country that Zhang came from. It includes a beautiful passage that begins, "If you walk to the west, you come to the glories of Chang'an. Zhang Yimou came from there. He didn't want to make a name for himself, but he had a sincere and honest ambition. That was to work for art, which is what his name means, not to work for material things."[10] It goes on to explain how Zhang took the camera he had sold his own blood to buy and left the glories of the Qin to realize his ambition. He left the ruins of the first Qin emperor's Efang Palace, along with the remains of Xingqing City, the stone carvings at General Huo Qubing's tomb, and the terracotta warriors in the Qin Emperor Shi's tomb. He put Liu's tomb behind him. Of the various Shaanxi specialties, he only remembers the rice wine. And he remembers the Empress Wu Zetian's tomb. Built in the shape of a reclining woman, it has lain on the earth for generations. The different kinds of scenery and legends from that region inspire a galaxy of emotions. Zhang built up his aspirations, learned about the ups and downs of life, and honed his ambition. As the years pass, nature goes through its cycles but humankind moves forward. Zhang Yimou has climbed Mount

Huashan ten times. He has witnessed many scenic splendors and many aspects of human society. But his greatest concern is the joy and woe of the common people, among whom he includes himself.

Chen Kaige's subject was Zhang Yimou, his determination to stand out from the crowd and his high aspirations. But between the lines one can detect Chen's own emotions, his empathy with Zhang, and his own ambitions. One can also see the great range of his literary ability. Other candidates for the academy shone when they were performing a small piece, and their directorial talents were recognized then. But this was certainly not the case with Chen Kaige. Long after he entered the Academy, his acting and his bodywork exercises still made the other students laugh. But most probably it was his literary ability, his intellect, and his silver tongue that caught the examiners' attention, and so, fortunately, he was included on the list of students admitted to the Directing Department.

■

Chen Kaige and Tian Zhuangzhuang were not the only applicants who had labored in the countryside and joined the production brigades as educated youths. Returned educated youths were not in the minority among those applying for the Academy that year. Indeed, unless we understand the implications of the term "educated youth," we cannot really understand the sources of Fifth Generation films or their historical content.

A candidate named Pan Yuanliang stood at the second exam site. He was a young man of medium build, stocky and energetic. One of the performance exams required the use of an object, and Pan Yuanliang used a shoulder pole and a length of rope in his piece. He was also allowed to perform the piece together with another candidate. The chief examiners, Professor Wang Suihan and Associate Professor Situ Zhaodun told him not to panic, to calmly think things over, and to prepare for five minutes. Pan Yuanliang performed the following story together with a young woman.

Two Beijing educated youths have recently arrived in the Great Northern Wasteland. As members of the advance brigades among those opening up the wasteland, they are scouts checking the way ahead and putting up signs. After using all the wooden stakes meant for making road signs, Pan Yuanliang tells his female comrade to take the shoulder pole and stand guard while he hurries back to camp and asks the others to bring more stakes. However, not long after he leaves, she becomes lonely and afraid.

She does not want to continue standing guard alone, so she tries to hurry back. But she does not follow the road signs and quickly finds herself in a swampy quagmire. As she slowly begins to sink, she calls for help, her piercing cries echoing across the wilderness. Pan Yuanliang rushes back to her side, but he cannot leave the area of dry land marked out with road signs and go into the swamp to save her. In crisis, he pulls out the rope and throws it out to the girl, telling her to tie herself tight to the shoulder pole. Only then is he gradually able to drag her out from the quagmire.

The performance was over. As the chief examiners silently looked at him, Pan Yuanliang became nervous. Was there something terribly wrong with his performance?

One of the teachers asked, "Was that based on your own experience?"

Pan Yuanliang said nothing for a long time, then slowly answered, "That girl sank into the mud less than half a mile from our camp, and she was never seen again."

There was a moment of silence.

"Which province did you go to work in?" asked a teacher.

"I was in the seventeenth brigade of the first division of the Northeast Production and Construction Corps," Pan Yuanliang answered. "It was on the banks of the Jinyang River in Heilongjiang Province, close to the border with the Soviet Union."

■

At the third exam site for the Directing Department, another candidate was being tested. His name was Bai Hong, and he was a worker with ten years experience in the Zhangjiakou Medicine Equipment Factory. Recently, he had been promoted to vice-head of his workshop. As he looked at all the props laid out on one side, Bai could not decide which one to use for his performance. His face was full of anxiety and confusion. Chief examiner Han Xiaolei told him not to worry. He could use an object of his own to make up the story. Bai tore a piece of paper out of his notebook and quickly folded it into two little white flowers. The piece he performed went as follows.

A worker joins the crush at Zhangjiakou train station ticket window, wanting to buy a ticket for Beijing. It is April 1976.[11] Tiananmen Square in Beijing is teeming with tens of thousands of people mourning the death of Premier Zhou Enlai.[12]

Peng Xiaolian and Bai Hong from the directing class of 1982 rehearsing a scene from *Early Spring in February*. Photo courtesy of Beijing Film Academy.

However, the train stations outside Beijing have received an order that no one is to be sold a ticket to Beijing unless they have a letter of introduction from the local Party political commissariat. The people throng around the ticket window, angrily demanding to know who has given this order and why they will not sell tickets to them. The door to the ticket office closes suddenly.

Bai Hong delicately fishes a little white flower out of his pocket and attaches it to his ID card together with the money for a ticket. He knocks patiently on the door until it opens, and then quickly slips in. He asks the people in front to let him put his money and ID card through the ticket window.

Soon after, a pair of hands stretches out from the ticket window, holding a train ticket, his ID, and, on top of them, two little white flowers. The ticket seller has added the second one.

All of the other passengers stand watching him with respect. Then they make a path for him. Solemnly carrying the train ticket and the white flowers, Bai Hong slowly walks out of the ticket hall.

The chief examiners' eyes were moist, and the other candidates watched Bai with bated breath. The atmosphere generated by this performance lingered for a long time.

■

At another exam site, a candidate named Jiang Haiyang was instructed to combine a wash basin and some postage stamps in his performance piece.

He placed a lot of household items into the basin, such as towels, soap, food, and medicine. Then he put the basin into a cloth wrapper, carefully sewed a small strip of white cloth on it, and stuck the postage stamps onto that. Taking a pen, he wrote, "Tangshan, Earthquake Disaster Area Command Post, Disaster Relief Supplies Administration. . . ."[13]

■

Back at the first exam site, the next student was answering questions.

A tape deck played Tchaikovsky's first piano concerto. The candidate, Xie Xiaojing, knitted his brows and listened intently to the lively melody, nervously preparing to answer the questions.

"Please tell us what this music makes you feel," the chief examiner asked amiably.

Xie Xiaojing was tall but shy and not good with words. Unconsciously, he began rubbing his hands together and beads of sweat appeared on his forehead.

"I feel there's a field of snow, sunlight, very bright, very wide." He gesticulated as he spoke, unable to express himself adequately. He smiled awkwardly, his eyes pleading for help. "I'm really no good at talking about music."

"Relax. You can talk about real feelings that you've experienced."

"Springtime! The snow on the ground still hasn't melted. My classmates and I are riding our horses. We're seeing off Xiao Liu from our educated youth cooperative. He's going back to Beijing because the brigade has recommended him for university. We only had a quota of one."

"Continue."

"The train is about to leave. He takes off his leather hat and presses it into my hands. All he says is 'Take care.' The minute he gets on the train it leaves, because it only stops at small stations for a minute." As Xie Xiaojing spoke, he gazed into the distance. "The train departs. Holding the hat he left behind in one hand, I undo the horse's harness and ride off after the train. The horse fairly flies across the snowy ground, the sunlight is piercingly bright, and the train disappears into the distance. When I hear this piece of music, I think of that scene then."

"And what else?"

"Since returning to the city, I have never seen a snow field so clean, so bright, and so wide."

■

The next candidate.

A petite young woman dressed in black stood in the center of the examination hall. Her face was pale and she seemed a bit nervous, but a cool, stubborn light shone from her eyes.

"Are you ready?" the chief examiner asked.

"Yes."

"Please begin."

As she began to recite, her voice was low but sincere and dignified.

> If there are some whose need for sleep is less
> Then our beloved Premier Zhou was such a one;
> For, throughout his whole life
> He slept so little, so little.
> The lamp in his office is all the proof we need.
> Is it an ordinary lamp?
> No, it burned on his life's energy,
> It was his loyal heart that shed such radiance.

According to the exam regulations, a candidate's recitation was not to exceed five minutes. However, none of the five supervising teachers interrupted the young woman, because the poem stirred painful but cherished memories in all their hearts.

> Never say that our beloved Premier Zhou has gone to rest.
> Great proletarian revolutionary that he was—
> Those brilliant, glowing eyes of his

Will never really sleep!
Never say his ashes lie inert upon our vast land,
Outstanding communist fighter that he was—
Whose life was so dynamic,
He will never halt and rest.[14]

After a total of fifteen minutes, she finished reciting the entire text of "The Lamp in Premier Zhou's Office." The examination hall was steeped in solemn silence.

As she stood quietly in the center of the exam hall, her simple black outfit made her look even more petite. Apparently she had not selected the color deliberately, but at this moment it appeared especially dignified, like a visual complement to the poem.

"Li Shaohong, are you still in an army medical team?" the chief examiner asked.

"I am a nurse with a community medical team in the Nanjing Military District."

"So why do you want to study film?"

"Because I like it!"

"What do you know about film?"

"From the age of fourteen to seventeen, I was a projectionist for four years in Sichuan Province. I projected hundreds of films in the countryside, for the military, and in factories. Back then, all the films we screened were based on the revolutionary model operas. Everyone would bring a stool with them and sit watching them in the open air."

"When did you finish school?"

"After the sixth grade of primary school."

"And then?"

"Then I taught myself. I borrowed all the literature and history books in the county library and read them one after another. Some I understood, others I did not understand completely."

"Name a couple of your favorite authors."

"Dostoevsky. I like his *Brothers Karamazov* and *The Insulted and the Injured.*"

"Why?"

"Because real people are just the way he describes his characters."

And so, because her grades were good in all the areas tested, this quiet

Li Shaohong during her time in the countryside. Photos courtesy of Li Shaohong.

young woman with the set expression made it onto the list of those admitted to the Directing Department.

However, no one saw the tenacity hidden deep inside this slight young woman, or her tortured and all-consuming awareness of historical and social contradiction. When she produced that most serious social issue film *Bloody Morning* thirteen years later, it took everyone by surprise. It also proved that Fifth Generation cinema was not just men's business.

■

At the site next door the exams were continuing.

On the program was the performance to be done with an object, and the object was a large bowl of the sort often used in the countryside. The candidate was a short, fat lad with thick glasses, and he started by industriously filling the bowl with grain. All of a sudden, he heard a mouse. Carefully, he began to search for it. Then he decided to prop up the edge of the bowl with half a chopstick, set a bait, tie a string to the chopstick, and tiptoe into a corner, where he squatted down and waited. When the mouse took the bait, he yanked the string and trapped it. Then he circled round the bowl, unable to think how to get the mouse out from under it. Suddenly he had an idea. He gripped the bowl and shook it around until the mouse's tail popped out. He grabbed the tail and flipped the bowl over, but when he moved to grab the mouse's body, it darted away from him.

It was a very lively little skit, well thought-out and well performed.

"Do you like comedy very much?" the chief examiner asked.

"I'm not sure how to put it, but I like ordinary events with a bit of humor to them."

"Did you go and work down in the countryside?" a teacher asked.

"No, I didn't. I'm a road worker in Beijing. I've been working on the roads for eight years, since 1970. Fuxingmen, Yuquan Road, the subways, Mentougou, Zhoukoudian—I've repaired the roads around all those places."

"What sort of work do you do on the roads?"

"I'm an unskilled laborer, second grade. In winter I have to grind down a lot of steel rods. After we've dug up the frozen ground, I can't even stretch my fingers out properly. I can only open my hands slowly after I've soaked them in hot water. I can't even hold chopsticks, they keep falling to the ground."

Xia Gang in the 1970s.
Photo courtesy of
Xia Gang.

"What sort of books have you read on film or theater?"

"Molière, Carlo Gordoni, *Selected Sichuan Comedies, Yuan and Ming Dynasty Dramas* . . ."

"Do you want to do comedy in the future?"

"Ordinary people work so hard, so they're always looking for someone to crack a joke or tell a funny tale to make life seem a bit easier." His eyes twinkled gently behind his glasses, and he seemed to have the air of a comedian or artist. He looked just like an account keeper in a shop or a purchasing agent running around after materials.

In fact, he was the future director Xia Gang, a talent that matured slowly like fine wine. His films from the early nineties, *Unexpected Passion* (1991), *After Separation* (1992), and *Nobody Applauds* (1993), are full of vivid scenes of the cozy intimacy of ordinary people. They are quick-witted and ironic city films widely welcomed by young audiences.

■

While the exams for the departments of directing, acting, sound, and production design were all busily underway, the chair of the Cinematography Department and several professors were poring over a photo album. In the album were forty or fifty shots of all types, including landscapes, portraits, still lifes, and photos of everyday life. There was no doubt that the photographer was remarkably talented, industrious, and painstaking, someone with rare prospects.

"Unfortunately, he's over the age limit," the chair said.

"How far over? Can't we bend the rules?" a professor who loved talent like life itself pleaded.

"He's twenty-eight years old. Our limit is twenty-two, so that's six whole years over."

"But if we let someone like this go by, we'll regret it for the rest of our lives."

"Are you suggesting we raise the age limit? If we increase it by two months, that would add two hundred more candidates. Six months, and that's another three hundred. A year and you've added another thousand just like that. How many people would we have to add to allow him to take the exam legally?"

"So what can we do?"

"What can we do? We have to bar him from the exam for now. Do you think I don't want him to take it?"

"Where's he from? What's his name?"

"He's from Shaanxi Province, and he's called Zhang Yimou."

As the site of the Qin dynasty palace and ancient capital of the glorious Tang dynasty, Xi'an, in Shaanxi Province, was once the flourishing center of China's feudal civilization. At that time, the ancient capital was called Chang'an. Famous far and wide for its bustling prosperity, it welcomed and bid farewell to merchants from the Silk Road and eminent monks from Japan, and stood as the economic and cultural center of Asia and even the Eastern Hemisphere. Although in recent years the area had been silently neglected, in the 1980s the historical glories of Xi'an were revived, especially when a force of New Wave Chinese filmmakers unexpectedly emerged from there. *Horse Thief, King of the Children, Black Cannon Incident* (1985), and *Old Well* (1987) were all made at Xi'an Film Studio. *Red Sorghum* raised the magnificent myth of the Chinese west to new heights, and in the eighth decade of the twentieth century Xi'an once again found itself the focus of national and international attention.

People know that the vastness of Shaanxi Province, along with its broad plains and the surging Yellow River, have given the Fifth Generation a wide canvas for their films. But they are less aware that the ancient city of Xi'an itself supplied an important number of young talents in all areas of Fifth Generation filmmaking, in particular in cinematography. Among admissions in 1978, Xi'an was one of the key sources for the Beijing Film Academy.

Zhang Yimou stars in *Old Well*. Photo from *The Stars Are Shining* (Kunming: Yunnan People's Press, 1996), 100.

That year, six hundred candidates reported to the Shanghai exam site for the Directing Department, and in the end six were selected from there. In Xi'an there were more than four hundred candidates, among whom only three made it through. In order to make the final decision on the three who would make it into the lucky twenty-eight selected for the department, the senior professors in charge of the entire admissions operation, Zhang Ke and Wu Guoying, flew specially to Xi'an. There they oversaw the final exam and selection procedure together with the Xi'an exam site teachers, Wen Lun, Wang Xinyu, and Situ Zhaodun.

The three successful candidates were Wu Ziniu, who later directed *Evening Bell, Big Mill,* and *The Last Day of Winter;* Zhang Junzhao, who directed *One and Eight;* and Liu Miaomiao, who went on to direct *Innocent Babbler* and *Family Feud* (1994).

Today, Liu Miaomiao is president of the Ningxia Film Studio. But when she talks about how nervous she was taking the entrance exams in Xi'an, her forehead breaks out in sweat just as it did back then. She was only sixteen, so young-looking that people assumed she must be a middle school student who had slipped into the exam hall to watch the fun. The candidates were divided into groups and squeezed onto benches in the corridor to wait to be called into the hall for their performances. Liu Miaomiao was in the excited throng, and heard Wang Xinyu calling out in a piercing feminine voice, "Zhang Junjian! Is Zhang Junjian here?"

A deep voice rang out from behind her. "Zhao, Zhang Jun*zhao!* It's 'zhao,' like in the name Li Dazhao!"[15]

Liu Miaomiao turned to take a look. She saw a sturdy young man wearing a military uniform bleached white from washing. His ruddy face shone. He seemed like a typical People's Liberation Army soldier.

"Wu Ziniu! Is Wu Ziniu here?"

A young man of medium build stood up in front of her. After answering, he turned to look at the other candidates around him. With a pair of dark eyes, he was vigilant and composed, like a wild animal crouched deep in the forest, waiting to attack. He would not move a muscle for hours in the quiet of the dense undergrowth. But when he found his target and the opportunity, he would shoot out at his prey like an arrow. Afterwards, he would not leave a scrap of evidence behind.

Liu Miaomiao took careful note of him. She saw his clothes were very old and worn. There was even a small hole in the back of his pants. But she could tell from the unusual look in his eyes that this was a man with a complicated past, making him a formidable adversary in the exam.

Indeed, Liu Miaomiao was right. Wu Ziniu was a tough guy. He had been through hell and high water but he had hung on and survived. Given all of his tribulations, he had no expectation of justice or sympathy from others, and he would be rather surprised if he succeeded this time. He had come with a cold and indifferent attitude, thinking that if he failed he could try something else again later.

■

Wu Ziniu was born in 1952 in the city of Leshan in Sichuan Province. Surrounded by water on three sides and hemmed in by mountains on the other, Leshan is celebrated as the site of a giant statue of Buddha. The Chinese say that it is not height but the presence of an immortal that makes a mountain famous, and not depth but the presence of a dragon that makes a stretch of sea renowned. Leshan is also famed for its scenic beauty. Wu spent his childhood in this place, in a loving and highly cultured household. Both his parents were teachers. His father was well known in Leshan as a middle normal schoolteacher who believed in friendliness as a pedagogical principle. Wu Ziniu was the second child, with an older sister and a younger brother. His sister was intelligent and nimble-witted, with a deep sensitivity to the world and to people born of experience. Were it not for the Cultural Revolution she would certainly have become an outstanding doctor or teacher. But the frenzied chaos in summer 1966 terrorized her, and soon she was put in a mental hospital. Her illness was triggered by her father's examination in solitary confinement. Every two weeks, she would bring him clothes and other necessities, but she could not comprehend or bear the idea of the interrogation of an ordinary and completely innocent man who was on the verge of collapse after many sleepless nights. Fate changed this excellent young woman's entire life, and it also changed Wu Ziniu's character forever. Once a lively and outgoing fourteen-year-old, he was no longer friendly and cheerful. He sealed his lips and his eyes grew colder and warier with every passing day. He deliberately became as fierce as a wild animal. It was as though he were a domesticated puppy who had been left in a wild forest on a mountain. Amid the howls of tigers and panthers, and as scorpions and spiders appeared and disappeared in the darkness, he gradually turned into a wolf cub.

The Cultural Revolution launched a second attack on Wu Ziniu's spirit when armed struggle broke out in Leshan in summer 1967. The armed struggle in Sichuan was different from elsewhere because the combatants used light machine guns and conventional weapons. It was not only workers but also fourteen- and fifteen-year-old Little Red Guards from middle schools whose blood flowed through the streets of the river city. Young lives were meaninglessly sacrificed to random bullets. Wu Ziniu himself witnessed the chilling sight of a young Red Guard on a high building hit by a stray bullet in the night as he tried to use a searchlight to pick out the enemy. The victim's face, pale after the loss of so much blood, was etched in Wu Ziniu's mind forever. Perhaps it was completely subconscious, or perhaps it was early maturity promoted by this massacre, but in his imagination the precious blood of young lives became like thick plasma ground under the millstone of history. In 1990, the adult Wu Ziniu poured all this into filming *The Big Mill*.

His parents had been transferred to a remote and poor area of the countryside. There was little hope of recovery for his sister, who was struggling in a ward of the mental hospital. On a foggy and overcast southern Sichuan day, carrying some clothes and a case of books, Wu Ziniu set off alone on 17 January 1969 to work and settle in the countryside. He lodged with an old and poor farmer in Angu Commune's No. 1 Red Flag Brigade. Wu Ziniu's annual ration was thirty-five pounds of rice and flour, along with some sweet potatoes, turnips, rice bran, and other miscellaneous grains. Each month he was allowed three and a half ounces of oil and seven ounces of meat. He gave over all of his allotted rations to the impoverished old farmer, who was in his seventies, because he had become the son in the household.

For a young man like Wu Ziniu, who had grown up in the city, carrying a 90 pound load of grain was no small thing. After only a few hundred yards he felt as though his shoulders were going to split open. But after a year, he could carry a 190 pound load for a mile without getting short of breath, and he carried a few dozen such loads back and forth every day. He had become a tough and sturdy farmer. History is a millstone and so is life. A tree stump has annual growth rings, and the calluses on our hands also show fine lines of growth. When Wu Ziniu first arrived in the countryside in 1969 his daily wage was only eight Chinese cents. But by 1972 it had increased to thirty-five cents a day, a princely sum back then.

An important job assigned to the educated youths who left the cities to labor in rural areas was the collection of human manure for the brigade. At first they scooped it out from the toilets in nearby towns and carried it, suspended from shoulder poles, several miles along a mountain path back to the village. That certainly made them learn how to use the shoulder pole! Later, a log from a raft that had broken up in strong currents came floating down the Dadu River. The educated youths turned it into a boat for transporting the manure, thereby increasing their efficiency severalfold in one step. They stood chest-high in the manure pits scooping it out for all they were worth. When they had emptied out the toilets from the communes and towns far and near, they sent the thick manure they had collected back to the village in boatloads. Once they got to the village, they would fill the boat with water to flush the manure out.

Given their efforts, they quickly reached and exceeded the target they had been set for manure collection, fulfilling the annual work quota in less than two and a half months. That meant they could sit in their thatched huts and read for the next eight or nine months. Books were their companions in the night, their friends in times of loneliness, their lamps in the darkness, and their charcoal fires in the chill of winter. By the light of a pine torch, Wu Ziniu devoured a pile of classics night after night, his shack filled with smoke. He could not afford cigarettes, so he rolled up the dust from tea leaves and smoked that. Later, he even smoked eggplant leaves and moss. Behind the mountain, not far from his home, lived a Rightist who wore glasses—a teacher who had been sent to the countryside.[16] Silent and wooden, he rose with the sun to go to work and rested when it set. People laughed because he had the thin appearance of a scholar but the tanned skin of a farmer. However, his demeanor also made them respect him. He had no possessions except for a room full of books. Although he did not say anything to Wu Ziniu, he opened his door to him and let him choose freely from among the volumes. From these works Wu Ziniu, who only had a middle school education, received a strict training in Chinese classical literature, especially in the classics of poetry.

> Parting from the dead, I've stifled my sobs,
> but this parting from the living brings me constant pain.
> South of the Yangtze is a land of plague and fever;
> no word comes from the exile.

> Now that you're caught in the meshes of the law
> how could you have wings to fly with?

> Where you go, waters are deep, the waves so wide—
> don't let the dragons, the horned dragons harm you![17]

The Cultural Revolution packed a lifetime of experience into a ten-year period. The twenty million educated youths studied wherever they happened to be in the countryside. They read the major classics of Chinese history and compared Marxism with all sorts of other political theories. But they did not only study written texts. They also learned Chinese history and pondered China's future through their experience of endless labor in slash and burn cultivation as the days and months passed by, year in and year out.

Being recruited as a laborer, enlisting in the military, going into the mines, and working on the railway—every job opportunity and hope of returning to the city turned out to be a mirage for Wu Ziniu. He despaired seeing the other educated youths around him go back one by one for school or through job transfers. He began binge drinking on the sly, drowning his sorrows behind closed doors, which made him wild-tempered and brutal. Getting into fights over the slightest reason, he was always determined

Wu Ziniu in the 1970s.
Photo courtesy of
Wu Ziniu.

to win whatever the cost; people would say, "There's an educated youth in Angu who can recite Tang poetry and who can fight. Whatever you do, don't get him mad!" But Wu Ziniu accepted his fate and prepared to spend the rest of his life on the banks of the Dadu River. When he got drunk, he would dream up schemes, saying, "I'll take my knife and go to Mount Liang! I'll become a bandit and live as a free man for the rest of my life!" But once he sobered up, he still had to take his hoe and go down to the fields.

During the season for transplanting rice seedlings in 1972, a brigade cadre came and called Wu Ziniu out from the fields. He said people had come from the Leshan Mao Zedong Thought Literature and Arts College looking for students, and he suggested Wu Ziniu go see them and give it a try. "No!" Wu Ziniu replied, "The work recruiters have been here dozens of times, and I've filled in countless forms already! Where did it get me?" He looked fiercely at the cadre like a wild beast alert to a dangerous bait. The cadre stepped back and said, "I'm just letting you know. It's up to you whether you go."

He was accepted into the college.

At the school they said he looked like the character of Hong Chang-qing.[18] Maybe one day he could do his bit for the model operas and take over from the battle-scarred, no-longer-so-young actor then playing Hong.

Wu Ziniu thought the idea was ridiculous. He did not think he resembled the saintly revolutionary pioneer Hong Changqing at all. But if it had not been for Hong Changqing, he would never have got out of the countryside, never mind back to the city. Because they said he resembled Hong Changqing, after all those missed opportunities when people came to recruit workers, now it was his turn.

At the Leshan Mao Zedong Thought Literature and Arts College, Wu Ziniu did everything from transcribing scripts to cutting stencils for mimeographs, playing musical instruments, taking part in crowd scenes, and joining the orchestra. Whatever the Mao Zedong Thought Propaganda Team needed, he gave it his all. He kept silent, put his head down, and went to work. This chance to return to the city had been harder to come by than a ticket into heaven, and so he intended to make the most of it. He took the opportunity offered by cleaning work to open the cultural troupe's library, which had been sealed at the start of the Cultural Revolution. Stored there were many teaching materials from the Central Academy of Drama that had been published before 1966. There were also works of literary history and theory, anthologies of Shakespeare and the plays of Yuan dynasty dramatist Guan Hanqing, and even the journal specially devoted to the translation of foreign theory, *Translations on Film Art* (later known as *World Cinema*).

On 6 October 1976, the Gang of Four was arrested in Beijing and the Cultural Revolution finally came to an end.

> Beyond Swords, we suddenly learn they regained North Thorn!
> When first I heard, falling tears flooded down my robes.
> Turning to see my wife and children—where is there any woe!
> Wildly roll up my verses and books—nearly crazed with joy.
> In broad daylight sing out loud, indulge yourself with wine!
> Green springtime will escort us, just right for going home.
> Once through Ophid Gorge, we'll thread Witch Gorge,
> Then straight down to Xiangyang, and on toward Loyang![19]

Wu Ziniu stood by the river alone. Facing Leshan's enormous Buddha, he looked at the turbulent river. The man who had not shed a tear for ten years was overcome with the emotions conjured up by the scenery, and wept.

■

Wu Ziniu sailed through all the elements of the Academy's admission exam, especially the story composition portion. For the latter, he spoke about a small event during the dark days of the long-distant past when he helped to protect a middle school teacher. When his seven minutes were up, he stopped of his own accord. But Situ Zhaodun looked at him carefully and said, "Go on, continue."

Wu Ziniu knew then that there was hope he might get the enrollment papers for the Academy. What he did not know was that the thin, sallow-faced, serious man in front of him had spent seven years, from 1967 to 1974, in a Gang of Four jail because he was caught flipping through a Shanghai pictorial from the 1930s that had some photos of Mao's wife, Jiang Qing, when she was a film star.

■

That year, Wu Ziniu, Zhang Junzhao, Chen Kaige, and Tian Zhuang-zhuang were all already twenty-six years old. They had already experienced the highs and lows of life. They faced the university entrance examiners as mature men, well prepared in their own areas of expertise and ready to compete for places on the list. Liu Miaomiao, however, was different. She was just sixteen—a decade younger than her opponents, who were like elder brothers to her. The professors hesitated over her age, but she argued that "in your regulations you only stated an upper age limit. There was never anything about a lower limit. You didn't say sixteen-year-old students couldn't apply or enroll. I might be too young, but I'll grow up!"

The professors decided they could not avoid the issue. They had to admit this girl from Ningxia because of her quick-witted enthusiasm, her verbal ability, the breadth of her literary knowledge, and her outstand-ingly imaginative performance in the acting piece. When Liu Miaomiao was instructed to take the role of one of Premier Zhou's nurses determin-ing how to talk to the sick premier, she gave a most vivid performance. A girl with only a fifth-grade primary school education, she had earnestly read *A Dream of Red Mansions* twice. Maybe it is hard to credit him now, but in Chairman Mao's teachings he says that no one has the right to ex-press an opinion unless they have read *A Dream of Red Mansions* at least five times. He also said that *A Dream of Red Mansions* was the history of a feudal society in decline and the story of class struggle. Liu Miaomiao's father had a friend who was an educated man in the Ningxia Autonomous Region, an elderly, non-Party personality. He had hundreds and thousands of books in his home, with ancient and modern classics overflowing the shelves. On her way home from school every day, Liu Miaomiao would go to this uncle's library and read for a couple of hours before returning home for dinner. Sometimes she'd forget the time because she was reading. Then the old couple would have her stay for a snack, something they called a "salad." It was there that her mind was opened and she received a real education. Of course, she not only read *A Dream of Red Mansions* in this home with its cosmopolitan atmosphere. She read many other works, too.

Ningxia has been a garrison province and a site for military campaigning since ancient times.

> Breaking the hoary grass, the northern wind whirls low,
> In the eighth month the Tartar sky is filled with snow.[20]

> Do you not see the Running-Horse River flow along the sea of snow
> And sand has yellowed sky and earth, high and low?
> In the ninth month at Wheel Tower winds howl at night,
> The River fills with broken stones fallen from the height,
> Which run riot with howling winds as if in flight.[21]

Beginning in the 1950s, armies of exiles were sent to Ningxia again. Many were highly cultured people disgraced in political movements. However, the locals are unsophisticated and forgiving, and in their distant hinterland receiving exiles was an age-old tradition. As a result, one wound after another healed and grief and indignation became a source of strength. An example is seen in the work of Zhang Xianliang, the representative author of the post–Cultural Revolution "literature of the wounded." His works include *Body and Soul* (adapted into the film *The Herdsman* by Xie Jin in 1982), *Mimosa,* and *Half of Man Is Woman,* where sorrow and joy mix together in vast deserts and soft expanses of winter snow.[22]

Liu Miaomiao was born and grew up in Ningxia. She was used to seeing the vast wilderness of the desert and to walking through high winds and deep gullies. Many years later, when her film *Innocent Babbler* was received with warm applause at the Venice International Film Festival in September 1993, she suddenly found herself weeping. People overseas had understood

Hou Yong on location in Xishuangbanna for *Red Elephant*. Photo courtesy of Hou Yong.

her Ningxia—her desert, her snowy mountains, and her story about children in the villages at the foot of those snowy mountains. And they were moved. At that moment she told herself that she had caught up with her elder brothers who were a whole decade older than her. "You always said I was young. But after ten years of obscure silence, now I've caught up with the pack. I've caught up with you."

While the intense exams for the Directing Department were underway, Cao Zuobin, an old teacher from the Cinematography Department, went to Xi'an Municipal Film Distribution Company to rent a print for the candidates' film analysis exam. In a room there he happened to see a wall full of sketches and gouache works. They seemed to be exercises by a beginner, but they had talent and spirit. Cao immediately asked who had painted them, and a technician in the company replied that they were by her son.

"Would your son like to try out for the Film Academy?"

"But of course!"

"Has he signed up for the exam?"

"We only just found out about it, so I'm afraid he wouldn't make it.

And besides, we don't know how to help prepare him for the other topics in the exam."

"Do you want to sign up now?"

"Can we? If you allow my son to sign up, then you'll be doing us a great favor. The whole family will be grateful."

"What's your son called?"

"His name is Hou Yong."

■

That is how the fate of the future cinematographer of *On the Hunting Ground, Horse Thief, Dr. Sun Yat-sen* (1987), and *Evening Bell* was decided. He joined the following list of candidates. Some of the works they later shot are given with their names.

GU CHANGWEI: *At the Beach* (1984), *King of the Children, Red Sorghum, Ju Dou* (1990), *Life on a String* (1991), *Farewell, My Concubine*, and *In the Heat of the Sun* (1995).

ZHAO FEI: *A Question for the Living* (1987), *Chief Eunuch Li Lianying* (1992), *Samsara* (1988), *Raise the Red Lantern* (1992), *The Sun Has Ears* (1995), *The Emperor and the Assassin* (1998), *Be There or Be Square* (1998), and *Sweet and Lowdown* (1998).

WANG XIAOLIE: *The Last Clue* (1985), *Troubleshooters* (1988), *Heaven's Blood* (1991), and *Story from Yunnan* (1994).

ZHI LEI: *At the Beach, Ballad of the Yellow River* (1989), *In Their Prime* (1986), and *On the Beat* (1995).

The first hurdle in the entrance exam was sketching. The sound of brushes on paper filled the room. Facing a plaster figure, a group of young men concentrated intensely on their work. No one could have imagined what they would bring to the Chinese cinema over the next decade. They seemed so shy and withdrawn. They were not at all like the candidates over at the exam site for the Directing Department. Among these quiet young men were Hou Yong, nervous and even timorous, and Gu Changwei, who kept to himself and was not a good talker. It is hard to understand what enabled them to transfer their strong and clear pictorial sense into the language of camera movement and light, and thereby transform the visual style of Chinese cinema. Were they influenced by the stone carvings of the Han dynasty and the kingdom of Wei? Or the terracotta warriors of the Qin dynasty? Or the Qin emperor's tombs? Or maybe the Chang'an school of landscape painting?

"I don't like Chinese painting and I rarely refer to it," Gu Changwei said not long after finishing *Farewell, My Concubine.* "Of course the films Chinese people make have a Chinese feel, that's for sure. But that doesn't mean we have to obsess about searching for our roots in traditional painting. There's no need for that. I like Western paintings because they have light. Light is so fascinating! When I was a kid, I liked to watch the clouds. They would block out the sun—slowly, slowly moving across it. Suddenly, a ray of light would burst through, shooting down to the ground like an arrow. All the ground was in shadow, but in the distance there was this one small spot of light. And as that spot moved, it suddenly felt as though the god of nature was beckoning. It felt sort of cosmic."

■

As the selection process at the Xi'an exam site was nearing an end, several teachers from the Cinematography Department met with a taciturn young man in an empty room. His eyes were attentive and his expression serious. Although he was only in his twenties, there were already two deep lines at the corners of his mouth. This was Zhang Yimou.

Right up to the day before the exam, the teachers at the Xi'an exam site had been doing their very best to think of a way he could enroll. But the order from Beijing was to proceed according to the regulations. The professors were still divided. One group was struggling to bend the rules and let him register. The other group was insisting the system could not be changed at will, or else a huge number of candidates past the age limit would demand the right to register and things would get out of control. However, regardless of which side they took, everyone agreed that Zhang Yimou had a rare talent for photography. He had to be supported—they absolutely could not let him fall by the wayside. But the exam was already almost over.

With deep sympathy, they told Zhang Yimou they wanted to help but there was nothing they could do. All they could try was to contact the *Shaanxi Pictorial* and the Xi'an Film Studio to see if either place would take him as a photographer or as an assistant to a cinematographer. They hoped that way he could learn to become a top photographer on the job.

Zhang Yimou was silently grateful. What more could he ask? They were showing great concern for him, and he was six years over the limit. However, in his heart he still wanted to go to college.

He would teach himself! He had already paid a price and struggled ten times more than anyone else, maybe even dozens of times more. But he still dreamed day and night of going to college. Surely his family background could not have predetermined that he would be excluded from the sacred halls of academe forever?

Zhang Yimou was born in Xi'an in Shaanxi Province in 1950. His father had been in the KMT Nationalist Army. The fact that his father and his two uncles had all graduated from the Huangpu Military Academy determined the political situation of the whole family after the establishment of the People's Republic in 1949.[23] Zhang's oldest uncle had gone to Taiwan before 1949. His second uncle had been killed by the KMT before he managed to make it to the safety of the Chinese Communist Party base at Yan'an. Nonetheless, he was labeled an "enemy on the run" for a long time after the Liberation. This added to his whole family's misfortunes. From the age of thirty on, for over half his life, Zhang Yimou's father carried problems from his past like a weight around his neck, and he could not throw them off. As a result, Zhang Yimou lived in his father's political shadow from childhood. His memories were completely different from those of other children. His problems did not start in 1966 but had been fated from birth. Many years later he recalled, "Some cadres' children were also attacked during the Cultural Revolution, and they suffered a lot. But after the Cultural Revolution they were rehabilitated. It was different for people like us. They say you spend thirty years on the bad side of the river then thirty years on the good side, meaning that your fate is always unpredictable. But I was always kept on one side of the river."

Perhaps it was precisely because of this that Zhang Yimou seemed more serious and mature than the others, and even more optimistic. In China, people like to say, "At thirty I stood firm, at forty I was free from doubts, and at fifty I understood the laws of Heaven."[24] But for Zhang Yimou, there was no "standing firm," only "the laws of heaven." To live is more important than anything else, more real. And only when you can live peacefully can you stand up on your own two feet.

When the Cultural Revolution began, Zhang Yimou's father was sent to herd sheep in the Shaanxi countryside. His mother, a doctor, was also sent to the country. On 26 December 1968, he went down to work in the countryside together with his classmates. They settled in the second team of Beini Brigade at Hangong Commune in Shaanxi Province's Qian County. And so Zhang Yimou became one of the educated youths sent down to the countryside. But he packed up and left home calmly, because to him this was an inevitable return to his roots. In fact, the conditions at Beini Brigade were even somewhat better than he had expected. Zhang Yimou was not the sort to take a bleak outlook on the world, blaming everyone but himself. He just accepted fate and took a positive attitude. He was physically strong, with legs like a soccer player's. He ate well, slept well, had energy, and was stoical. He could perform any kind of heavy labor. He took red and white paint, brushes, a straightedge, and all manner of Chairman Mao images and badges with him to the countryside. The very day he arrived, ignoring a heavy snowfall, he painted an enormous image of Chairman Mao on the door to the production brigade's livestock pens. He wrote a couplet down the sides of the image. On one side it said, "Limitless Loyalty to Mao Zedong Thought!" And on the other side, "Firmly Implement Chairman Mao's Revolutionary Line!" The news that the livestock pens had taken on a new look flashed around the whole village. The brigade leaders were very pleased, praising Yimou as a good educated youth who followed Chairman Mao's words. "How about this?" they said. "You're talented. Take your time and paint our brigade offices, the threshing ground buildings, and all the houses. That way the commune members can look up and see Chairman Mao wherever they go."

Zhang Yimou worked in the countryside for three years as an agricultural laborer and painter. He painted the image of Chairman Mao on all the houses in Beini Brigade one after the other, working hard to win the praise and love of the country people. "Yimou is a good son of our Beini Village," they said. Zhang Yimou represented this personal experience very vividly in his 1994 film *To Live*.

In 1971, state-owned cotton mill No. 8 in Xianyang in Shaanxi Province was looking for workers. Zhang Yimou was selected because he could paint and play basketball well.

Every day, for several hours at a time, he hauled bales of raw material weighing more than 100 pounds into the workshops, or he would tear

Etchings of Mao Zedong by Zhang Yimou. Photo from *The History of Art in New China* (Beijing: China Youth Press, 2000), 30.

The Abyss, by Isaak Levitan. Photo from *Landscapes in Oil Masterpieces* (Shenyang: Liaoning Fine Arts Press, 2000), 130.

apart thick layers of materials. He would do this repetitive physical labor patiently, working so hard that sweat soaked his back. But when the day's work was over and he had cleaned up, he stretched out on his wooden plank and stared up at the darkened old ceiling, wondering, "Surely my life can't go on like this forever?"

It was 1974. Even the most imaginative person in the world would not have indulged the wild fantasy that a young worker from a cotton mill in Xianyang in Shaanxi would one day stride out onto the stage to accept awards at international film festivals in Europe. But in fact, this mythlike narrative began to unfold one day in 1974. For that was when twenty-four-year-old Zhang Yimou decided to save his money for a Chinese-made Seagull brand camera.

It all started when he went to see a friend who was a student in the Oil Painting Department of the Xi'an Academy of Fine Arts. A landscape in oils hung above the head of his bed; it was a copy of a painting called *The Abyss* by the late-nineteenth-century Russian painter Isaak Levitan. Because it was a real oil painting, not a print, Zhang Yimou was awestruck. The dusk light, the pool and the inverted image in it, the dense forest, the mesmerizing power of the colors, and even the sense of the fresh smell of the air in the forest all had an enormous impact on him. He sat there staring for a very long time, not wanting to tear his eyes away. Bitterly he recognized that it was too late for him to attain such a level of artistic skill in painting. But photography was still completely possible. He would study photography! Absolutely! That was what he would do! And so it was decided.

He did everything, through hard labor, to save money, and eventually he bought the Seagull camera made in Shanghai. He also borrowed tomes on the art of photography written by the famous photographers Huang Xiang and Xue Zijiang before the Cultural Revolution. He buried his head in the books, but when the time to return them arrived and he had to relinquish them, he acted on the saying: "Reading a thousand times does not compare with copying once." And so Zhang Yimou copied by hand the entire text of the two books, word by word and sentence by sentence, including the diagrams, legends, and even the photos themselves. From this point on, he formed the habit of laboring by day and copying out books and developing photographs by night.

Zhang Yimou climbed Mount Huashan eleven times to shoot landscape photographs. The trip to Mount Huashan from Xianyang takes more than ten hours, and requires travel through Xi'an, Mengyuan, and Huayang counties, followed by a bus ride to Mount Huashan. Taking the traveling into account, Zhang Yimou could only spend a few hours on the mountain. On each of the eleven trips, he was restricted to the period between Saturday afternoon and Monday morning, because he could not skip work and dared even less to ask for a leave. Through four years of crazy obsession and repeated effort, working under extremely simple and crude conditions, he learned film developing and printing. His black-and-white work reached a level of mastery exceptional even for a professional photographer. When he sent his album of neatly mounted prints to the teachers of the Cinematography Department, everyone realized that a student like this was the find of a lifetime. But nobody could change the rules for admission.

When the process of selecting the students for the Academy in 1978 was complete and the letters of notification had all been sent out, it seemed that Zhang Yimou's fate was sealed. However, there was a light at the end of the tunnel, and he was unexpectedly rescued.

The then Minister of Culture, Huang Zhen, sent two directives to the

Academy concerning the selection of students. The first stated that because there was such a large number of outstanding candidates that year and because art colleges had not been able to accept students for so many years, there was clearly a large pool of talent. Therefore, he hoped they would consider increasing their admissions, which would be good for the development of film personnel and the industry itself. Second, he had heard about the especially talented photographer Zhang Yimou, and the fact that he had not been able to take the entrance exam because he was over the age limit. He hoped they would enroll him and let him study for two years, with an emphasis on still photography. Then, after the two years, they could consider sending him to work at the Central News and Documentary Film Studio as a news and still photographer.

As far as the first directive was concerned, the leaders of the Academy were delighted to implement it. They increased the enrollment from the original 120 to 150. But they found the second directive hard to accept. What were the implications of a tertiary-level institution accepting a student who had not taken the entrance exam? How would it be able to maintain its reputation and prestige or its system and rules in the future?

The faculty in the Cinematography Department developed a strongly resistant attitude. "Surely we are as clear as you are about the talent and standard of this applicant, Minister? Are we cold and unfeeling and only you have great foresight? And now you arrive like a hero on a winged steed?"

The standoff continued for several days. In the end, the Academy made a decision. It was a decision with unforeseen results for art in years to come. They sent an official letter—but not a letter notifying a student of a place—to cotton mill No. 8 in Xianyang in Shaanxi. It said: "According to a directive from above, we have decided to accept your worker Zhang Yimou as a student in the Cinematography Department at our college. Please ask him to come to our college on 30 October with his ID, household residence permit, and your ration coupons to complete enrollment procedures."

■

Never before and never since has Beijing Film Academy accepted a student who did not take the entrance exam. How will history judge the merits and demerits of this breach in the enrollment rules?

Zhang Yimou did complete four years of classes with excellent results.

Not only were his graduation results outstanding, but his later triumph in the international film scene also proved on all accounts that he could have a clear conscience about his irregular enrollment, in regards to both the Film Academy and Chinese film history.

Victors are not bound by rules, and history is a record of victors. But what about the system? What about justice? What about giving equal opportunities to all? Certainly, no exam can be completely fair. But especially in the unforgettable year 1978, when fate created opportunity and prospects for some people did it also close the door for others? Was another Zhang Yimou left out from history? Still, that is the way history develops.

Happiness and unhappiness, justice and injustice, fate and chance, will and accident, suffering and joy all flow together in the river of life. In just the same way, heroes overcome all difficulties and acquire battle scars on the way to their triumphs, while ordinary people are fated to live and die in obscurity.

■

Zhuxin Village, September 1978.

All over the country, the successful candidates for the Beijing Film Academy were saying goodbye to their loved ones. They were shouldering their bags and traveling from the north and the south toward the Academy, toward a college outside the city, surrounded by fields.

But this time was different from their earlier journeys up into the mountains and down to the countryside. This time every student's heart was beating with hopes and dreams for the blossoming of Chinese cinema.

Zhuxin Village, are you ready for us?

CHAPTER 2

NOSES TO THE GRINDSTONE

■

September 1978—the autumn sky was clear and boundless and the air crisp and fresh, as Zhuxin Village welcomed more than 150 Beijing Film Academy freshmen. Full of excitement, they burst through the green, shady entrance. Although the Beijing Film Academy sign was on the concrete gatepost, the site was once the Beijing Agricultural Labor University. Therefore, the campus was large and surrounded by over eighty acres of fields, along with nearly fifteen acres of experimental orchards and about one hundred acres of dairy cattle pastures opposite the campus. It was a veritable arcadia.

How did a film school come to occupy an agricultural college campus? It is said that Mao Zedong remarked that it was absurd for an agricultural university to be close to the city. So, in 1969 the entire faculty and student body of the Beijing Agricultural Labor University were transferred to counties outside the metropolitan area for work and study. It was a vast campus, completely empty and padlocked. Only a small team had been left behind to look after the clutch of buildings huddled in the fields.

In 1970, Mao's wife Jiang Qing wanted to set up a university of the arts modeled on the Lu Xun Academy of the Arts in Yan'an for her model opera

The cinematography class of 1982, photographed on entry to the Academy. First row: first from left, Zheng Ming; second, Xiao Feng; fourth, Zhang Huijun. Second row: first from right, Zhang Yimou; sixth, Deng Wei; first from left, Gu Changwei. Third row: third from right, Hou Yong. Photo courtesy of Hou Yong.

The campus of the Beijing Film Academy was at Xiaoxitian in the fifties and sixties. Photo courtesy of Beijing Film Academy.

reserve forces.[1] The teaching of music, opera, dance, and film was to be brought together. The students in this new institution would both study and engage in labor, and it would be called the Central May Seventh University of the Arts.[2] On the recommendation of one of her subordinates, Jiang Qing was chauffeured to the outskirts of Beijing. There, she selected this campus and ordered a total reconstruction of the original buildings into dance rehearsal studios and acting classrooms. Next to the orchards she had a dozen new music studios built, and requested the transfer of pianos from the city to the conservatory. She also had two film studios built for the academy's use. Then instructions to move out to Zhuxin Village and start teaching were issued to four art colleges: the Central Conservatorium, the Beijing Dance Academy, the Beijing Opera College, and the Beijing Film Academy.

There is no going back to the past, however, and Beijing in the seventies could not be the border town Yan'an in the forties. The students of the music, opera, and dance schools did not spend a single day on this rural estate far from the city center. Their heads were swimming with Jiang Qing's model opera concoctions. How could they tough it out in these lonely fields? Jiang Qing's trusted followers headed the colleges, and one

On the Xiaoxitian campus of the Academy. Photo courtesy of Beijing Film Academy.

after another they complained to her, begging to move back to the city. Their requests were approved very quickly, and the music, opera, and dance colleges returned to their original city addresses.

Therefore, the Beijing Film Academy was the only college left at the so-called Central May Seventh University of the Arts in Zhuxin Village. It stayed put, alone, in glorious isolation. Soon, orders were given for its original address in the city to be taken over by a cultural organization under Jiang Qing's direction, and courses in filmmaking began on the campus of the Agricultural Labor University.

The tragedies of history sometimes become the first steps toward happy endings, just as mistakes in the editing room often produce unimagined montages. Chen Kaige and Tian Zhuangzhuang later pried off the locks of the neglected music studios and used them as private studies in which to read and debate into the small hours. The abandoned dance studios were insulated for sound and converted into film studios. Zhuxin Village, seen as a wild and barren place by Jiang Qing's followers, went on to become the cradle of China's New Wave cinema. Every cloud has a silver lining.

In fall 1978, the cluster of buildings jutting out of the fields filled with noise and bustle. The lights in the library and the student dorms were often lit well into the night, sometimes until dawn. Gone forever was yesteryear's scene of a solitary light in the janitor's room casting one old man's shadow. On the campus beneath the towering poplars, students hurried back and forth clutching books and cameras, their eyes sharp and alert and their demeanors serious and responsible. In fact, most of them knew little about film and some were even complete beginners.

Between 18 and 22 December 1978, the Third Plenum of the Eleventh Central Committee of the Communist Party of China was held in Beijing. This was not a routine session. It put an end to the incorrect "Two Whatevers" policy and the use of the slogan "Take class struggle as the key link."[3] It also made the decision to shift the entire focus of the Party's work to economic construction, and it launched rural experiments in economic reform. Even more important, it decided to reverse the incorrect verdicts on the 1976 Tiananmen Square incident and against Deng Xiaoping,[4] and it began the wholesale rectification of all sorts of misguided policies and unjust and erroneous judgments of individuals during the Cultural Revolution. This meeting was a historic watershed that brought an end to the calamitous Cultural Revolution and ushered in a new era of socialist construction.[5]

The Beijing Film Academy class of 1982 undertook their program of

Wu Ziniu in front of the Zhuxin campus gate. Photo courtesy of Wu Ziniu.

study in this unusual period. The four years between 1978 and 1982 were truly the liveliest in the movement to liberate thought.

The teachers in charge of the directing class of 1978 were Wang Suihan and Situ Zhaodun. Wang greeted the new students with solemn words: "We were forced to stop teaching during the Cultural Revolution decade. But now with your class everything has started over again. However, having stopped for so long, we're not so sure how to teach you. Still, we promise to do our very best and we hope you will, too. There's something I want to say to you from the bottom of my heart. Being a film director is a heavy responsibility. A film costs millions, enough to build a medium-sized hospital. While the country is still so poor, that really is a lot of money. Regardless of whether it's a hit or not, shooting a film is a major undertaking. I hope you will always bear this in mind." Situ Zhaodan added, "The twenty-eight of you must resolve to be original and not copy your predecessors. If twenty-eight little Situs hatch after your graduation, that will be very disappointing! I trust that will not happen."

These were the first admonitions addressed to the students.

The Beijing Film Academy was set up in 1956 according to the Soviet educational model. The three core courses in the Directing Department were "The Art of Film Direction" (which included acting classes), "Film Montage Theory," and "Screenwriting," and they were designed after consulting Soviet teaching materials. All pre–Cultural Revolution classes of directing students had been taught using this model. Now, with the directing class of 1982, the method was revived.

First, the Directing Department asked Chen Wenjing, Tian Jinfu, Xu Tongjun, and two other Acting Department teachers to organize an instruction and research group to systematically teach acting. Standard texts included Cao Yu's *Thunderstorm, Sunrise,* and *The Peking Man,* Lao She's *Rickshaw Boy* and *Teahouse,* and Tian Han's *The Death of a Famous Opera Performer.*[6] There was also a list of foreign standard texts, including Ibsen, Shakespeare, and Chekhov.

Thunderstorm is a 1930s Chinese play set in a city. It describes complex entanglements in the household of a mining company board chairman called Zhou Puyuan. The elderly Zhou and his beautiful second wife, Fanny, are mismatched and do not get along. In Zhou's labyrinthine mansion the days pass like years for Fanny, but she has a secret affair with his eldest son, Zhou Ping. However, Zhou Ping tires of his stepmother and

The directing class of 1982 rehearsing Cao Yu's *Thunderstorm*. From left: Geng Xiaozhen, Li Shaohong, and Tian Zhuangzhuang. Photo courtesy of Beijing Film Academy.

wants to dump her. He plots to elope with the servant girl, Si Feng. Si Feng's mother, Lu, was Zhou Puyuan's lover in his youth. She was a Zhou family servant who had a secret affair with the young Zhou Puyuan and was later expelled from the household. Si Feng and Zhou Ping are thus half-brother and half-sister, with the same father but different mothers. Once all of these relationships are unexpectedly revealed by various coincidences and reunions, a tremendous battle breaks out in the Zhou household, causing the disintegration of the rich and powerful family. This play, which combines Western classical drama and Chinese family melodrama, has maintained its popularity over half a century, exciting one generation of audiences after another. The tragic figure of Fanny has long been an important role for leading actresses of the Chinese stage, and many have become stars through their performance of the role.

When the directing class of 1982 rehearsed a scene from *Thunderstorm*, Li Shaohong played Fanny, Tian Zhuangzhuang was Zhou Ping, Liu Miaomiao was Si Feng, and Xie Xiaojing was Zhou Puyuan. The teacher in charge, Chen Wenjing, is very fond of Li Shaohong and to this day remembers the scene in the classroom. However, Li Shaohong maintains that she has no talent as a performer, because she is so rational and controlled she is only good at directing others. Indeed, it was asking a lot of a girl who had grown up in People's Liberation Army housing during the sixties and seventies to develop a thorough and subtle grasp of the emotions and psychology of a woman in a capitalist household in the thirties!

Many of his classmates remember Tian Zhuangzhuang as someone who just muddled through the acting classes. It was not that he did not care about the class. But he wondered about the importance of such a stage-centered class for a film director. He felt that it was not even good material for the theater—it was so exaggerated that it made your flesh crawl. So he always appeared compliant but only on the surface, and he often left his partners on the stage completely at a loss.

What follows is one particularly passionate and moving scene in *Thunderstorm*, in which Zhou Ping decides to elope with Si Feng:

The directing class of 1982 rehearsing Cao Yu's *Thunderstorm*. From right: Xie Xiaojing, Tian Zhuangzhuang, and Li Shaohong. Photo courtesy of Beijing Film Academy.

The acting class of 1982 rehearsing Lao She's *Rickshaw Boy*. Standing on the left is Fang Shu, who went on to star in a film version of *Thunderstorm*. Crouching is Xie Yuan, who went on to star in *One and Eight*. From left, the other actors are Zhang Chao, Zhao Yong, Zhang Zhiqiang, and Wang Yuzhang. Photo courtesy of Beijing Film Academy.

SI FENG: (*incredulous*): What, go this minute?

ZHOU PING: (*tenderly*): Yes. I was intending to go alone and then come back for you later, but there's no need to wait now.

SI FENG: (*still incredulous*): You really mean it? We'll go together?

ZHOU PING: Yes, I really mean it.

SI FENG: (*delirious with joy, she seizes Zhou Ping's hands and kisses them wildly, while tears stream down her cheeks*): So it's true! It's true, then! Oh, Ping! You're the best man in the world! You're my—I love you! (*She continues to weep*)

ZHOU PING: (*wiping her tears away*): Feng, from now on we'll always be together!

SI FENG: (*drawing herself into his embrace*): Yes, once we get away from here, we'll never be apart again.

Liu Miaomiao played the role of Si Feng in a sincere, heartfelt manner, strictly according to Stanislavsky's method: "Truly listen, truly look, and truly feel." Tian Zhuangzhuang was the young master, and as Liu knelt before him again and again, he almost taunted her.

"OK, OK," he said. "Near enough'll do. You don't need to pretend it's for real, do you?"

Liu Miaomiao was stunned and did not know what to do.

"So, are you telling me to act or not to act?" she asked.

Perhaps because his own parents were very accomplished actors, Tian Zhuangzhuang had long ceased to be awed by the mysteries of the stage. He had seen so much since childhood that he had become alienated from the pretentious and exaggerated world of stage and film acting. He had a particular aversion to hamming it up and was so opposed to contrived melodramatic plots that he rejected dramatization altogether. This fascination with life in the raw had a direct impact on the style of his early works. When he made the short exercise films *Our Corner* (1980) and *The Yard* (1980), his aesthetic preference for documentary-style realism and nonfiction narratives was already quite apparent.

Another group in the acting class rehearsed Lao She's 1940s novel *Rickshaw Boy,* which was adapted for the stage in the 1950s.

Lao She is an outstanding representative of modern Chinese literature, as well as the standard bearer for the Beijing school of literature. His early works, including *Black Li and White Li, Crescent Moon,* and *Rickshaw Boy,* established his place in China's literary pantheon with their combination of rich Beijing flavor and lucid social critique. His later works—the plays *Dragon Beard Ditch* and *Teahouse,* together with the novel *Beneath the Red Flag*—displayed his skillful and smooth mastery of language.[7] When New China was established in 1949, Lao She resolutely broke off his studies in the United States to return home and sincerely sing the praises of the new society. He wrote many simple, elegant, and moving short stories and plays. However, during the Cultural Revolution in summer 1966, the sudden flood of violence swept away his sincere faith and snapped his proud and upright personality.

Early in the morning of 25 August 1966, on the shores of Peace Lake in the suburbs, someone found Lao She's corpse. In the pocket of his sodden clothes, there was a handwritten copy of a Mao Zedong poem. The day before he died, the Red Guards had humiliated him and conducted a brutal struggle session against him.

Peace Lake is only one hundred yards from the original site of the Beijing Film Academy, and it would be no exaggeration to call it the Academy's own lake. With its light-dappled ripples and shady footpaths, it was fondly

The directing class of 1982 rehearsing Lao She's *Rickshaw Boy*. Chen Kaige (left) plays Fourth Master Liu. On the right is Xia Gang. Photo courtesy of Beijing Film Academy.

remembered by former students who had wandered its shores and opened their hearts to each other there. So, when the staff and students heard that Lao She's corpse had been discovered beside this charming lake, they were shocked and distressed. People went to the quiet lakeside and stood there for a long time, mourning him in silence.

During the sixties, *Rickshaw Boy* was a standard text for exercises in the directing class at the Beijing Film Academy. Now, rehearsing it again after the end of the decade of chaos, students and faculty thought about the past and were overcome with emotion.

When the directing class of 1982 rehearsed *Rickshaw Boy* under the direction of Geng Xiaozhen and Zhao Jinzuo, Chen Kaige played the role of Fourth Master Liu and Zhang Jianya was Xiangzi, the rickshaw boy. Hu Mei played Tiger Girl, Xia Gang was Second Master Feng, and Jin Tao was Big Guy.

Both Zhang Jianya and Hu Mei were professional actors before they entered the Academy, and they could be said to have had plenty of acting experience. Zhang Jianya was a member of the Shanghai Film Studio's acting troupe. Every bone in his body was comic. After graduation, while his classmates were concentrating on tragedy and exploring deep and serious historical themes, he directed one comedy after another. As is evident in *Royal Heart and Soul* (1991), *San Mao Joins the Army* (1992), and *The Romantic Adventures of Mr. Wang* (1993), his style is marked by broad physical comedy, historical satire, and parody of film classics.

Hu Mei came from the theater group in the song and dance ensemble of the People's Liberation Army Central Political Department. She was a young but experienced performer who had acted in plays such as *Ten Thousand Crags and Torrents,* which is about the Long March. But army life had not turned her into a typical model cultural soldier. On the contrary, after graduation she went on to direct the women's films *Army Nurse* and *Far from War,* both of which were full of subtle psychology.

At nearly six feet tall and fully kitted out in a long robe and a mandarin jacket, Chen Kaige was a striking presence in the center of the stage, full of lordly arrogance and rolling a couple of walnuts in the palm of his hand. "Tiger Girl!" he called. "Over here!" His voice rang out like a copper bell, commanding and powerful.

The following exchange occurs at the beginning of the fourth act of *Rickshaw Boy.*

> TIGER GIRL: My hair ribbon?
>
> XIANGZI: It's on your shoulder, isn't it?
>
> TIGER GIRL: (*holding her braid out to Xiangzi for him to tie*): Tie it for me.
>
> XIANGZI: (*making a clumsy effort*): OK.
>
> TIGER GIRL: Forget it. (*Snatching the ribbon away and tying it herself*): I'm telling you, you've been really on the ball the last couple of days. [Fourth Master Liu]'s birthday's coming up and he's really excited. So, if you keep buttering him up, there's hope for us yet.
>
> XIANGZI: We'll see.
>
> (*Fourth Master Liu calls from outside*)
>
> FOURTH MASTER LIU: Tiger Girl! Tiger Girl! Get out here and give me a hand!

"Stop!" shouted Professor Zhang Ke. The room fell silent.

Drawing in his considerable stomach, Zhang Ke strode across and remonstrated, "Hu Mei, you're not playing this scene right. There has to be a teasing and flirtatious undercurrent in your attitude to Xiangzi, a combi-

The directing class of 1982 rehearsing Lao She's *Rickshaw Boy*. Hu Mei plays Tiger Girl and Zhang Jianya plays Xiangzi, the rickshaw boy. Photo courtesy of Beijing Film Academy.

nation of kindness and a desire to control him. You have to use the look in your eyes to lure him over and get him to tie your hair ribbon for you. Let's do it again."

But despite several attempts, Hu Mei was unable to communicate Tiger Girl's teasing and flirtatious undercurrent.

"Stop!" ordered Zhang. "Come over here, Hu Mei. Pick up the thermos and pour out a glass of water, real hot water, and take it over to Xiangzi."

Hu Mei hesitated for a long time, then timorously ventured, "But that's not one of the stage directions, Professor!"

"I know it isn't. I want you to forget about the passage you've just performed and actually pour out a glass of water for Xiangzi and take it over to him."

Hu Mei did as she was told, and Xiangzi took the glass.

"Do you believe in yourself? Do you two believe in the relationship between you?"

Silence. The class waited for Zhang Ke's directions.

"You don't even believe in yourselves. When you tie your ribbon, your movements are utterly mechanical, without any inner meaning. At a time like this, a director has to enable the actors to find a way out of their confusion and to rediscover their confidence. It's true that pouring a glass of

Shen Danping from the Acting Department together with Professor Zhang Ke on an Academy spring outing. Photo courtesy of Zhang Meng.

water isn't in the play. But pouring a glass of water would be a normal everyday exchange between you and Xiangzi. Only when you've discovered how to work together in a truly believable way can the play proceed smoothly. Come on, let's do it again."

Today, years later, Hu Mei still has not forgotten that rehearsal session.

"The point wasn't to turn us into actors," she says. "It was to make us realize what a director must do for the actors when they're rehearsing; how he or she can make them believe in themselves and develop their technique. When I see my classmates' films, like Chen Kaige's *Farewell, My Concubine* and Tian Zhuangzhuang's *Blue Kite,* I see life in the performances. To put it another way, they've directed the actors to underact. When I direct my own films, I often help the actors through their difficulties like that, too. Whenever that happens, I cannot stop myself from thinking of Professor Zhang and the detailed directions he gave us. He was such a skillful and patient old teacher!"

Professor Zhang was short, plump, and elderly. Although he was overweight he was nimble and quick. He was always bright and cheerful, and when he spoke he was crisp and precise. He had high blood pressure and heart disease, but he never let it show and never asked for special treatment. When the school moved out of the city, he took the work bus to and from the Academy. The bus stop was a mile away from his home, but he happily walked the last stretch. He said that this exercise kept him limber and helped him to teach well. Indeed, Chairman Mao's basic principles for maintaining good health were eating lots of vegetables, making the effort to walk, remaining calm in the face of adversity, and being open-minded.

Many members of the Fourth Generation of Chinese film directors were Professor Zhang's students. Wu Yigong, Ding Yinnan, Huang Shuqin, and Wang Haowei all went on to become key players during the transformation of Chinese cinema. Wu Yigong directed *My Memories of Old Beijing* (1981), which won the Best Film award at the Manila International Film Festival. Ding Yinnan directed *Dr. Sun Yat-sen* and *Zhou Enlai* (1991), and Huang Shuqin's *Woman, Demon, Human* (1988) won an award at the Rio de Janeiro International Film Festival. Xie Fei, Zheng Dongtian, Zhang Nuanxin, and Han Xiaolei all remained at the Academy after graduation to teach, but they also continued to direct films. Xie Fei's *Black Snow* (1989) won a Silver Bear award at the Berlin International Film Festival, and his *Woman from the Lake of Scented Souls* (1992) shared the Golden Bear. They were all impressed by Professor Zhang's dedicated teaching and held him in high esteem, addressing him as "Master Ke." Zhang Ke had been a director himself at the Shanghai Film Studio in the early fifties. In his prime, full of vigor, he had directed films such as *The Great Start* (1954), which was about the lives of steelworkers, and the Cantonese opera film *Poem on a Red Leaf* (1962). He was a rising star. But then, because of the demands arising from the establishment of the Beijing Film Academy, he reluctantly gave up his directing career and took up a teaching position. He trained one group of graduates after another and sent them out into the world. He was proud and pleased as he saw one familiar name after another appear on the screen, but he also harbored a quiet sense of loss. Of course, it was a great personal achievement to have students everywhere, but Master Ke was also an active, enthusiastic director. He longed to be rushing around on a film set again, making a few more films of his own.

However, faced with the first undergraduate class after the Cultural Revolution, Zhang Ke put his all into teaching again. He not only trained the acting class but also lectured and tutored the montage class.

The Soviet Union is the birthplace of montage theory and, as founders of the montage school, Eisenstein and Pudovkin made an enormous contribution to film art.[8] In the 1950s, because the Soviet Union was the model for everything, montage became one of the more developed courses at the Beijing Film Academy. It was taught by a woman called Xu Guming, who spoke fluent Russian and had acted as a translator for the Soviet experts. She was very impatient and spoke very rapidly. She often carried a capacious basket in which she kept her lecture notes, reference books, diagrams, and a big tea mug. After she had set all these things, one by one, on the desk, she delivered her lecture at breakneck speed, as fast as a string of firecrackers going off. As she lectured, she looked straight ahead and up, never making eye contact with the students as the words poured from her mouth without a pause. She left many of the students dumbfounded. They could not keep up with her nimble train of thought, to say nothing of being able to take notes. Some people said she looked up as she spoke because she was so short, and the Soviet experts had been so tall that she became used to looking upward. Her machine gun delivery was so rapid and concise because of her experience as an interpreter; she had to jump in and speak quickly in either Russian or Chinese as the Soviet and Chinese experts questioned and answered each other. As a result, when she became a montage expert herself and wanted to take her time expressing herself in the classroom, she found she could not change her ways.

Despite the strange style and speed of her delivery, the students held Xu Guming in the highest esteem. She analyzed every montage technique in detail. Her practical examples were drawn from the classics of early Soviet cinema, such as Pudovkin's *Mother* (1926), Eisenstein's *Battleship Potemkin* (1926), the Vasiliev brothers' *Chapayev* (1934), and Dzigan's *We from Kronstadt* (1936). The students eagerly tried to copy every word she said, carefully noting the composition of every frame and the editing rhythms. They felt that this was a real directing class at last, and that they were getting much more out of it than the endless acting classes.

But not long afterward, the situation changed again.

A student asked a question in class.

"During the last lesson, you said the prime example of metaphorical montage was Eisenstein's *October*. Could we see the film rather than just rely on the written text?"

"I'm so sorry," the teacher answered. "We don't have *October* at the Academy, and neither does the Film Archive."

"Recently, we saw Godard's *Breathless* at the archive. He doesn't edit in the regular manner. How should we classify his montage?"

"We saw a Franco-Greek coproduction by Costa-Gavras called *Z*. There were several new editing techniques in it. Could you analyze its montage methods for us?"

"I read an essay by the French critic Bazin in a magazine recently. He says that if you want to express the relationship between two bodies in the same space, you should not use montage. How should we understand this? Could you explain it to us, please?"

Zhang Ke came to the classroom in person to supervise the montage techniques class.

In the late seventies, video equipment was not yet widely distributed in China, and the Academy was not yet using camcorders for teaching practice. When they reached their third year, students made short film exercises using black-and-white 16mm stock, but in the first and second years, diagrams composed of still photos were used for exercises analyzing the language of montage. Both of these exercises had been derived from the Soviet teaching methods. During the stage rehearsal process, they used wooden frames. As the actors moved, the frames were held up in front of them at various distances so that long shots, medium shots, and close-ups could be observed. This constituted a sort of visualization tool for montage analysis.

However, no one could have foreseen that when the directing class of 1982 used these methods in their montage class, it would lead to absurdity and farce.

"Full shot!" A large frame was placed a long way away from the two actors.

"Medium shot!" A frame was placed in front of one of the two actors, framing his head and chest.

The plot reached a moment of high drama. The student director yelled out, "Close-up!"

The frame outlined the actor's face.

Then a student raised a tricky question.

"So what do we do if we want an extreme close-up of a pair of eyes?"

"You do this!" The comedy expert Zhang Jianya bounded up. He slapped two pieces of wood over the top and bottom of the frame, and put his own face up against them, his eyes twinkling through the chink that re-

Professor Zhang Ke surrounded by his students. Front row from left: Xu Tongjun, Zheng Dongtian, and Han Xiaolei. With glasses: Jiang Shixiong. Behind Professor Zhang Ke: at left, Ding Yinnan; at right, Situ Zhaodun. Apart from Ding Yinnan, all of these former students became teachers in the Academy's Directing Department. Photo courtesy of Zhang Meng.

mained. While performing this little skit, Zhang Jianya had no idea where it was leading.

A gale of laughter swept through the classroom. The students fell about.

Professor Zhang sat quietly by himself, like a stone Buddha.

The laughter died away quickly as the students realized how they were behaving.

From then on, the wooden frames were never used again to compare shot sizes in montage exercises.

These were two generations at once close and yet light-years apart.

They did everything they could to develop deeper mutual understanding, but there was a huge generation gap between them. The older generation sincerely hoped the younger generation would continue their artistic ideals, bridging the gap opened by the Cultural Revolution. The younger generation not only repudiated the Cultural Revolution but also fixed their gaze on new paths ahead. Filled with a deep sense of responsibility, the older generation passed on their accumulated wisdom. Tolerant and understanding, the younger generation nonetheless regarded that knowledge as outmoded. The older generation wanted to recover the dignity and nobility of purpose lost during the farce of the Cultural Revolution. The younger generation participated in that effort, but felt that in the final analysis it was a preposterous project. Good intentions clashed with sincere intellectual differences and left everyone unsure about what to do. In this mixture of mutual respect and tolerance, they spent four years together in Zhuxin Village.

When the Fifth Generation directors recall their lives in Zhuxin Village, they always remember their teachers with gratitude. Regardless of academic status or teaching ability, every teacher took an equally serious, responsible, and generous attitude to the students. "The teachers were very understanding of our independent research and free thought, and they left us alone to get on with it. This enabled us to make the most of being at the Academy, and ultimately it led to our creative individuality. Maybe that's the main thing we should be grateful to the Academy for."

Compared to the Directing Department, the first steps taken by the cinematography students in the class of 1982 were more conventional but also tougher.

The Beijing Film Academy's Cinematography Department was established in 1956, and under the leadership of veteran cinematographer Wu Yinxian it developed a disciplined and demanding course of study.

Wu Yinxian was a famous cinematographer from the left-wing films of the 1930s. *Street Angel* (1937), which he shot, is a classic of the black-and-white era that represents very vividly the joys and sorrows of the Shanghai underclass. By then Wu Yinxian was already an original and expert still photographer and cinematographer. In 1939, he went to Yan'an and became one of the most prominent documentary filmmakers of the revolutionary base area. He used the 35mm camera and the very limited amount of film stock that had been presented as a gift by the Dutch filmmaker Joris Ivens to shoot precious footage of Chairman Mao, Commander-in-Chief Zhu De, and other revolutionaries.[9] He also recorded the historic Seventh National Congress of the Communist Party of China, historic scenes from the reclamation of the Nanniwan wastelands during the Yan'an era, and many other

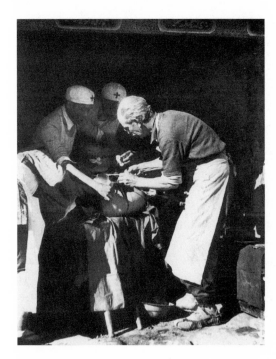

(left) *Dr. Bethune,* photographed by Wu Yinxian in Hebei, 1939. Photo from *Collected Photographs of Wu Yinxian* (Beijing: Central Documents Press, 1983), 49.

(opposite) Wu Yinxian teaching. Photo from *Wu Yinxian: 100 Years* (Beijing: China Film Press, 2000), 77.

historic events during the most difficult stages of the Chinese People's War of Resistance against Japan. In the extremely tough conditions of those times, all of this film was developed by hand in the caves of Yan'an. Wu Yinxian also used an old-fashioned still camera to take many valuable photographs, including a photo of Norman Bethune, the Canadian doctor who sacrificed his own life saving Chinese lives during the War of Resistance. The shot of Bethune calmly performing an operation while risking gunfire under the eaves of a small temple in north China has become one of the mostly highly esteemed works of Chinese photojournalism.

In the fifties, Wu Yinxian was made vice-principal of the Beijing Film Academy and was put in charge of the Cinematography Department. From the first day he demanded very strict basic training for the students. He also saw still photography as a core element of that training, and one that could not be treated lightly. In their first and second years of study, he insisted that all students get such a thorough grasp of framing and lighting that they became second nature. These teaching methods were handed down to become a tradition in the Cinematography Department.

When the students in the class of 1982 enrolled, Wu Yinxian had already retired. But his pupil and assistant Zhang Yifu was in charge of the first- and second-year still photography classes, and he maintained Wu Yinxian's artistic legacy.

Because only one class had been admitted in 1978, supplies of photography equipment in the department were more than adequate for the twenty-six students. Neither the cameras nor the enlargers were the most technologically up-to-date, but they were not in short supply: There was a camera for each student, and for every two students, there was an enlarger, printing equipment, a light meter, and other equipment. Film was also supplied by the Academy, and there was no charge for the use of the equipment, a fact that would distinguish the Beijing Film Academy from many schools in other countries. But although it was all free, no one wasted a single foot of film; it was treated as a precious resource.

According to Zhang Yifu's exacting demands, students began working with artificially lit plaster figures, still life tableaux, and portrait photographs so as to practice all manner of ways to use light. Many students had

Wu Yinxian photographed on
the Great Wall. Photo from
Wu Yinxian: 100 Years
(Beijing: China Film Press,
2000), 93.

Wu Yinxian and the famous
Dutch documentary filmmaker
Joris Ivens in Yan'an. Photo
from *Wu Yinxian: 100 Years*
(Beijing: China Film Press,
2000), 122.

never taken a photograph before. When they saw Zhang Yimou's beautifully presented photo album, many of his fellow students muttered to themselves in amazement, "When will I ever reach that standard?"

Zhao Fei was the youngest student in the class. At first, his photography grades were a mediocre "three plus" on the Soviet-style five-point scale in use then. He was worried. Overcome with anxiety, he would often walk alone around the fields of Zhuxin Village. Even now, this young man, who went on to become a highly skilled cinematographer and shot *Raise the Red Lantern* in 1990, is overcome with emotion when he remembers his difficult beginnings. "I had never taken a photograph in my life. I had no idea how they were produced. The others took such a rich variety of shots from all kinds of unusual angles—especially Zhang Yimou. From the day he walked into the Academy, that beautiful photo album of his became an object of veneration for all of us. We went to his dorm to look at his photos, one little group after another. It was as though he was having a one-man show. When he came back after spending one of the winter breaks in Xi'an, he showed us a lot of new photographs. They were just marvelous. For example, there was a back-lit picture of the Great Wild Goose Pagoda. And there was a shot of a girl from behind that had been overexposed so that the white color of her clothes and the white background became one. Only her long braid stood out. It was really striking, you couldn't get enough of it. I was very unsure of myself then. When would I ever be as good as Zhang Yimou? The only thing to do was to get up early, take my camera, and go practice. Sometimes, once I'd set out, I'd walk for hours in search of an interesting scene to shoot. To get some dramatic shots with unusual angles, I even went all the way to the top of the high furnace at the Capital Iron and Steel Works. I waited there at the top of the smokestack for the rush hour crush of people and bicycles. I waited for hours!" He laughed softly. "Thinking about it now, it seems so naive, but I was deadly serious back then."

Another cinematography student, Xiao Feng, went on to shoot *One and Eight* together with Zhang Yimou before shooting *Black Snow* for Xie Fei and Ning Ying's *For Fun* (1992). When he thinks back to those days his emotions stir: "There were several people in our class who could draw and paint very well. Gu Changwei, Hou Yong, and I all had that kind of background. With painting and drawing, you use your skill to capture things the way you see them; it's a living process. But that's impossible with pho-

Professor Kong Xiangzhu teaches the cinematography class of 1982. Photo courtesy of Beijing Film Academy.

tography. One click of the shutter and that's it. It's very constraining. For a long time, I didn't feel comfortable with this line of work and preferred painting and drawing. You could say that during the two years of still photography training, I was very resistant. I only truly began to love this art of the cinema when we started real cinematography, relying on movement and complicated changes in lighting to represent a scene."

There were classes in dark-room technique twice a week then, and when those days came around students jammed up against the doors to the two Cinematography Department dark rooms. Before opening time everyone lined up, pushing against the doors. When the teacher in charge of the dark rooms opened them, the students crashed in and took up their positions in front of the enlargers. Once there, they stayed put. Some brought steamed buns and pickled vegetables with them and ate their lunches in the dark room. When the afternoon came around and it was time to end the class and lock the doors, there were always stragglers who were unwilling to leave and would not put down their photographs.

"Time to finish! Please put your things away. We're locking up!"

The teacher in charge of the dark room repeatedly urged them to hurry up. But by the time the last student left the dark room it was almost dusk.

■

Whenever those cinematographers nostalgically recall their time at Zhuxin Village, they all remember spring 1979. That was when they went to shoot landscapes at Tenth Ford on the outskirts of Beijing. They spent an entire month there climbing up hills and wading through streams, and as a result everyone's technique improved enormously.

Tenth Ford is a famous scenic spot southwest of Beijing. It is located in the southwestern part of Fangshan district on the upper reaches of the Juma River. The river valley meanders, making the near seem distant and the far close. To get from First Ford to Tenth Ford, it is necessary to cross the river ten times, which explains the name. Precipitous hills form a forest, and the river beaches are wide. The ten-mile long river valley is just like a landscape picture gallery. Although Tenth Ford is not too far from the city, the mountains there are sharp and high, giving the place a majestic atmosphere. These features made it a favored location for students from the Academy's Cinematography and Production Design Departments to come for practice.

At Tenth Ford, everyone was divided into pairs and groups of three to lodge with the local farmers. They ate with them and shared their houses, and they also helped out by fetching water, sweeping the yard, and doing some light work in the fields. Because they were like members of the family, when they shot portrait photos of the farmers, the results were relaxed and natural. Hou Yong says, "I took so many artificially lit portrait photos for class assignments at the Academy, but I can't say I ever felt really satisfied with any of them! We weren't filming living people, just endlessly studying light. I agree it's a basic skill that must be practiced thoroughly, one without which no great cinematographer can emerge. But I still prefer taking pictures of real living people, all kinds of living people. The old farmer and his little daughter whom I photographed in the village look completely at ease. Even the use of light was straightforward and natural. I put everything I had learned in the classroom to work. It was great. But it's impossible to shoot such lifelike photos in the classroom."

Along the river beach at the foot of the high mountains there is a river

Cinematography students at Tenth Ford. From left: Gu Changwei, Zhang Yimou, Zhi Lei, Hou Yong, Zhao Fei, and Wang Xiaolie. Photo courtesy of Hou Yong.

crossing every half mile or so. Each crossing point has its own special charm. But if you want to reach the more distant crossings such as Third Ford and Fourth Ford, then you have to walk for a long time indeed. If you want to take the shortest route, then you must follow the railway line along the cliff tops or take the train and get off two small stations down the line; that is a much quicker way to reach your destination crossing. Here, the railways bore through one mountain after another in quick succession. The pitch-black tunnels can run for hundreds of yards or even half a mile before there is light at the end. Carrying a camera through a tunnel as a clattering and whistling train brushes past is certainly a scary experience, but it is the sort of scare that all the students wanted to try. And the shots they took inside and outside the mountain tunnels came out wonderfully as well.

Once, Xiao Feng set up his camera beside a railway line in front of a tunnel. He had also set up several warning mirrors ahead, because he wanted to take an action photograph of a speeding train roaring out of the tunnel as it swept past. He lay down on a little path by the track and waited quietly. When he heard the distant whistle and the echoing of the rails from inside the tunnel, he got really excited. But unexpectedly, when the train conductor spotted Xiao Feng lying down by the rail with his equipment just as the train shot out of the tunnel, he panicked and slammed on the brake. With a terrible clanging, the train heaved a great sigh and came to a sudden halt. The driver jumped down in one enormous bound, intending to seize the "criminal." The minute Xiao Feng saw him hit the brake, he knew he was in big trouble. So he grabbed his camera, leapt up, turned, and ran. He was familiar with the territory and agile, so he jumped down under the bridge, then ran into the bushes and quickly disappeared.

"We were all crazy back then. We'd freeze for hours on a mountaintop just to get a photograph, or we'd wait until dusk for some shots then walk back several miles after taking our photos. By then, all the village families were about to put out the lamps and go to bed. They go to sleep early in the countryside, you know." Deeply moved, Xiao Feng looked away into the distance, as though the endless strings of mountain peaks at Tenth Ford were right in front of him. "Quite a few of us used our savings to buy a dozen or so rolls of film, which we quietly added to the rolls allocated us by the Academy. We shot a lot of film then. In particular, we took a lot of spontaneous shots. Quite a few good ones came out of that. When we came back and developed them, we hung them up one after the other in the dark rooms, and they were like a forest. After they were enlarged, we held an exhibition of scenes from Tenth Ford. Hou Yong, Lü Yue, and several other students took some really great shots. Zhang Yimou wasn't out in front by himself anymore."

Hou Yong remembers, "That time, after we'd returned, developed the film, and hung the rolls up on the wires in the dark rooms, Zhang Yimou came and took a few turns, looking around. Finally he came to a halt in front of my negatives and looked at them for a long time without uttering a word. Pointing at a shot of a grain field, he said, 'This one's really good.' Right then, I felt elated. It was taken looking down from high up on a mountain. In the field below, the grain stretched far and wide, and in the middle there was a little road with a hand tractor on it. It was very picturesque." Warming to his theme, he continued. "After that, we shot many famous old places around Beijing. In addition to Thirteenth Ridge, we went to the Great Wall, Fragrant Hills, and Vulture Peak. One winter morning we woke up to find an expanse of silvery white outside the windows. The whole of Zhuxin Village was covered in a thick blanket of snow.

Professor Zheng Guoen teaches the cinematography class of 1982. Photo courtesy of Beijing Film Academy.

Everyone leapt up excitedly, running from one dorm to the next with the news. Then the whole class decided to ask for a day's suspension of classes so that we could go out and shoot snow scenes. The department agreed. We loaded our cameras at once, grabbed them and some spare film, and all headed off in different directions. Together with some of the other students in my dorm I went off to Badaling. The snow on the Great Wall made our hands and feet numb with cold, but we got what we were looking for. One of the snow scenes we developed was analyzed and critiqued by Professor Zhang Yifu in class as an outstanding work with exemplary use of light. My heart was bursting. I can remember it even now."

However, the cinematography technique and design classes were specialized courses that only came after the second year. The then chair of the Cinematography Department, Professor Zheng Guoen, taught them both. He was a big, strong man from the northeast with an open and outgoing personality. His Russian was good, so he had been to Moscow twice for advanced cinematography training and had a systematic grasp of contemporary Soviet film teaching methods and materials. Furthermore, he adapted the course to Chinese conditions.

Once they got to the cinematography classes, the students were divided into three groups and took turns shooting scenes suitable for the three sets available at Zhuxin Village. The large shooting stage had two sets constructed on it, one of a village compound and cottages and the other of a courtyard home in the city. A third unit was a naturally lit exterior. A different teacher took charge of set lighting. Each student shot a five- or six-minute dramatic short, while the other students helped with the lighting or worked as assistants. The students and teachers from the Acting Department performed the roles. The atmosphere was one of great teamwork; nobody ever just went through the motions when doing the lighting or acting as an assistant for somebody else.

Zheng Guoen lived in a student dormitory at Zhuxin Village. Every evening he would work together with students on their assignments, and he often told anecdotes from his filmmaking days in the Soviet Union. Two 16mm developers at the Beijing Film Laboratory were dedicated to the students' black-and-white films, and there was a constant shuttling back and forth between the Academy and the lab. At the beginning of the economic reforms instituted in the late seventies, the planned economy continued to operate and the lab could take on developing for educational purposes at very low rates. This gave every student plenty of opportunities to practice. Sometimes they even got a chance to repeat their exercises. From the fifties to the early eighties, the state covered the major costs of education. For the students, most of whom were conscientious, hardworking, and poor, this was essential to their successful graduation. When the class of 1982 were burying themselves in their studies, everyone worked together to ensure success and achieve the desired results. They were permitted to shoot their exercises three, four, and even five times, and the teachers did everything they could to help. But today, society has become completely enveloped in a commercial atmosphere and students view study and work as ways to get rich, and where homework is sometimes seen only as a task to be completed and nothing more. Will the atmosphere in which collective talent like the Fifth Generation flowered ever return?

■

The students in the Production Design Department's class of 1982 were as dedicated and committed as those studying cinematography. The Production Design Department enrolled students for two courses of study. The first was production design itself, and the aim was to train film set designers. The other was an art direction course, training set builders and decorators. Art direction was not originally a major at the Beijing Film Academy; however, in the seventies, due to Jiang Qing's promotion of Beijing opera and other kinds of opera films, every film studio placed more emphasis on theatrical set craftsmanship. Soon, art direction came to be treated on an equal footing with production design in the film school of the Central May Seventh University of the Arts, and this continued until the end of the Cultural Revolution. When undergraduate students were admitted in 1978, production design and art direction were of equal stature, and so two classes with twenty-seven students overall were enrolled.

The art direction class included many people who had an excellent foundation in painting and who had originally aspired to become artists. After graduation, these people went on to become capable production designers in the Fifth Generation cinema. For example, He Qun's sterling work on *Yellow Earth* made a great contribution to the visual style of the new film movement's aesthetic. But later, many of the students not only went in for production design but also became directors in their own right, producing a considerable number of distinctive films and television dramas.

A simple list indicates their achievements:

HE QUN (as production designer): *One and Eight* (1983), *Yellow Earth* (1984), *Big Military Parade* (1986), *Widow Village* (1988), and *The Bride* (1990); (as film director): *Mutiny* (1989), *Prison Car to the West* (1990), *A Tried and Tested Warrior* (1991), *Conned* (1992), *The Vanished Woman* (1992), and *Country Teachers* (1993).

YIN LI (as production designer): *Neighbors* (1981), *The Cool Clear Stream* (1983), and *Come On, China* (1985); (as film director): *My September* (1990) and *Apricot Blossoms in March* (1993).

FENG XIAONING (as production designer): *Teenage Years* (1984) and *The Imp* (1988); (as film director): *The Virus, the Gold, Sunday* (1988), *The Ozone Layer Vanishes* (1990), *Meridian of War* (1991), and *Red River Valley* (1997).

However, back then, when the art direction students were using spray guns and big brushes on enormous backdrops day in and day out, they were not certain about what they would do when they finished studying. "You could say you are another kind of artist," one of their teachers told them, "the kind of artist who paints on the largest canvasses in the world and whose work is ultimately expressed through the film screen."

Every day, after all the other students had already gone to the cafeteria, collected their meals, and sat down to eat, a bunch of "E.T."s would appear and file in. They wore overalls and work hats and were splattered with paint in every color of the rainbow. Some even had their faces covered in different-colored paint, with only the whites of their eyes and their teeth showing through. When they put out their red and green "claws," they could scare the girls into dropping their food onto the floor. These were the art direction students. They hurriedly washed their hands, took their food, and sat down together with an exhausted look in their eyes.

Zhang Jianya and Jiang Haiyang from the Directing Department took their food trays over and began to set the "E.T."s straight.

"He Qun!" said Jiang Haiyang. "Know what work you're going to do once you get to a studio?"

"No idea!"

"You'll each be issued two buckets, two big brushes on long poles, and a spray gun. Then you'll be sent to the backdrops that go hundreds of yards around the back of the big shooting stages, and you'll slowly paint them."

"No way!" Their spoons came to a halt in midair.

"Don't be stupid! We've both spent time at the Shanghai Film Studio. Each profession sticks to its own job. Art directors make sets, production designers design the production. What do you know?" Jiang Haiyang spoke like an older brother.

He Qun put his bowl down on the table.

All the "E.T."s put their bowls down.

"Trying to fool us all, are you? Who do you think you're kidding?"

■

Within a week, the art direction class dorms were under guard and shrouded in mystery. No one from the other departments could get in, no matter how hard they tried.

"What the hell are they up to?" asked directing student Jin Tao resentfully as he carried his food tray in front of him.

In fact, the art direction class was drawing up a petition for a change of major. They selected six representatives, who drafted and redrafted the petition until they arrived at a final version. In spring 1979, they formally sub-

The days at Zhuxin Village. From left: Zhao Jin, Geng Xiaozhen, Xia Gang, Chen Kaige, and He Qun, photographed in 1980. Photo courtesy of Geng Xiaozhen.

mitted the document to the Education Bureau of the Ministry of Culture, requesting that their major become production design. The reply came back very quickly, and the Academy was directed to change the class from art direction to production design. From then on, the two classes proceeded with the same syllabus.

Officially, only the art direction class changed, but the ripples radiated out to affect every department in the school. The general feeling was, can we go on studying like this? Are old teaching methods good enough?

As students, you have to study the knowledge, experience, and methods of your predecessors. Study provides a foundation, and the more solid the foundation the more free and original you can become. That's the way it's always been; it's a rule that has stood the test of time.

But what did the foundation consist of?

Was acting part of the foundation? They rehearsed day in and day out for two years. Was it really necessary? Dramatic exercises were part of the foundation, with different exercises for different components, such as working without dialogue; relying on the gaze alone, listening, and tone of voice; using props; and work on detail. But when would they ever put it all together? Montage was part of the foundation. But many contemporary films were not edited according to classical montage techniques, so what should they do?

Certainly, as a student, one had to get a grasp of the basic language. However, we were facing a difficult choice between using an established language and finding a new one.

■

Building a new culture in any era always involves a new language of expression.

Operating under the umbrella of the May Fourth Movement, China's New Culture Movement of the 1920s took up *baihua* vernacular Chinese language and launched a linguistic revolution to promote it.[10] Without the elimination of the age-old classical Chinese language system and its replacement by modern *baihua* Chinese, which was closely linked to Western linguistics, it would have been impossible to even think about modernizing ideas and popularizing them. Similarly, the dividing line between the nineteenth-century and twentieth-century modernism in Europe marked a rupture with the past and new forms of expression that composed a comprehensively modern cultural landscape.

Likewise, a sort of linguistic revolution necessarily accompanied the birth of the culture of China's new era after the Cultural Revolution—without it there could not have been a complete break with the Cultural Revolution era. Between 1979 and 1982, just when China's Fifth Generation of film artists were studying hard at the Academy, the thorough overhaul of social and cultural discourse was beginning.

An enormous billboard above Xidan Street in central Beijing reads, "Practice is the only test for truth."[11] A black-and-white television set is broadcasting live the special trial of Jiang Qing and the Gang of Four by the Supreme People's Court.[12] Xu Chi's reportage piece "The Goldbach Conjecture" extols the almost religious devotion to science of a young mathematician, who works day and night in a tiny sixty-four square-foot apartment adapted from what used to be a bathroom.[13] The news of the spirited victory over Japan of the Chinese women's volleyball team ignites the thunder of firecrackers, following the custom for celebrating public holidays. Crowds mill around Democracy Wall, where people who have just stepped off bustling Xidan Street find themselves confronted by passionate words and cool thoughts.[14] Lectures and poems recited on university campuses make young people's blood run wild with excitement.

> I don't believe the sky is blue,
> I don't believe in the sound of thunder,
> I don't believe that dreams are false,
> I don't believe that death has no revenge.[15]

The publication of the devastating facts concerning Zhang Zhixin, a female Communist Party martyr from Liaoning Province, exposes the inhuman tortures practiced by the Gang of Four and stuns the public.[16] Hundreds of thousands of Rightists are filled with mixed feelings as the verdicts against them are belatedly rectified. And twenty million educated youths are packing up and returning to the cities from the icebound north and the steamy forests of the tropics. Sanyo "boom boxes" have just gone on sale and people form lines to buy them so long that one cannot see the end of them. This simple machine multiplies the enthusiasm for learning English. And, of course, it is also used to enjoy the lilting tunes, over and over again, of Taiwanese pop singer Teresa Teng.

What sort of an age was this? Everyday life was changing drastically, demanding equally drastic changes in literature and language.

The first ripples were being generated by "scar" literature that denounced past injustices—works like "The Scar," "Hong Yulan under the Wall," "Body and Soul," and *The Legend of Tianyun Mountain.*[17] In the dormitories out at Zhuxin Village, the lights stayed on all night and tears were shed over this moving writing that was such an integral part of the era. But once the output of scar literature began to level off, attention turned to linguistic innovation in fiction and poetry. Literary language is directly linked to cinematic language, so efforts to transform the dull and outmoded Chinese cinema often turned first to literature for answers and ideas.

Around 1980, Wang Meng published a series of short stories that formed a fresh discursive stream. In succession, he published "The Eyes of Night," "Voices of Spring," "A Dream of the Sea," "Kite Streamers," "Deep Lake," and "Light of the Heart," as well as the novellas *Bolshevik Salute* and *The Butterfly.*[18] He went beyond methods such as Western stream-of-consciousness to create a kind of free-association narrative voice and linguistic rhythm. Moreover, he freely combined colloquial language and dialect to form fresh idioms, and so the dialogue in his works was full of colorful vernacular expressions. People were attracted to this fresh linguistic style, which employed lively satire, strong metaphors, and striking imagery. In the short story "The Eyes of Night," he writes:

> All the street lamps were switched on, of course, at the same time. However Chen Hao felt as if there were two streams of light shooting out in opposite directions above his head. There seemed to be no end to them. Locust trees cast their simple, yet stalwart shadows on to the pavements, as did people waiting at the bus stop, each having more than one shadow.
>
> Everywhere, there were heavy vehicles, cars, trolley buses, bicycles, and the hooting, voices and laughter typical of a big city at night—full of life. He saw occasional neon lights and barber's poles. Also permed hair, long hair, high-heeled shoes, and frocks. In the air hung the fragrance of toilet water and face cream. Though the city women had just begun to pay a little attention to their appearance, they had already outraged certain people. This was interesting.
>
> Chen Hao had left this city more than twenty years before, to live in a remote small town, where one-third of the street lamps were never lit and the rest had no electricity for part of the month. Nobody knew whether this was through neglect or lack of coal. However, it did not matter much, because people began their work at dawn and finished at dusk, like peasants following the customs of their ancestors. After six o'clock when all the offices, factories, shops, and halls were closed, people stayed at home, looking after their children, smoking, washing, or chatting.[19]

The linguistic inventiveness of Wang Meng's fiction ultimately can be traced to changes in the author's cultural outlook. This followed the shift in Chinese literature from being a vehicle for politics to being an assertion of the free individual. The satire and witty banter of his language flowed from his reflections on all the absurdities of the Cultural Revolution. They mocked worn-out ultra-leftist politics bitterly and with a modern attitude, and they also opened a large gap between him and his literary peers. Wang Meng had already thrown off the past completely, and this made him extraordinarily significant. With a new linguistic style, he pointed toward the arrival of a new literary era.

Indeed, after 1985, a new school of urban literature did appear. Wang Shuo was its representative author, and in honor of his short story "Masters of Mischief" it was called "mischief masters literature."[20] Innovation was found everywhere in this literature from character construction to the use of language. This produced the mischief masters' dialect and the image of the "lout," a flippant type who pretended to be a real gangster. It attracted a lot of attention. Of course, Wang Meng and Wang Shuo are like chalk and cheese. Nonetheless, in the late seventies and early eighties, Wang Meng's series of short stories had already pioneered linguistic innovation, colloquialism, and flippancy to the point of the sacrilegious. I have no intention of blurring the differences between the two of them here, but just wish to trace the discursive transformation back to the turning point of the late seventies and early eighties. Discussing Wang Shuo later, Wang Meng pinpointed the historical origins of linguistic "play" brilliantly. He said, "First life itself became flippant, for example when Jiang Qing and Lin Biao eliminated masterpieces and performed clumsy and nauseating farces. Our political movements repeatedly made jokes out of sacred things such as beliefs, loyalty, Party membership, titles, and even life. They started this cruel play! And now it's Wang Shuo's turn!"

Such a sharp insight! And to a certain extent, it forms a footnote to Wang Meng's own linguistic style in the eighties.

Perhaps it was this linguistic playfulness and vitality that struck a chord with the women students Peng Xiaolian and Li Shaohong in the Directing Department. They eagerly adapted Wang Meng's *Kite Streamers* into a film script in an attempt to transfer it to the screen.

The new generation of poets went even further than Wang Meng in their experimentation. They began the modern poetry movement as early as the late seventies. Among them was Chen Kaige's friend, the poet Bei Dao. He and all the other "Misty Poets" constituted a literary phenomenon. Although the number of people involved was quite small, their influence among young people was considerable, which soon led to criticism and envy directed against them. In fact, these dense and difficult verses did touch the restless, yearning, and sensitive souls of the young.

Bei Dao wrote:

Baseness is the password of the base,
Honor is the epitaph of the honorable.

Look how the gilded sky is covered
With the drifting, crooked shadows of the dead.

The Ice Age is over now,
Why is there still ice everywhere?
The Cape of Good Hope has been discovered,
Why do a thousand sails contest the Dead Sea?

I come into this world
Bringing only paper, rope, a shadow,
To proclaim before this judgment
The voices of the judged.

Let me tell you, world,
I—do—not—believe!
If a thousand challengers lie beneath your feet,
Count me as number one thousand and one.[21]

Another young poet, Gu Cheng, wrote:

I'm convinced.
I try to stare with steady eyes.
I pause by a shimmering fountain,
glancing at bypassers.
When
I blink, the fountain turns
into a disembodied snake.

I rest in the temple,
quietly whiling away the time.
The bell turns when I blink
into a bottomless well.

Blossoming on the screen,
nodding cheerfully in the breeze,
the red flowers turn when I blink
into a streaming pool of blood.
Holding fast to my convictions,
I try to stare at it without blinking.[22]

The young poet Shu Ting was even more individualistic and subtle in the expression of her moods:

Fog has drenched my two wings
But the wind will not allow me to dally
Oh land, land that I love
Only yesterday I said goodbye to you
Today you are here again
Tomorrow we will
Meet again at a different latitude

It was a storm, a lamp
That held us together
It was another storm, another lamp
That parted us to the east and west
Even to the edge of the sky and the farthest shore
Surely every morning and evening
You will be on my route
I will be in your sight.[23]

In comparison with traditional Chinese cinema, one of the important breakthroughs of the Fifth Generation was in film language. The substitution of poetic language for parablelike narratives was one of the important hallmarks of early Fifth Generation cinema. Chen Kaige has a particularly poetic temperament. His writing is highly poetic, sometimes even more lyrical than his film language, which is full of literary metaphors and poetic allusions. He reads, writes, and recites poetry, and in classroom discussions he repeatedly turned to poetry to support his arguments.

■

Early in April 1979, an amateur photography exhibition was held in Beijing's Zhongshan Park. It was called "Nature—Society—Humanity." A group of young photography enthusiasts organized the event themselves, and there were more than one hundred works on display. The main focus of the work was on everyday life, with many shots of common sights, ordinary people, old people, and children. The waterside pavilion in which the exhibition was held was small, and the crowds that attended the exhibition washed through it like a flood tide. Some people came again and again,

Farmers exiting from the photography exhibition "Nature—Society—Humanity," held in Beijing in April 1979. Photo courtesy of Wu Peng.

while others stood transfixed, gazing at a single photo and showing no inclination to leave.

The majority of the young photographers' works were black and white. Drops of rain dangling from electricity wires. A fleet of bicycles jostling through the rush hour. Unmelted snow heaped up on a pile of bricks by the roadside. A few lonely geese in the winter countryside outside Beijing. Lovers on the snow beside a lake, oblivious to the cold. Little monkeys in a zoo, quite unafraid of human beings. A relaxed and contented father with two youngsters pushing an infant in a stroller along in front of them. Old men on the side of the road, lost in thought as they focus on a chessboard. From today's perspective, in terms of both subject matter and artistic execution, these photos would be deemed commonplace—nothing more than clearly focused and technically competent. But in April 1979, when art had only recently been liberated from the stale clichés of ultra-leftist political formulas, they were like a spring shower. Utterly realistic and fresh in tone, they filled visitors with warmth and sympathy.

A powerful demand for realism, a return to nature, and the expression of ordinary people's honest feelings sprang up from every sector of society. This encouraged artists to change their imagery and their language even more in order to restore and rebuild the relationship of mutual trust and equality between art and audiences.

"Nature—Society—Humanity" was a small photography exhibition, but it elicited a strong response across the whole country and even overseas. The Cultural New Wave Press of Hong Kong published an album of photographs in response to the energy generated by the independent activities in mainland China, and to introduce to overseas readers the new language being explored by mainland artists.

The "Stars" art exhibition, had a similar impact. In the language of painting it was avant-garde, and it created a sensation. "Stars" was held in a pavilion in Beijing's Beihai Park from 23 November to 2 December 1979.[24] Twenty-three practitioners, most of them young nonprofessionals, organized it. There were 163 works in the exhibit, including Chinese-style paintings, oil paintings, etchings, and wooden sculptures. The works basically fell into two categories. The first group tackled contemporary injustices in an incisive fashion, touching on everyday life and social problems. The second group was formally innovative and emphasized painting form. The introduction to the exhibition directly addressed this double focus: "The shadows of the past and the brightness of the future overlap, creating the multifaceted nature of our lives today. It is our duty to resolve to live on but at the same time to remember every lesson. We will also strive to explore new forms in art. The world offers boundless possibilities to those who explore." Wang Keping, a representative participant in the exhibition, said, "Käthe Kollwitz was our mascot, and Picasso was our pioneer. But we placed greater emphasis on the former. We could not be like some of the literati of the Ming and Qing dynasties who isolated themselves and engaged in art for art's sake when the social struggle was most intense."[25]

Wang Keping's wooden sculptures, *We Wish You a Long Life, The Backbone of Society,* and *The Silence* used absurdist symbolism to produce metaphors for the Gang of Four's political dictatorship, their policy of keeping the people in ignorance, and ideological imprisonment. He used the natural twists and movements in roots and branches to develop a language of wooden sculpture that was very modern and creatively expressive. Ma Desheng's black-and-white engraving *Rest in Peace* represented the anonymous self-sacrifice that China's farmers made to the soil. And Huang Rui's oil paintings *Will and Testament* and *New Life* depicted the ruins of the old Summer Palace, the Yuanmingyuan outside of Beijing, as a symbol of the ebb and flow of national history. The symbolism of artists such as Bao Pao, Ai Weiwei, and Qu Leilei was rudimentary but sincere and bold, and their works moved visitors who had only just been liberated from the Gang of Four. For a time all of these artists were the talk of Beijing, with people falling over themselves to either censure or praise them.

Clearly, the appearance of the "Nature—Society—Humanity" and "Stars" exhibitions in 1979 was closely connected to the movement to liberate thought that followed the smashing of the Gang of Four. Most of China's professional artists were still struggling to restore and use realist techniques to portray history and depict political leaders, as well as to convey the sufferings of the Cultural Revolution. But the avant-garde "Stars" exhibition had already taken the first steps away from the existing language of drawing and painting. Although the technique of these artists was immature, the influence of new language was already impelling them, and future artists would take it further. The oil painting *Father,* exhibited in the 1980 "Sichuan Youth Art Exhibition," is an important example. The image of an old farmer who had spent his whole life laboring on the land was painted on an enormous canvas using photorealist techniques by Luo Zhongli, a young graduate from the Department of Oil Painting in the Sichuan Academy of Fine Arts. All of the elements combined well to form a boldly executed whole, like a stone carving, and the work communicated the force and stoicism of the Chinese farmers. Because the painting was so large, every wrinkle, deep as a ravine, and every bead of sweat was full of life's bitterness and the unyielding quality of fate. This farmer, extremely concrete yet also very abstract, expressed generations of life and work spent close to the soil. Through his technique and the language of oil painting, the artist magnified "ordinariness" and "the individual," as well as millions of usually ignored "worthless lives," to challenge history and the viewer. This enormous "ordinariness" took people by surprise. It disturbed them and made them stop and think.

When it was exhibited at the China Art Gallery, *Father* created a stir and provoked immediate debate. The discussion became quite heated. Critics pointed out that the painting depicted farmers of the new society just as those of pre-Liberation times were painted. For one thing, it was impos-

Father, by Luo Zhongli (left), created a sensation when it was exhibited at the "Sichuan Youth Art Exhibition" in 1980. *Photos from China New Arts Series 1976–1982, Fine Arts Anthology* (Beijing: China Literature and Arts Association Press, 1985), 34. Still of the father in *Yellow Earth* (right). Photo from the 1985–1986 volume of *China Screen.*

sible to tell if he was a tenant farmer from the past or a liberated commune member. However, day after day a crowd of people milled around *Father* without dispersing. They stood there gazing, silently lost in thought. This proclaimed both the bankruptcy of ultra-leftist thought and also the establishment of a tacit agreement between the new language of painting and the public.

At this moment, the significance of artistic imagery transcended what can be measured by empirical social science. Aesthetic beauty had reestablished the independent dignity of art and humanity, and "language" had produced its own autonomous significance and value.

As a result, *Father* won wide sympathy in the art world, students at the Film Academy included. After the long trek from the outskirts of the city to the art gallery, they too lingered in front of *Father* and many other works, clutching bread and steamed buns, soaking up the atmosphere of their contemporaries' achievements. Their palpable patriotic longing for cinematic creativity was being expressed in the powerful language of their painting peers, stirring up indescribable emotions. Four years later, the film *Yellow Earth* shows the image of the character Cuiqiao's father sitting on a platform bed like a statue. Chen Kaige, Zhang Yimou, and He Qun frankly acknowledge that this image was based on *Father*. "We filmed those long takes where he sits talking to Gu Qing on the bed platform or sings 'sour tunes' for him employing the tone and mood of the painting *Father*."

Zhang Yimou was introduced to Wang Liping, one of the organizers of the April exhibitions, by a classmate in the Production Design Department, Yin Li. Wang wanted Zhang to include his photos in one of the annual April exhibitions that followed the "Nature—Society—Humanity" exhibition. Of course, this was a wonderful opportunity, and as a result he had seven large photos shown in the third April exhibition under the title *This Generation*. Yin Li also exhibited a group of four photographs called *Lovers' Symphony*. Zhang Yimou's series depicted the relationship between the educated youths and the land in the countryside. The composition emphasized flatness, absence of vanishing point, and a feeling of grace and strength. The visual style of the films he shot and directed later was fully displayed in these early photographs, clearly showing the beginnings of an auteur's style.

Zhang Yimou told Yin Li that if the photos were going to be exhibited, the prints must be large. Largeness was important because it communicated a certain significance by itself. So, they asked someone to buy a whole roll of uncut photographic paper from the Baoding Film Plant. Then they laid it out on the floor of the dark room, exposed the film, and printed it there. There was no developing dish large enough to hold the images, so they soaked cotton with developing fluid and fixative and patiently rubbed it bit by bit over the photographic paper. It was spring 1980, and the sweat poured down their backs all through the vacation right up to their exhibition debut. However, when in one of the exhibition halls of the art gallery they looked at what had seemed like a big photo in the dark room, it was small and inconspicuous. Indeed, in the feast for the eyes at the April exhibition, they were almost overshadowed.

"The movie screen! Only when we can get our images onto the screen will we really be able to show people what we can do!" Zhang Yimou told himself as he stood among the endless flow of visitors and closed his lips tightly.

■

While the language of literature, poetry, and painting was being transformed, what was happening to the cinema? Without doubt, film language had also joined the tide of innovation discussed earlier.

During 1979 and 1980, Fourth Generation directors shot *Reverberations of Life, Troubled Laughter,* and *Xiaohua,* followed closely by *The Drive to Win, Neighbors,* and *As You Like It.* All these films were significant in terms of linguistic innovation. At the same time, the publication of the theory article "The Modernization of Film Language" set off a large debate.[26] As the Fourth Generation directors were taking this great step forward, Chen Kaige, Zhang Yimou, Tian Zhuangzhuang, Gu Changwei, and the others were still studying hard in Zhuxin Village. The Fifth Generation cinema was still in its infancy.

The new climate stimulated the young creators as they studied and prepared. How should they develop their own language? How should they find their own creative perspective? How should they increase their knowledge and improve their technique? Because they were in a time of great change, when the class of 1982 was in Zhuxin Village they did not simply follow the conventional pattern of reproducing everything straight after they had finished studying it. Instead, as they studied they also examined, critiqued, and modified film language. This independent thinking was spurred on by developments in the outside world. It meant that although they followed the innovative movement launched by the Fourth Generation, they also developed their own distinctive artistic position. The expressive and image-based film language of *One and Eight* and *Yellow Earth* was poles apart from the realism of the Fourth Generation.

As they absorbed and selected film language, which movements did they encounter and what processes did they experience? Social history had made them the direct products of the Cultural Revolution and the movement to send educated youths up into the mountains and down to the countryside. But in regard to culture and film language, which traditions did the Fifth Generation tap into?

First, during their four years at the Academy the entire class of 1982 received an extensive grounding in classical cinema. During their first and second years of study, their major models were Chinese classical cinema, Hollywood film of the thirties and forties, and the Soviet classics. Two evenings of screenings per week were organized for the whole school. One evening followed the thread of world cinema history with a double bill of classics, and the other featured two contemporary Chinese films. These productions were often the best of those most recently completed. After four years, the students had seen a very large number of films indeed.

Later, some Chinese film critics objected to the heavy emphasis on the visual at the expense of plot in early Fifth Generation films. They questioned the young artists: "How many film classics have you seen? Have you studied classical Hollywood feature films? What about Chinese traditional cinema?" "They don't understand plot or acting, and they think they know it all on the basis of a minimal introduction. They're clearly not up to scratch. It must be because they haven't studied enough of the classics."

In fact, the models for study at the Academy included a great many classical and traditional films. During the two years between 1978 and 1980, the American films of the thirties and forties supplied by the China Film Archive constituted an almost comprehensive survey of tendencies over a dozen or so years. Among the many titles were *Random Harvest* (1942), *Gone with the Wind* (1939), *Rebecca* (1940), *Waterloo Bridge* (1940), *Stagecoach* (1939), *Citizen Kane* (1941), *The Best Years of Our Lives* (1946), and *Gaslight* (1944). They included several highly commercial films. At the beginning of their training, everyone developed an enormous interest in the twists and turns of the plots. "But after the second year," explained more than one Fifth Generation director, "we were no longer so fascinated by them. With very conventional Hollywood films, we'd even walk out halfway through." Their cinematic field of vision had become wider. They were paying much greater attention to modern art and, besides, Hollywood itself was undergoing great change.

The second major tradition was Soviet cinema. Soviet film had a very strong influence on China in the fifties and sixties, and many of the professors at the Academy were direct descendants and disciples of Moscow Film University. Of course, the influence of the montage school was very great. Apart from early silent films and famous classics, such as Eisenstein's *Battleship Potemkin,* Pudovkin's *Mother,* and Dovzhenko's *Earth* (1930), greatest emphasis was placed on the Soviet films of the fifties and sixties. This was the period of the thaw that followed the death of Stalin in 1953, and it was characterized by literary and filmic works exposing and criticizing the past.[27] Chen Kaige, Zhang Yimou, Wu Ziniu, Zhang Junzhao, Hou Yong, and Xiao Feng have all claimed that the Soviet cinema of this period had a direct influence on their own early works. The strong emphasis on visual

Documentary filmmaker Joris Ivens came to Beijing to teach at the Academy in the early eighties. First on the right is the director and Academy professor Xie Fei. Photo courtesy of Beijing Film Academy.

language in *One and Eight,* the wrongly treated Communist Party member who remains steadfastly loyal, and the theme of vows and faith were all almost completely derived from Soviet cinema of the thaw period. In the rooms of Zhuxin Village then, the Soviet films *The Cranes Are Flying* (1957), *Destiny of a Man* (1959), *Ballad of a Soldier* (1959), *Ivan's Childhood* (1962), and *Clear Skies* (1960) provoked much heated debate deep into the sleepless night. These films communicated the grief and indignation kindled by opposition to war and the rounding up of counterrevolutionaries, and they displayed humanist sympathy for individuals who had sacrificed so much because of the incorrect political line. The movement for the liberation of thought and the redressing of past injustices made the situation in China around 1980 very similar. However, the Chinese cinema of the time did not possess the realism and visual style of the Soviet films. Naturally, this elicited a positive response and an eager use of these films as models.

The third and most important tradition was Chinese classical cinema.

One pattern emerged clearly. The class of 1982 was indifferent toward the films of the fifties and paid more attention to the films of the thirties and forties. Wu Yonggang's 1934 film *The Goddess* and Fei Mu's 1948 film *Spring in a Small Town* were especially well received, causing the class of 1982 to respect and ponder Chinese film history.[28] In the mid-eighties, some foreign film critics said that the Fifth Generation both broke with tradition and maintained it, because they skipped the fifties to pick up the humanist philosophy of classical China and to extend the nonmainstream tradition of thirties Chinese film. Later developments proved the prescience of this assessment. *Ju Dou, Raise the Red Lantern, Farewell, My Concubine,* and *Blush* truly demonstrate a link to the tradition of the thirties. However, both Tian Zhuangzhuang and Chen Kaige have repeatedly expressed their respect for the Third Generation directors of the fifties and sixties. Tian Zhuangzhuang says, "Shui Hua is a first-rate director; *The Lin Family Shop* and *Regret for the Past* are classics of the Chinese cinema." And Chen Kaige has paid homage to "the crisp and fluid narrative in Chen Huaikai and Cui Wei's *Song of Youth,* which is of a standard unsurpassed to this day."

However, their research interests soon turned to contemporary cinema.

Song of Youth, directed by Chen Huaikai and Cui Wei. Photo from *China Film Album, 1949–1979.* (Beijing: China Film Press, 1983), 81.

In the late seventies, the first foreign films to be imported into China were Japanese. Chinese audiences were introduced to films such as *Sandakan No. 8* (1974), *A Dish of Sand* (1974), *Love and Death* (1971), and *Swan Song* (1975). Initially the audiences came in droves and found the Japanese works very novel. The names of stars such as Takakura Ken, Kurihara Komaki, and Yamaguchi Momoe were on everyone's lips. The editing methods and narrative structures of Japanese films became a model for film directors in the newly opened China, even though they were already becoming outmoded overseas. Contemporary American and European cinema followed in quick succession, and China's opening up led to an influx of movies. Information excluded for many years was hurriedly assembled, almost overnight, and Chinese filmmakers found themselves before a feast of modern European cinema after the long dearth of the Cultural Revolution. This and the influx of literature in translation became the two main sources for the Fifth Generation's modernist consciousness.

Filmmakers such as Bergman, Resnais, Godard, Truffaut, and Antonioni, and writers such as Kafka, Sartre, Camus, Wolfe, Garcia Marquez, Faulkner, Bellow, and Hemingway all became objects of intense fascination and half-comprehending worship. "We were more taken with the modernist movement in literature and art than with the vast volume of Western film theory translated at that time. Themes of absurdity and loneliness resonated very strongly with our own experiences. We had wasted nine or ten whole years in isolation, being humiliated and experiencing the drudgery of primitive rural labor in the mud and storms. That's why realism seemed too timid for us."

In the rush to see new or "taboo" films, there were many amusing incidents. One such incident, popular in the reminiscences of the class of 1982, concerns the forging of film tickets.

At first, it was the clever handiwork of one or two people who forged the occasional ticket and slipped unnoticed into the small viewing rooms of the Film Archive. But this activity soon developed into a technically skilled operation, so much so that it became hard to tell the real tickets from the false ones.

Why did the class of 1982 forge movie tickets? Was not brazenly breaking the law like that a dreadful thing to do? To understand their motivations, we need to begin with the "internal reference material film" system established by Mao's wife, Jiang Qing.

During the Cultural Revolution, there were no films produced between 1966 and 1970. After 1970, the eight model operas began to be transferred to the screen. Around 1974, the production of a few feature films began. By that time, hundreds of millions of ordinary Chinese had, countless times, seen Beijing opera films such as *The Red Lantern* (1970, 1975), *Taking Tiger Mountain by Strategy* (1970), *In Praise of Longjiang* (1972), and *On the Dock* (1972, 1973).[29] However, Jiang Qing and her privileged inner circle had special private screening rooms in which they watched American and European films, creating two different worlds with two different cultures in the one country. To improve the taste and the skills of cinematographers, directors, and screenwriters from the film studios, dance troupes, and model opera troupes, Jiang Qing gave them special permission to see Western films. The understanding they gained of European and American directors' most up-to-date methods and technological standards would enable them to lift the quality of films made from the model operas. This was what the "internal reference material film" system was all about. In the West, any ordinary citizen just has to buy a ticket and they can watch a film in a movie theater as they please, or they can rent it on video. But during Jiang Qing's time, watching films was turned into a special and mysterious privilege. Access to "internal reference material films" became a special social prerogative and a kind of hidden currency. During the Cultural Revolution, a ticket to an "internal reference material film" could open a lot of doors. If you had steady access to tickets for "internal reference material films" you could use them to buy meat and sugar, go on trips, see a doctor, and even gain admission to schools or change your residence permit. It may sound unbelievable, but to ordinary people in a closed society who were desperate for a peep at Western life, it was absolutely real.

The "internal reference material film" system continued into the eighties, making the forging of film tickets a deliberate breach of the rules by the Film Academy students. However, it was not that they were cheap or that they wanted to look at the taboo and the obscene. They just wanted to be able to see films by Fassbinder, Schlöndorff, Coppola, Oshima, and Scorsese as early as possible.

The forged film tickets were the handiwork of a team from the Production Design and Cinematography departments, and they looked just like the real thing, down to the smallest detail. They were even stamped with the appropriate day and date and a session number. They were works of art, and the small screening rooms were jammed with people. However, it blew up in their faces because of a small accident.

The problem originated with the use of advertising pigment to print the tickets. In summer, the weather was hot and the ticket collector's hands were sweaty. One day, the collector discovered to his surprise that his hands were covered in ink, and the tickets were smeared. The entire audience was asked to leave the theater and their ticket stubs were checked again. It was discovered that there were many young students in the audience to whom tickets for this "internal reference material film" had not been distributed.

Once the word spread that Academy students were forging tickets, it caused a great deal of embarrassment. The school leaders reprimanded them severely and insisted that nothing like this should ever happen again.

However, more skilled techniques were developed. After manufacture, the tickets were coated with a thin layer of wax. It was smooth and glossy and felt very good. Even if you put it in water, it would not run, never mind in the sweaty palms of summer.

In response to this incident, the range of people permitted entry was widened and the number of screenings were increased, allowing the students to see new films representative of all the current trends. It was not long before the Fifth Generation directors were coming and going from international film festivals all over Europe and America, where they had plenty of opportunities to see new films from all over the world that were in competition that year. But often they had too many appointments to see many films, or else they saw so many that they got tired of them. When they recall those years in Zhuxin Village and how they broke the rules and racked their brains for ways to see a new foreign film—or what passed for a new foreign film—as early as possible, their behavior seems absurd and they do not know what to think about it.

When they went into the city to view films at the China Film Archive, they were crammed into two large buses. Over one hundred students from every department went, as well as some members of the faculty. People were packed in so tightly they could hardly breathe, but no one grumbled. As long as they were going to see a new film, no one wanted to be left behind. Regardless of whether it was bitterly cold or unbearably hot, once the bus was on the road between Beijing and Changping, songs and jokes flew out of the windows. A continuous barrage of good-natured teasing relieved the tedium of the journey. A loaf of bread, a couple of griddle

From left: Wu Ziniu, Hou Yong, Zhou Wei, and Jin Tao at the Zhuxin Village bus stop. Hou Yong was in the Cinematography Department at the Academy and the others were in the Directing Department. Photo courtesy of Hou Yong.

cakes, or even a couple of steamed buns from the canteen were often the only dinner they ate as they watched the films. They became accustomed to watching film after film of all genres in these austere conditions, writing up one detailed set of notes after another.

Chen Kaige's father, the director Chen Huaikai, gave his son a notebook. On the cover he wrote, "Write up every film." He told Kaige that he himself remembered analyzing films like that. Kaige took his father's advice very seriously, and after every film he saw he wrote an analysis in his immaculate handwriting. He was not the only one who did this; almost every student had notes of some sort. Students in the Cinematography Department took the front row seats at the screenings. Many had cameras and took photos of particularly well-composed shots. Of course, there was not enough light for the photos, so the results were not technically distinguished. However, the students were at the beginning of their studies and fascinated by the films, so they closely examined the materials they gathered in an effort to gain an understanding of the distinctive composition and visual language of different directors.

When I interviewed the Fifth Generation directors and cinematographers about their studies of film language and the influences on them, their answers were very illuminating.

WU ZINIU: The Soviet director Tarkovsky's *Ivan's Childhood* and *Andrei Rublev* went straight to my heart. He has a fatalistic, tragic quality that really grabbed me and shook me, filling me with a kind of yearning. *The Dove Tree* tried to reproduce that tragic quality, but we didn't have the right conditions yet. *Ballad of a Soldier* and *The Forty-First* both moved me very much.[30] Later, Antonioni's *Blowup* made me feel I was being let into the secret of life and existence. I felt I'd made a connection.

XIE XIAOJING: Ermanno Olmi's 1978 film *The Tree of Wooden Clogs* and the Japanese director Shindo Kaneto's *The Island* attracted me the most. They were in the style Tian Zhuangzhuang and I were aiming for: an on-the-spot realism where all meaning flows from the processes of life itself, with no need for dramatization and embellishment. Meaning is right there in the original appearance and authentic movements of life. That was the style we were trying for in *Our Corner* and *The Yard*. Tian Zhuangzhuang's later films *On the Hunting Ground* and *Horse Thief* actually took that style to new heights.

TIAN ZHUANGZHUANG: Martin Scorsese was my favorite—a very important director. I've seen *Taxi Driver* eleven times. The French director François Truffaut's *The Four Hundred Blows* is real cinema. The Japanese director Ozu Yasujiro's powerful flavor of life and silent, implicit meanings are quintessentially Oriental. Among Chinese directors, Shui Hua's accomplishments and profound knowledge are quite extraordinary. Skill is not a matter of superficial techniques. It lies in one's character and learning and one's understanding and command of the Way.

ZHANG YIMOU: First, films must be enjoyable, and their deeper meanings must be experienced by the audience through their enjoyment. That's the kind of film I like, and that's why I never was particularly taken with Italian neorealism. I like Truffaut's *The Four Hundred Blows*. It made an enormous impression on me. Fei Mu's *Spring in a Small Town* was tremendously important. To have achieved that level in 1948 makes it a magnificent film. And it makes him a magnificent director. It's still

Spring in a Small Town,
directed by Fei Mu. Photo
from *The Film Art of "Spring
in a Small Town"—A Tribute to
Fei Mu* (Taipei: Taiwan Film
Archives, 1996).

very important today. Its doubts about the human condition run very
deep. Its language is simple yet it had deep and lasting appeal. Back then,
we really didn't like modern Chinese film because so many films lacked
realism and were phony. But a film like *Spring in a Small Town* has not
been surpassed by many urban films to this day. It's a rare masterpiece
in Chinese film history.

GU CHANGWEI: I liked *Barry Lyndon, Days of Heaven,* and *Lovers' Symphony.*[31] I like grand, mysterious, even ghostly lighting. I go for a rich
variety of complex and subtle changes. I don't like,flat or simple compositions or excessively stark contrasts. Lighting effects should be like a
complex symphony. I'm fascinated by that rich and fluid, ever-changing
feel.

NI ZHEN: You women students all loved Italian neorealist films such
as *Bicycle Thieves, Umberto D,* and *Shoeshine.* However, your own later
works did not necessarily have that look. Why is that?

LI SHAOHONG: At that time what we hated most was falseness in art.
We absolutely couldn't bear it. And which cinema most closely reflects
reality? Italian neorealism. However, I also like things that are very dynamic. Kurosawa moved me a lot. *Rashomon* made me think for a long
time. After that, I moved further and further toward films concerned
with individual psychology. So, I wrote a very detailed analysis of *Julia,*
looking at the connection between its editing and its expression of psychology. Truffaut's *The Four Hundred Blows* and *Shoot the Piano Player*
also had a great impact on me.

Li Shaohong in the dormitory. Photo courtesy of Li Shaohong.

HOU YONG: Kurosawa's *Dersu Uzala* was very important for me. As a shot passes, time becomes a kind of accumulation of the real. It expresses the conflict and the interaction between the human and the natural worlds. The aestheticism and focus on the individual in Lamorisse's 1956 film *The Red Balloon* and Resnais's *Last Year at Marienbad* were very inspiring. As far as Chinese films are concerned, Wu Yonggang's *The Goddess* from the thirties is without equal. Ruan Lingyu's acting really amazed me. *The Goddess* changed my opinion about many other films from the thirties. To pass the test, films have to make the grade on artistry alone.

CHEN KAIGE: I found the philosophical implications of Alain Resnais's *Hiroshima, Mon Amour* and *Last Year at Marienbad,* for which Robbe-Grillet worked on the screenplay, very thought provoking. Their visual aesthetic is also extremely unusual. I was very struck by the moving scene in *Hiroshima, Mon Amour* of that French girl who had been shaved bald by her compatriots because she'd had an affair with a German soldier during the war, and was therefore a victim of prejudice and humiliation. This sort of dilemma, between humanitarianism and responsibility, is eternal and universal. This film is like a heart monitor pouring out enormous quantities of data. It makes me feel its vibrations.

Citizen Kane's detailed revelation of human complexity and the Russian melancholy of *Ivan's Childhood*, with its combination of hatred and helplessness in the face of war, both made me come to a realization that our films are about human relationships and not about the human individual. Films like ours tend toward order and morality, and they lack an examination and expression of the existential condition of the individual. They lack real attention to the individual.

Of the Chinese films, at that time I was very fond of *The Goddess*. No other work can compare with it. It stands out from other left-wing films of the thirties. Ruan Lingyu's grief is both moving and exceeds the immediate circumstances. She lives her part completely.

When we were at the Academy, we all shared the desire to develop film language. That was a responsibility that our generation had to accept. Our film language had to be different from previous Chinese cinema. We had to completely eliminate falseness in film, along with emptiness and pretension. We had to use a transformed language to tell history anew.

Traditional Chinese cinema was in need of successors, and the future Fifth Generation was also examining tradition and taking from it selectively; the nonmainstream appearance of Fifth Generation film and its continuation of the thirties cinema tradition have their particular cultural roots.

Even though I have called this chapter "Noses to the Grindstone," there were many little comedies and happy times during the days at Zhuxin Village. Bittersweet love, long heart-to-heart talks deep into the night, noisy parties with drinking and dancing, and the delights of "naughty children" getting into trouble: freedom in the countryside was completely different from freedom in the city. Life at the Academy, which was part Beijing and part countryside, was a unique mix, half solemn and sacred and half fun and games. From eight in the morning, when the staff bus bearing the Academy's administrators and faculty rolled sedately onto the campus, until four-thirty in the afternoon, class order and discipline were strictly maintained. But after the bus left at five in the afternoon, the happy children took over the campus. Although a teacher from each department remained on campus and some faculty members lived in the student dorms, their presence could not alter the overall nighttime atmosphere of free-

Women members of the directing class of 1982 at a sports match on the Zhuxin campus. From left: Liu Miaomiao, Hu Mei, and Li Shaohong. Their slogans encourage the women competitors. Photo courtesy of Beijing Film Academy.

dom. Of course, "freedom" here does not mean acting wildly, but instead an alternative order was established by the students themselves.

A special space produces special behavior and molds special character, psychology, and confidence. The edges of the city were also the edges of order, far from the center, and perhaps this contained the seeds of a new center. Outmoded teaching materials and methods motivated self-directed reading and gathering of new data. The pranks they played on village cadres during their time of working and living in the countryside extended to unrestrained derision directed against false passion, false respectability, and woodenness in films.

■

If the Academy had not been moved out of the city by Jiang Qing and the campus had remained at Xiaoxitian on Xinwai Street in Beijing, perhaps the full significance of the Fifth Generation would never have made itself felt, either. The city would have tamed them and cozy families and comfortable lives would have absorbed them, making them yield completely to mainstream culture. But Zhuxin Village was a world unto itself, a community on the edge, half inside and half outside. It created a distance from the city, and the students' strong antiauthoritarian impulses, together with the pride born out of experiences of injustice felt by all members of the tribe of educated youths, laid the basis for strong alienation from mainstream film. Ultimately, Jiang Qing and Western cultural trends worked together to produce a group of rebels for the Chinese cinema.

Although they revered Chinese cinema of the thirties, the class of 1982 treated contemporary films as occasions for frivolity and jokes. The false plot twists, obvious flaws, and especially the sentimental love scenes of modern films made the theater erupt into laughter. The students would clap and even stomp their feet in unison. Very few directors could tolerate such dismissive laughter; even the most self-controlled could not help but slam their fist down, stand up, and storm out.

However, this reaction did not make the group of highly critical students in the least bit inclined to compromise. They were firm in their belief that they were attacking falseness in art and not the directors personally.

On one occasion extreme laughter forced the screening to a halt, and the house lights were turned up.

Sun Yuezhi, a teacher in the Academy and vice-secretary of its Party Committee, stood at the front and lectured them. "This is the Film Academy, not some provincial teahouse. You're going to make films yourselves in the future. How can you treat other people's films so rudely? You haven't got any manners or refinement, so how on earth are you going to become filmmakers?"

"It wasn't deliberate. We couldn't control ourselves."

"Nice try. If you continue to willfully flaunt the regulations like this, we'll have to stop showing Chinese films altogether."

"No, don't do that. We promise to behave ourselves. However, they'll have to stop being so fake, too."

Of course, not all contemporary films met with such misfortune. *The Corner Forgotten by Love* (Li Yalin and Zhang Qi), *The Legend of Tianyun Mountain* (Xie Jin, 1980), *My Memories of Old Beijing* (Wu Yigong), and *The Drive to Win* (Zhang Nuanxin) were all received with warm and sincere applause, and numerous analyses were written about them.[32] The screening room of the Academy was harsh and cold, but it was also a place of respect for real art. The problem was that the students were not willing to

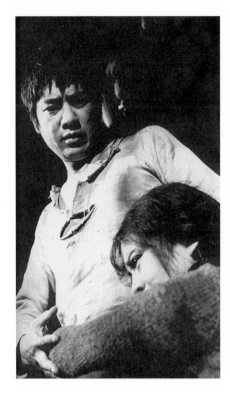

The Corner Forgotten by Love, adapted from Zhang Xian's novel of the same name. Photo from the 1985–1986 volume of *China Screen.*

pretend or to compromise, or to blur the distinction between the true and the false in art. In particular, they did not want to violate their own artistic judgment, which was born out of their own life experiences and their reflections on history. Maybe it was precisely this quality that formed the core of the future Fifth Generation.

It was easy to forgive breaches of discipline inside the Academy screening rooms, but such rash outbursts on public occasions would have much greater consequences.

In early summer 1979, the choir from the Academy caused a small incident at a singing contest for schools under the direct control of the Ministry of Culture. The event focused on revolutionary songs, and the list of songs was specified. It included tunes like "We Are Marching on the Highway" and "A Million Lei Fengs Are Growing Up." However, after the women's choir of the Academy, led by Hu Mei and Wang Ziyin, finished two revolutionary songs, they launched into a popular tune. The soft melody and the gentle swaying of their bodies to the accompaniment of their male classmates' guitars and percussion transformed the atmosphere in the auditorium instantly. Some people wanted them to stop and return to the specified songs, but they pressed on, spiritedly singing one song after another. They sang "The Bubbling Brook" and then a Japanese tune called "Red Is the Sunset":

> I went back to the little town again today
> And saw the sunset turn red once more
> The water gurgles as it flows under the bridge
> All the pedestrians are long gone
> Head down, I walk back to the little town
> Vaguely dreaming of the city

The students from the other schools in the audience were both shocked and delighted. But the teachers assumed very severe expressions.

Suddenly, a woman teacher got up and barked, "Beijing Dance Academy, stand and exit the hall!"

On the Zhuxin campus. From left, the front row includes Lü Yue and Hou Yong from the Cinematography Department and Wang Ziyin from the Directing Department. The back row includes Zhi Lei (second from left) and Zhang Yimou (far right). Photo courtesy of Hou Yong.

The directing class of 1982 at a sports match on the Zhuxin campus. Standing in the back row: second from left, Xie Xiaojing; fourth, Wu Ziniu; fifth, Chen Kaige; and first on right, Xia Gang. Photo courtesy of Beijing Film Academy.

Then another teacher stood. "Opera Conservatorium, exit the hall!"

It caused a big fuss. A critical report was circulated. The disruption of the revolutionary song contest by rock and roll music was a serious issue in 1979. Now, in the nineties, the universities see karaoke and MTV as perfectly healthy recreational activities for students, and these musical forms are quite acceptable. But back then, popular songs were not performed in refined auditoriums. It was a controversial event in cultural circles.

Although because of Hu Mei, Wang Ziyin, and the other girls, the choir of the Academy got into hot water, the Academy's basketball team won back Zhuxin Village's honor as it swept through the capital. With Chen Kaige at center, and Tian Zhuangzhuang, Zhang Yimou, and others on the team, they carried all before them. Battles among the ten major art colleges were fought out on one basketball court after another, but in the end it was these future leaders of the film world who always won. It must be noted that when Chen Kaige, Tian Zhuangzhuang, Zhang Yimou and the others were transferred from the countryside and the production brigades into the factories and the armed forces, they all relied on their basketball skills to get approval for transfer. The boys from the Film Academy took on every art college in the capital without a single loss, and the college leaders lurched between horror and delight at the behavior of these willful students.

Climbing the Great Wall, wading across Tenth Ford, joining the armed forces, or going to the countryside—wherever they went, they were a lively and unruly bunch that inspired both concern and delight. In spring 1980, all twenty-eight members of the directing class of 1982 went to stay with a naval unit in Dalian, where they were put up in a convalescent hospital that was not in regular use. They interviewed the sailors and performed free plays, both in Dalian and on outlying islands. They completed all the tasks they were given very well. The young officers paid special attention to the female students, and the female marines and nurses made a big impression on the male students from the Academy. In the convalescent hospital's radio station, a female marine worked as a broadcaster. She was skilled in her work, but appeared to stay aloof from the university students. However, unbeknownst to them all, she and Zhang Junzhao had sworn in greatest secrecy to spend their lives together. I gather that after the students returned to Beijing, she soon dropped out of the navy. She started to hang out with the class of 1982, and she became Zhang Junzhao's closest assistant.

Ah, distant Zhuxin Village, and those unforgettable student days in the clutch of buildings in the fields! Traces of my hard work and study, writing deep into the night, remain there, and it etched many marks of happiness and sorrow into my soul, too.

During that time everyone withdrew into their own space and studied hard, writing essays or filming, competing intensely against each other. However, if that group had not been thrown together in such unusual circumstances, I don't think the Fifth Generation would have appeared later.

Graduation photo for the directing class of 1982. Front row (faculty): first on the left, Situ Zhaodun; seventh, president of the Academy and famous director Cheng Yin; eighth, Zhang Ke; tenth, Wang Suihan. Middle row: third from left, Peng Xiaolian; fourth, Li Shaohong; fifth, Xia Gang; sixth, Wu Ziniu; fourth from right, Professor Zhou Chuanji. Back row: third from left, Liu Miaomiao; first at right, Tian Zhuangzhuang; second, film director and professor Zheng Dongtian; third, Xie Xiaojing; seventh, Chen Kaige. Photo courtesy of Beijing Film Academy.

CHAPTER 3

FIRST STEPS

■

In summer 1980 three students from the Directing Department—Tian Zhuangzhuang, Xie Xiaojing, and Cui Xiaoqin—were told to make a short film. This was a rare opportunity; normally group work of this kind did not happen until the fourth year of study. This team effort was an unscheduled experiment prompted by the need to check the technical performance of some newly arrived video equipment. Most importantly the students had found a very moving short story to adapt into a film script. Called "The Sunless Corner," it had appeared in the literary journal *Lake No-Name,* which was published by Beijing University students. The avant-garde work published in the journal had given it a large following among students and young people, and the author of the short story, Shi Tiesheng, had recently rocketed to fame. The characters in "The Sunless Corner" were vivid and its length was ideal for adaptation as a short film, so Tian Zhuangzhuang and the others decided to produce it as a short television drama.

The story focuses on three young men with lower limb disabilities who work together in a small factory located in the alleyways of Beijing. Beisheng, Kejian, and Tiezi have dull, repetitive jobs painting flowers onto lacquerware. One day, out of the blue, a girl called Wang Xue comes to their reproduction antiques factory. She enters their lives like a warm ray of sunshine, awakening hope in the three men's hearts. Their antisocial attitudes, low self-esteem, and dejection are all transformed by her arrival. Quietly, she cleans up the corner where they work, tidying their brushes and inkstones and the tables where they paint, and moving the drawing boards and stools for them. Her actions make them feel cared for and respected. After she gets to know them, she uses the pretext of her birthday to invite the young men home. In fact, she wants her father, who is a famous doctor, to examine their legs and treat their longstanding illnesses. When he tells her their conditions are incurable, she is choked with tears and deeply saddened by the unfairness of it all. In 1978, when the university entrance examination system is restored, Wang Xue alone is able to register to take the exam. The three young men help her to prepare round the clock, and she passes. However, this also means that she will leave the painting workshop and this unforgettable little corner forever.

Tian Zhuangzhuang, Xie Xiaojing, Cui Xiaoqin, and the cinematographer Zeng Nianping interviewed the author, Shi Tiesheng, and discovered that this young man was himself confined to a wheelchair. He had lost the use of both legs because of an illness he contracted down in the countryside ten years earlier.

■

Shi Tiesheng was a Beijing educated youth who was sent to work in the countryside of northern Shaanxi Province. His destination was a tiny mountain village more than twenty-five miles from Yan'an, and it formed the setting for the novel that established his reputation, *My Far-Away Qingpingwan*, which is a story about a cowherd on the loess plateau.[1]

> They said that place of ours was still the loess plateau, but actually it was all loess and no plateau. There was no level ground to be seen. Because of the annual floods the flat ground was always caving in, and rivers poured down ditches and gullies to the Yellow River. From Luochuan north, it was one yellow slope after another without a break.
>
> The old man who rounded up the cattle with me was called "Bai." But in northern Shaanxi dialect his name was pronounced "Po," which means "damned" in Mandarin. So, we all called him the "damned old man."

He loved to sing, but his voice was like a cracked whistle. When he drove the cattle back to the village in the evening, the last rays of the sun would glance off the slopes, turning everything red. The old man picked up a bundle of firewood on his pickaxe and sang as he walked along. "The flowers blossom and the hills are tinted red. A downtrodden man walks through a beautiful landscape."

Shi Tiesheng became ill while he was living in a damp cave in northern Shaanxi. At first, his back and his legs simply ached. However, his condition deteriorated with every passing day until he had no choice but to return to Beijing to see a doctor. Tragically, he ended up paralyzed from the waist down and completely unable to walk.

However, his bad luck did not make him lose the courage to live.

Secretly, he began writing short stories. One story after another about the lives of the disabled flowed from his pen. Everyone knows Chen Kaige later adapted *Life on a String* from Shi Tiesheng's novel of the same name.[2] But not everyone knows that over a decade earlier his story "The Sunless Corner" had already been made into a television drama by Tian Zhuangzhuang and his classmates.

In the heat of summer 1980, Tian Zhuangzhuang, Xie Xiaojing, Zeng Nianping, and several others went every day to fetch Shi Tiesheng. They pushed him in his wheelchair to the home of a professor of acting called Lin Hongtong, where they would discuss the script together. The Lin family lived in the city, quite close to Shi's home, and Lin and Shi were good friends. Tian Zhuangzhuang always lifted Shi Tiesheng in and out of his wheelchair, and with each passing day they all grew very close.

In one of the dorms out at Zhuxin Village, Tian Zhuangzhuang took up his pen. Ignoring the summer heat and the mosquitoes, he ground out a fourth, fifth, and sixth draft, bent over his desk with the sweat pouring down his back. Only after the eighth draft did his teachers Zhang Ke and Situ Zhaodun give him their nod of approval; they felt that the script was fundamentally sound and preparations for the shoot could begin. Through countless revisions, Zhang Ke carefully checked the script scene by scene, stressing the importance of detail. This work was vital to ensure a smooth shoot later. The title of the final draft was changed to *Our Corner.*[3]

Because Sony video equipment was being tried out on this short film, a young Cinematography Department teacher, Zeng Nianping, had been

On location for *Red Elephant*. From left: Tian Zhuangzhuang, Zhang Yimou, Zeng Nianping, Lü Yue, and Hou Yong. Photo courtesy of Hou Yong.

sent over from the Academy's video center to shoot it. Zeng had studied in the Cinematography Department from 1975 to 1977. He stayed on at the Academy after graduation and was assigned to the newly established video center as an additional member of their staff. He was tall, grave, said little, and seemed shy, but he had a particular propensity for moving camerawork, and he edited his shots into complex and striking sequences. Over a two-year period, he shot two films with Tian Zhuangzhuang, *Our Corner* and *Red Elephant* (1982). Later, after he married the director Li Shaohong, he shot *The Silver Snake Murders* (1988), *Bloody Morning, A Man at Forty*, and *Blush* for her. He became a consummately skilled and highly valued cinematographer.

The first conflict during the production of *Our Corner* concerned casting. The Academy wanted to use students from the acting class of 1982; a joint production required the departments to work together, and this way everyone would get to practice. However, Tian Zhuangzhuang, Xie Xiaojing, and Zeng Nianping had decided on non-actors from outside the Academy, because they felt the acting class students were too good-looking. They were fine for calendar work but no way could they pass as disabled people. Both sides dug their heels in for a long time, but in the end the decision was to be made by the directors.

Ultimately, using non-actors was the right decision. It transformed the old look of student films from the Academy, and it gave *Our Corner* the feel of a documentary about the lives of disabled people. Although a work of fiction with a fictional narrative, the characters were just like real people acting out real events.

First, there was the search for the female lead, Wang Xue.

■

According to the original story, Wang Xue was petite, had a little upturned nose, and loved to laugh. There really was no one so ordinary among the Acting Department students. After the semester began, Tian Zhuang-zhuang, Xie Xiaojing, and Cui Xiaoqin went to Beijing University, where they staked out the entrances to various dining rooms on campus, prepar-ing to ambush their "prey." There were at least ten thousand students at Beijing University at the time, and they poured in and out of the entrances in endless streams, so surely they could find a suitable person? Two, three, then four days passed and at least two thousand girls must have walked in front of them, but they still could not find a plausible Wang Xue. Under the blazing sun, Tian Zhuangzhuang's heart began to pound. If they really couldn't find someone, would they have to go back and do it the way the Academy had suggested after all? He lit up a cigarette, squatted down in the shade of the trees at a dining room entrance, and continued to search.

"We'd looked through the crowds countless times. Then suddenly we turned round and there she was in the dusk."

Out of nowhere, three or four women students approached the din-ing room, chatting and laughing as they walked. One of them was full of giggles. As she passed by in profile, they could see that her nose was slightly upturned. If she was not Wang Xue, who was?

Negotiation, persuasion, obtaining official stamps of approval, signing of documents, more negotiation, more stamps of approval, more research, and yet more signing of documents. That is the way things get organized in China, slowly talking round and round in circles. This time the process included persuading that giggling woman student. She was a sophomore studying foreign languages, and the minute she heard the word "film" mentioned, she shook her head and backed off as fast as she could. Fortunately, Tian Zhuangzhuang has a way with women, and in the end, with a sigh of relief, they were able to return to Zhuxin Village with the ideal person for the role.

In much the same way, they found Lei Han in the Athletics Department of Beijing Normal University. Gentle, refined, shy, and attractive, he would play Kejian. He looked so delicate that when he dithered on Xizhimen Street leaning on a crutch, passers by crossing the road would come up and try to help him. He looked as though he was only fifteen or sixteen years old. From *Our Corner* to *Our Fields,* he became a favorite of the class of 1982 and acted in one film after another. Indeed, he soon changed professions, which had never been part of the original plan.

Tiezi, who used a pair of crutches, was played by the son of old Zhao who looked after the water tower on the campus at Zhuxin Village. Young Zhao played basketball and swam with the students every day, so he knew them very well. He looked very fierce, a bit like a gangster with his eyes glaring out from beneath two straight brows; in fact, he appeared later as the bandit called Eyebrows in *One and Eight.* Although of medium height he was a tough guy, and with only his two rough hands to hoist himself up on a pair of crutches he was like a chained snow leopard and the spitting image of a frustrated disabled person.

The only leading role left to fill was that of Beisheng, who sat in a wheelchair. Who would play him?

Shi Tiesheng! No one else would do. Someone said that no able-bodied person could ever get the look in the eyes of a disabled person. However, in the end they had to abandon the idea because Shi Tiesheng's health was too weak. Xie Xiaojing took the part of Beisheng and much to everyone's surprise, because he seemed withdrawn and awkward, he did it perfectly.

The shoot for the television drama began in the middle of fall 1980 and continued until the first snow, three months altogether. The first scene was shot in a wooded area next to the water tower on the campus at Zhuxin Village. It was set during Beisheng's teenage years, when his legs were still fine, and depicted a charming scene of young love. All the students from every department came over to watch and encourage the work. Everyone had something to suggest, eager to display their talent.

Tian Zhuangzhuang tried for the objective look of a documentary film: sad but not sentimental, simple and restrained. Even in this debut, one can see Tian Zhuanzhuang's adaptability and willingness to try new things. Shot like a documentary, the film realistically and sensitively depicts the silent and lonely suffering of three disabled friends as life flows past, along with their resistance to their fate and their sadness in the face of society's failure to understand them. One day, there is a sudden storm on the way to work. Beisheng's wheelchair cannot move fast and the rain gets heavier and heavier. His two friends want to push him under some eaves and take shelter, but there are steps and it is impossible to get the wheels up them. All three are stuck out in the rain. Their clothes are soaked through, but they press on, heads held high. At this point, Wang Xue comes running up with raincoats and umbrellas. But Beisheng and the other two are so dejected they cannot accept her good intentions, and their pride drives them to put on a display of bravado. Proud and aloof, they stick it out in the rain, mistaking her sincerity for pity. Closing her umbrella, Wang Xue follows them, joining the "wheelchair tribe" and letting the storm drench her. Finally, her silent actions win their trust. This is a particularly moving scene from *Our Corner*.

At the end of January 1981, *Our Corner* was in the can. The first student work from the directing class of 1982 was actually finished. They sent it off to China Central Television, hopeful that it might be aired. At that time there had not yet been a television drama on the lives of the disabled, but, much to everyone's surprise, it did not get past the censors. They felt that the tone was too depressing and negative, and some refused to believe that the whole of society would ignore these three disabled people and only one girl would come to their aid. What about the Communist Party? What about the People? "Then one of the high-ups in the China Television Drama Production Center, an old veteran called Jin Shan, came and sought me out for a chat," remembers Tian Zhuangzhuang.[4] "He said, 'It won't be easy to put *Our Corner* right. Why don't we just put it to one side for now? We'll give you another script and you can shoot a bright, uplifting TV drama.'" That was the future *One Summer*. However, Tian Zhuangzhuang and the other students were not yet ready to abandon *Our Corner*. They had sweated blood over it. It was meticulously crafted and tried hard to be original. Bright or dark, why not air it and let the audience be the judge?

There have been cultural clashes on this earth since the splitting of the first amoebae started life. Over the next decade, from *One and Eight* and *Yellow Earth* through *Farewell, My Concubine* and on to *Blue Kite,* tempests

On location for *Red Elephant*. From left: Feng Xiaoning, Zhang Jianya, Tian Zhuangzhuang, Zhang Yimou, Hou Yong, Lü Yue, and Zeng Nianping. Photo courtesy of Hou Yong.

followed the Fifth Generation. The fate of that little television drama back in 1981 almost seemed to foretell their future, that trials and tribulations were destined from the moment of their inception.

Although China Central Television did not broadcast *Our Corner,* the work did have a great impact at the Beijing Film Academy because it encapsulated the last two years of study. Its assured cinematic voice and distinctive on-location style expressed the ambitions and strengths of the students in the Directing Department. Every student in every department was quietly eager for a chance to work; they were all hoping for the opportunity to display their own talent. Fortunately, it was not long before that chance came.

The fourth year began. In summer 1981, the entire student body began working on graduation productions, supervised by Professor Xie Fei. The majority of students from all departments were divided up into six short-film production teams and started preparing for their shoots, while the remainder were sent to the film studios to work on feature films either as production assistants or as director's assistants. All the departments in the Academy combined to select the teams. Overnight, the students changed from classmates into contestants in a talent competition for film crews.

■

"Tian Zhuangzhuang's group! What more is there to say? Who can compare with him?"

"He's him and you're you. Everyone should just do their best. Right now, you're just practicing, aren't you? We'll only really find out how good you are when you're in the studios later."

Tian Zhuangzhuang had become the focus of all the classmates' attention, and he was the one to beat.

Later, it was Chen Kaige and Zhang Yimou who made Fifth Generation cinema famous internationally. But in terms of their cinematic prehistory as students, Tian Zhuangzhuang was indisputably the central figure. He not only directed *Our Corner, The Yard,* and *Red Elephant,* forming a series of works, but he also gathered Zhang Yimou, Hou Yong, and Lü Yue around him, showing strategic foresight and an eye for talent.

The students of the class of 1982 used to say that their classmates could be divided into "three worlds," according to their family backgrounds.

The "first world" consisted of the children of high-ranking cadres. They enjoyed social privilege and had opportunities that ordinary people never enjoyed.

The "second world" came from families in the arts. They had educational advantages and an extensive network of social connections in the film world. They were assured of a future in the arts.

The "third world" consisted of people from ordinary family backgrounds. They had none of the advantages of either of the other two groups. Only hard work and more hard work would give them any chance of making a name for themselves in the arts.

It is true that Tian Zhuangzhuang came from an arts background. However, it was not just his "aristocratic background" that gave him so many opportunities to make films. His experience and filmmaking skills were probably even more important, and they were entirely the result of his own hard work.

Tian Zhuangzhuang, Chen Kaige, Zhang Junzhao, and some of the other students were all born in the same year and entered the Academy in the same year. But Tian had much more experience in film and photography than the others. After spending a year working in the countryside in Jilin Province in northeast China, he joined the army in Dingxing County in Hebei Province from 1969 through spring 1970. He was a literature and arts soldier, responsible for darkroom work in a propaganda department.

Shooting *September*. From left: Hou Yong, Acting Department Professor Jiang Yunhui, actor Wang Jian, and Tian Zhuangzhuang. Photo courtesy of Hou Yong.

His main job was to photograph the troops while they were studying quotations from Chairman Mao, explaining how they put Mao's thoughts into practice, being selected as model soldiers in the Five Good Points Movement, and putting up honors lists. Of course, he also took photographs of the officers. He was busy in the darkroom for five years altogether. When he was demobilized and returned to Beijing in 1976, he went to the Agricultural Film Studio and became a camera assistant. He had to measure the light, carry the camera, pull focus, and set up the lights; working for a cinematographer, he learned a great deal. By the time he entered the Academy, he was more or less familiar with what happened on the set.

Therefore, once he was in the Academy, Tian Zhuangzhuang could pour all of his energies into screenwriting and montage. Shooting a forty- or fifty-minute short film was not a problem for him. On the set, when there was something wrong with the cinematography or lighting, he could suggest a way to fix it on the spot and could even do it himself. As a result, everyone felt they could rely on him.

Tian Zhuangzhuang keeps his promises and places great emphasis on friendship, which helps him to maintain good working relationships over the long term. He is especially close to Hou Yong, and they have worked together for many years. Everyone in the Fifth Generation is aware of this relationship, and it was one of the factors guaranteeing the achievement of his documentary realist style. From *The Yard* to *Red Elephant, September* (1984), *On the Hunting Ground, Horse Thief,* and *Blue Kite,* whenever Tian Zhuangzhuang encountered an important artistic problem Hou Yong was always there by his side as his faithful cameraman. Among Tian Zhuangzhuang's classmates, Zhang Jianya, Xie Xiaojing, Li Shaohong, Liu Miaomiao, and Zhang Junzhao all got along with him especially well. Whenever they ran into a problem, they would think of Zhuangzhuang and go and talk it through with him. Down in Guangxi Province in 1983, when Zhang Junzhao, Zhang Yimou, Xiao Feng, and He Qun were sweating over the script of *One and Eight,* they bumped into Tian Zhuangzhuang. He was working as Ling Zifeng's assistant director on *Border Town* (1984), scouting for actors in the south.[5] As soon as he found out what was going on, he pitched right in.

"Let's do this," he said. "He Qun and I can take care of the meals—the shopping, the preparation, and the cooking. You can spend the days writing, and in the evenings we can all talk it over together. After two weeks, I think the script should be more or less finished."

Tian Zhuangzhuang pursues a relaxed, simple, and natural film style. He does not put on airs and can seem rough, but he is able to distinguish between the elegant and the crude when he needs to. Maybe because he is so easygoing, sometimes his films are outstanding and sometimes they are just ordinary. He is not as highbrow as Chen Kaige, nor is he an all-round talent like Zhang Yimou. Tian Zhuangzhuang makes films, but he has a life, too. He is easygoing and can take the rough with the smooth. This is both an attitude to art and a kind of philosophy of life.

If we are discussing his philosophy of life, maybe we should also discuss his "aristocratic" pedigree. Although both Tian Zhuangzhuang and Chen Kaige come from film families, Chen Kaige's father came from the KMT Nationalist-controlled area whereas Tian Zhuangzhuang's parents were artists in the Communist base in Yan'an. They both grew up in Beijing Film Studio housing and went through the storms of the Cultural Revolution, but there were also vast differences in their attitudes to both life and film. Tian Zhuangzhuang has the best family credentials—his family was both politically revolutionary and active in the arts. His background may even have had a greater impact on him than Chen Kaige's had on him. Although Tian wanted to experiment and break with tradition, by nature he

The Lin Family Shop, directed by Shui Hua. Photo from *China Film Album, 1949–1979* (Beijing: China Film Press, 1983), 69.

was calm, mild, sociable, and easygoing. He did not need to struggle for every little bit of success with a film or worry about his own future, let alone see a single opportunity as something that would determine his destiny. The others had to take on *One and Eight* without being able to weigh the risks, and they felt their whole futures were riding on it. Tian could display his talent in relatively relaxed and calm conditions, entering the hall of fame by stacking up one achievement after another.

■

Tian Zhuangzhuang has enormous respect for the veteran director Shui Hua. He admires him both as an artist and as a person. Although Tian Zhuangzhuang can seem brusque and undisciplined, his respect for Shui Hua is based on their common Yan'an cultural background, and these historical roots go very deep indeed. This makes understanding the work of Tian Zhuangzhuang more complicated. His cinema is not only an important part of Fifth Generation cinema but also the conscious continuation of the Third Generation of Chinese directors, adding to its significance in the evolution of Chinese cinema. A detailed comparison of Shui Hua's *The Lin Family Shop* (1959), *Regret for the Past* (1981), and *Blue Flower* (1984) with Tian Zhuangzhuang's *Blue Kite* reveals similarities in narrative, camera position, rhythm, style, restrained attitude, and tone. If *On the Hunting Ground* and *Horse Thief* exhibit vigor and youthful passion, then *Blue Kite* expresses more restraint and a return to orthodoxy.

This perspective helps us to see the connection of Fifth Generation cinema to tradition and its cultural roots and that it is not a cultural aberration that came out of nowhere.

During the early stage of Fifth Generation cinema, between 1983 and 1985, its creativity erupted on three fronts.

First, there was *One and Eight,* directed by Zhang Junzhao and shot by Zhang Yimou and Xiao Feng in 1983, followed by *Yellow Earth* and *Big Military Parade,* directed by Chen Kaige and shot by Zhang Yimou in 1984 and 1985. They were all made at the Guangxi Film Studio.

Second, there was *September, On the Hunting Ground,* and *Horse Thief,* all directed by Tian Zhuangzhuang, shot by Hou Yong in 1983, 1984, and 1985, and produced at the Beijing, Inner Mongolia, and Xi'an Film Studios respectively.

Third was *The Probationary Team Member* and *Secret Decree,* directed by Wu Ziniu at Xiaoxiang Film Studio in 1983 and 1984.

It should be acknowledged that Tian Zhuangzhuang was at the center of this three-part structure, because he had already pioneered a path with *Our Corner, The Yard, Red Elephant,* and *September* long before the others made their debuts. The first work of this series also marks the source of the river that the Fifth Generation became. But the appearance of *One and Eight,* like a gushing stream, was sudden and unstoppable. It changed the original river's course and direction, creating a new flow that spilled over into a torrent.

That is why we have given so much attention to Tian Zhuangzhuang's background and his place in the prehistory of the Fifth Generation.

■

In spring and summer 1981, Tian Zhuangzhuang and his crew first shot the black-and-white short film *The Yard,* and then went to Yunnan to shoot the children's fairytale feature film *Red Elephant.* Other teams were working on Pan Yuanliang and Pan Hua's black-and-white short *Our Fields,* and Lin Daqing's black-and-white short *The Last Shot.* Starting in spring 1982,

Shooting *September*. Behind the camera is Hou Yong, and Tian Zhuangzhuang directs. Photo courtesy of Hou Yong.

Xia Gang and Geng Xiaozhen began work on *We Are Still Young*, Bai Hong on *The Target*, and Jin Tao on *The Wedding*. By now, everyone's work was underway.

While this was happening, Chen Kaige and several other students went to the Children's Film Studio to work for the woman director Wang Junzheng on the full-length feature *My Brother the Yes-man* (1982). Li Shaohong and Peng Xiaolian became director's assistants on the Youth Film Studio production *The Apprentice Lawyer* (1982). And Wu Ziniu joined Wang Xinyu's crew as an intern at the Xiaoxiang Film Studio on *Chen Huansheng Comes to Town* (1982). This meant that these key Fifth Generation figures did not direct anything by themselves as graduation works.

The Yard was adapted from a short story called "Life in a Small Courtyard" by the young writer Wang Anyi. By focusing on the gossip and trivia in the lives of a group of neighbors in courtyard apartments belonging to a cultural troupe, it offers a cross-section of life that details the small storms and carefully nursed grievances of married life. It feels like searching in hidden corners by candlelight and has a distinct aftertaste, like a piquant tea. For a new young woman writer, this was a remarkable effort.[6]

The directing team on *The Yard* was Tian Zhuangzhuang, Xie Xiaojing, Zhang Jianya, and Cui Xiaoqin. The cinematography team consisted of Zhang Yimou, Hou Yong, Lü Yue, Zhang Huijun, and several others. This crew was considered the strongest shooting graduation works.

The Yard details everyday life among the young members of a cultural troupe living in a typical Beijing courtyard, including an orchestra conductor, a violinist, a trumpeter, and stage set designers. Although each individual story is quite small, the film required a large cast—about a dozen in all. Among the actors chosen for the film were Li Ling, Zhu Lin, Wang Yongge, and Ma Jing. All were greenhorns then, especially Zhu Lin. She was an acting student in the Chinese Amateur Arts University, a girl attending night school. However, her charisma and her delicate face mesmerized everyone, and they all agreed that she should play Sangsang, the female lead. Zhang Yimou and Hou Yong shot a great range of close-ups and portrait shots of her in this black-and-white film, capturing every detail of her striking appearance and sparkling personality. She shot to fame with *The Yard,* and soon became a professional actor with Emei Film Studio.

But when Zhu Lin was working on *The Yard,* she was still an inexperienced actor and often handled complicated or strong emotions poorly. In one scene, Sangsang accosts her composer husband, Ah Ping. He ignores her, busying himself with his work. Sangsang is then supposed to turn around and start to sob, but Zhu Lin could not make the tears flow no matter how hard she tried.

They took a break. All twenty-plus people on the crew stopped work, waiting for the actor to get in the mood.

Tian Zhuangzhuang instructed everyone to wait quietly. No one was to make a sound or leave the set.

He called Zhu Lin over to one side and the two of them talked for a long, long time. The whole crew watched their intimate talk from a distance, with no idea of what they were actually talking about.

Ten minutes passed, then twenty. . . .

The actor playing Ah Ping was Zhang Jianya, who was also a member of the directing team. He walked over and drew Tian Zhuangzhuang aside, whispering that if she really could not cry naturally then maybe they should use glycerin tears.

Tian Zhuangzhuang rejected this method. He lowered his head, went back, and continued to talk quietly with Zhu Lin.

Zhu Lin in 1985. Photo courtesy
of Beijing Film Academy.

The director's patience enabled the actor to get into the mood gradually.

Zhu Lin came to the set. All the lights were turned on and the actors took up their positions.

As the camera turned and whirred, Zhu Lin found two streams of tears trickling down. She carefully controlled her emotions, turned around, and went over by herself to stand with her back to Ah Ping, suffering the sorrow of a young wife by herself.

Tian Zhuangzhuang does not like formal meetings. Nor does he like standing by a camera barking out orders. When the supervising teacher Meng Qingpeng could not stand it any longer, he came over and demanded, "Don't you know where the director should stand? Where's the director in your group?"

"Tian Zhuangzhuang likes people to work out his directorial vision from his behavior and from conversation," Zhang Jianya explained later. "You can't be slack when you're working with him. You have to think hard, get in tune with him, figure out what he wants and then do it. When he's directing on the set, his strengths as a director and cinematographer come out naturally and invisibly, and he draws you into the work."

Something especially well worth recalling occurred during production of *The Yard*—an event that was the catalyst for the three cinematographers to work out their future directions.

The Yard was shot in a real courtyard by Houhai Lake in the western district of Beijing. Because the shoot was going to take several weeks, it was too much trouble to keep moving the lights and cameras in and out. So they borrowed an empty room in the yard and piled the equipment into it at night. Then they would just shoot again the next day. However, someone had to stay to guard the equipment. Zhang Yimou, Hou Yong, and Lü Yue volunteered. They passed the nights beside their cameras and did not go back to the Academy.

It was early summer then and the nights were extremely hot. It was too stuffy to sleep, so all they could do was lie back on their mats and chat about this and that. The conversation turned to what they wanted to do after they graduated.

"I want to become a director," said Zhang Yimou. "As a cinematographer, you don't have enough control. No matter how good your ideas and

The Yard. Zhang Jianya (left) and Zhu Lin. Photo courtesy of Beijing Film Academy.

technique are, you're still shooting for someone else, expressing their ideas. That's no good. I'm determined to work for myself."

However, for the present, he still had to try and shoot every film well. No matter if it was a big project or a small one, he had to mind every little detail. Only if his cinematography were so good that no one could pick holes in it would he gain recognition and be able to start talking about taking the next step. So, how was he preparing to become a director?

"I already had the hang of still photography before I went to the Academy," Zhang says.

> After I got there, I got the hang of cinematography, too. The teachers worked very hard. That goes without saying. But I studied directing on the sly. I read all kinds of books, squirreling away knowledge bit by bit. Kuleshov's *The Four Fundamentals of Film Direction,* Eisenstein's *The Film Sense,* Pudovkin, and Kracauer were all very important to me. But I'm a very practical person and I wanted to learn how to do it. There was one book I found especially useful and that was the Uruguayan Daniel Arijon's *Grammar of Film Language.*[7] That book's so good! He doesn't waste a single word. It talks about how to position the camera, how to determine the axis, how to cross the 180 degree line, and how to edit a scene. It's extremely down-to-earth, and it was just what I wanted. I already had stories I wanted to tell, but what I didn't know was how to direct. I was shooting *The Yard* by day but at night I was thinking about how I'd do it if I were directing. However, that was all in the future.

That future was not far away. Six years later, Zhang Yimou took the helm and directed his first feature, *Red Sorghum.* For him, the regular way of doing things was only a reference point. He took romantic passion to the extreme with an extremely stylized look, intricate rituals, intense colors, and all the clamor of a wild life. The gush of freedom and release from restraint was combined with the passionate color of red to issue an all-out challenge to staid, worn-out, traditional ethics and customs. It was as though Zhang wanted to explode all the constraints of his earlier life.

Since then, almost every film Zhang Yimou has directed has attracted wide attention and been welcomed in international film festivals. At a social event during one European film festival, he spotted a scholar who was getting on a bit in years. Someone told him the man was the Uruguayan film scholar Daniel Arijon. Zhang eagerly asked his interpreter to intro-

Shooting *The Yard*. From left: Hou Yong, Lü Yue, and Zhang Yimou. Photo courtesy Hou Yong.

duce him, and he told Arijon, "When I was a young student, your book was a great help and inspiration to me. Your clearly presented techniques have been of great practical use to me as a director, so I really must thank you for writing that book."

■

Hou Yong revealed that he did not have any ambitions outside of cinematography. "In the future, I want to be a real cinematographer," he told Zhang Yimou and Lü Yue. "I want to shoot a series of top films. I'm going to shoot one film after another with the greatest of care."

Hou Yong's father committed suicide during the Cultural Revolution when Hou Yong was only six years old. His mother and elder sister brought him up. In order to protect the sole remaining male of the family, Hou's mother took special care with his upbringing. From an early age she taught him to be obedient, hard working, cooperative, and morally upright. As a result, he was sensitive, extremely diligent, and reliable. The basic training he received in the cinematography class made him proficient in the use of the camera, ensuring a thorough command of lighting and focus. His earlier grounding in fine art shines through in his films; comparing his work with that of equally well-trained cinematographers, Hou Yong's is more varied, richer, and better detailed. He uses his mind well, too: whenever the crew confronts a problem on the set, a light bulb goes off in his head and he sees a way out. This happened again and again during the filming of *The Yard*. Once, when they were shooting in the limited space of a very tiny room, the light directed on the actor seemed too strong. But if they used a filter, it was too dark. Because the room was so small that the light could not be moved back, it looked as though they would have to give up. Hou suddenly remembered that there was a transparent plastic bag hanging on a clothesline in a corner of the yard. He ran and got it, tore it open, and put it in front of the light. Now it was just right. Everyone was delighted, and the director yelled, "Camera! Action!"

Tian Zhuangzhuang was observant and noted this retiring young man's dedication to his craft. He feels that he and Hou Yong are opposite extremes fated to meet, and they have worked together for a long time. When Tian shot *On the Hunting Ground* with Hou Yong and Lü Yue, they were overawed by the spartan beauty of the Inner Mongolian grasslands. Hou Yong stood there enthralled by the last rays of the setting sun. He watched the herds of horses being brought in, the smoke curling up from the yurts and turning red in the sunset, and the hamlets gradually settling into the dusk. "I must find a way to film the real atmosphere of the grasslands," Hou Yong said. "I want to make everyone breathe in the air of the grasslands and sense the fragrance of the dew."

In 1986, the French Cinéma du Réel International Film Festival showed *On the Hunting Ground* as their opening night film, and it was selected for competition at the 1987 Locarno International Film Festival in Switzerland. After the Dutch documentary filmmaker Joris Ivens saw *On the Hunting Ground,* he said, "I've been searching for years without success to find cinematographers for my project *Tale of the Wind*. But now I've found them—Hou Yong and Lü Yue. I hope Tian Zhuangzhuang will lend them to me so that I can realize my dream of making what may be my last film."

When the Ministry of Culture received the request from Ivens, they agreed that Hou and Lü could be lent to him. However, Tian Zhuang-

On location for *On the Hunting Ground*. From left: Lü Yue, Hou Yong, and Tian Zhuang-zhuang. Photo courtesy of Hou Yong.

zhuang was about to start work on *Horse Thief*, and he really could not afford to let Hou Yong go.[8] After lengthy negotiations, Lü Yue alone was lent to Ivens to shoot his art documentary *Tale of the Wind* (1988).

For Lü Yue, this turn of events was ideal. He had told the others that he hoped to go overseas and spend some time there studying foreign film culture so that he could understand where film art was headed and then put that understanding to work on his return to China. Lü Yue realized his dream. After he finished shooting *Tale of the Wind* for Ivens, he stayed on in Paris to study. Over the next six years, he developed a very thorough understanding of French cinema and European culture, and professionally this helped him enormously.

In their later lives, these three successful men all fondly remembered their nighttime talks together in the yard. You need a dream before you can motivate yourself and turn the dream into reality.

The crew of *Red Elephant* on location in Xishuangbanna in Yunnan Province, 1981. From right: Zhang Yimou, Tian Zhuangzhuang, Zeng Nianping, Zhang Jianya. Crouching in the foreground with his back to the camera is Lü Yue. Photo courtesy of Tian Zhuangzhuang.

■

Before the shoot on *The Yard* was finished, Tian Zhuangzhuang's mother Yu Lan sought out her son and asked him if he could shoot a feature film for the Children's Film Studio. She put the script for *Red Elephant* on the table. Yu Lan had been given the task of building up the Children's Film Studio. The script was about three children searching for a sacred elephant in the forests of Xishuangbanna in Yunnan Province. The plot was simple and the budget low at about RMB300,000 (approximately US$167,000). Given that the whole thing had to be shot in the forests, the working conditions would be tough. "With such poor conditions, I'm afraid most people wouldn't want to do it," said Yu Lan. "But you boys share a vision, so you may be able to make a good film despite the conditions."

While *The Yard* was still in postproduction in summer 1981, Tian Zhuangzhuang and Zhang Jianya took RMB500 (approximately US$275) from the Children's Film Studio and went to Yunnan to scout for locations and work on the script of *Red Elephant*.

From the north to the south of China is a long journey. Even though prices were very low in China in 1981, RMB500 certainly was not enough. So once they got to Yunnan, they went to the Dai Autonomous Region and borrowed bicycles. They covered fifteen and sometimes as many as twenty-five miles a day. Sometimes when they crossed mountains they could not ride the bikes and had to carry them on their backs. Fortunately, they were young, strong, vigorous, and afraid of nothing.

In late fall, Tian Zhuangzhuang and Zhang Jianya returned to Yunnan with Xie Xiaojing, along with Zhang Yimou, Hou Yong, and Lü Yue from the Cinematography Department and Feng Xiaoning from the Production Design Department. They moved through Yunnan, up hill and down deep into the forests, shooting *Red Elephant*.

■

The Yard won attention because there were so many talented people involved. But *Our Fields* and *The Target* are the two graduation works that best represent the background of the class of 1982.

Pan Yuanliang from the directing class of 1982 wrote the script of *Our Fields*. He was the student described in the first chapter acting the little piece for his entrance exam about rescuing a woman from the quicksand. As far as he was concerned, he would never be at peace with himself until he wrote the story and filmed it.

> If I were a seedling,
> I'd sing out in a hoarse voice:
> This land is soaked in blood, sweat, and torrential rain.
> This river tumbles eternally with our feelings and thoughts.
> These magnificent mountains lead from the past into the future.
> And that sublimely soft and gentle dawn light comes from the
> forest . . .
> I am the embryo of this land
> Even if I die
> My lifeless cells will melt into this land.

Pan Yuanliang used this poem to guide his script. *Our Fields* is about five Beijing middle school students and the opening up of the Great Northern

Wasteland in Heilongjiang Province in the northeast. They are all members of an advance party for the Wasteland Reclamation Army, sent to a vast and marshy tract of virgin land to set up a forward position with a campsite and to establish a new reclamation site. The team leader is Xi'nan, who is smart and sturdy—an elder-brother figure everyone feels they can rely on. Qulin is a quick-witted mischief-maker who often gets into scrapes. On one occasion, he goes on an errand and returns with a hen. When he cooks it, the smell is so enticing that all their mouths start to water and they gobble it up in no time at all. Only then does he tell them he stole it from a family in the village. But Qulin is a hard worker and so helpful that the team cannot do without him. Ningyu and Qiyue are the two girls on the team. Ningyu is refined and introverted, and she and Xi'nan are secretly in love with each other. However, Ningyu cannot cope with the tough life on the wastelands. She is crippled with indecision, but in the end she gets on a truck and abandons Xi'nan with a heavy heart, leaving forever. Qiyue is a feisty girl. She comes from a cadre family and is a typical child from an exemplary class background. She firmly believes that the movement to send educated youths up into the mountains and down to the countryside is correct, and she despises Ningyu's weakness and selfishness. She is determined to serve Chairman Mao's line by working and settling in the Great Northern Wasteland permanently. The final member of the team is Little Brother Xiao. He is the son of an overseas Chinese, and everyone says he is spoilt and unable to bear hardship because of his family background. However, in an arduous battle to extinguish a grassland fire, he sacrifices his life, alongside Qiyue.

Two new graves in a peaceful spot by a birch tree forest; the wasteland reclamation team members stand at the headstones mourning their comrades-in-arms. The magnificent natural beauty makes seeing off the young people all the more difficult. One after the other, Xi'nan and Qulin leave the Great Northern Wasteland and go back to Beijing. They find that Ningyu has already married and become an office worker with a settled life. Qulin becomes a driver, and Qiyue's parents are gradually forgetting about their daughter's death in a strange place. The whole of society has changed completely. Grappling with the enormity of his loss, Xi'nan boards a northbound train again, hurrying to "our fields" to hold a memorial ceremony for the young people who lost their lives.

In May 1981, an advance team composed of Pan Yuanliang and Pan Hua from the Directing Department, along with Gu Changwei, Mu Deyuan, Xiao Feng, and others from the Cinematography Department, set off to the Great Northern Wasteland State Farm to select locations for the shoot on their graduation work.

The earth looked as if it were covered with a green carpet, undulating with the terrain to the horizon. The pure white branches of the birch trees in the forest were sprinkled with leaves fluttering in the breeze and the air was fragrant. Gu Changwei, Mu Deyuan, and the other students were rapturous. "Under this wide sky, we're sure to be able to shoot something as brilliant as the Beijing-based competition."

One morning they set off along a path through the swamps to find an island in the marshlands. They had a map with them but they weren't prepared when, after walking for a couple of miles, a thick fog descended and visibility was reduced to a few yards. They could not go forward, but they could not retreat either. They had to hold on tight to each other and cross the swamps by stepping on the protruding roots and advancing one step at a time. After quite a distance, the fog gradually lifted and a beautiful stand of birches appeared before them. Beside it was a charming patch of open land. It was impossible to imagine a better site to set up camp for the film shoot. But none of them could figure out where they were. Suddenly they were overcome with an indescribable fear. Pan Yuanliang told everyone not to panic, to stay together, keep calm, and study the map. By tracing along the marshlands from the farm they would find this forest. From there, they could find the stream alongside the forest. Following that, they would be able to get to a bridge on which there should be a simple road, and once they got to the road they would hitchhike. So there was no possibility of not finding their way back to the farm.

Eventually they were able to follow the route indicated to the stream by the forest and find their way back. Although no real disaster had occurred, it was a true test of character for everyone except Pan Yuanliang. The script of *Our Fields* describes a dramatic situation when the educated youths were struggling through the marshlands in the rain and got lost as it turned into a blizzard. Now that they had been in a similar predicament themselves, they felt they had had a taste of what it was really like. This was an unexpected bonus for the production of the film.

With Professor Xie Fei in command, the rest of the team soon reached the Great Northern Wasteland from Beijing and filming got underway in the normal fashion. However, when the team followed the route laid out by the earlier survey and reached the patch of empty ground by the birches in the swamplands, they found that there were bushes and saplings growing amidst the grass. "So, this is the spot you've chosen?' asked Xie Fei. "The overall setting's fine, but with all these saplings in the foreground, how are you going to shoot?"

"When we came here to have a look," said Pan Yuanliang and Mu Deyuan, "there weren't so many saplings and bushes."

Actually, a heavy fog that day had obscured all the saplings and bushes that were more than a few yards away.

Pan Yuanliang and Mu Deyuan said, "We're shooting dusk scenes, aren't we? It's only midday now and there are quite a few hours before sunset, so we'll be able to shoot by five for sure."

The two of them went and got the sharpest axes and saws from the farm. Without further ado, they went over to the birch forest and set to work chopping and clearing. They got rid of all the scrub and saplings within camera range. The sweat poured off them as they labored through the whole afternoon, but by five o'clock a patch of grassland had been cleared completely.

The crew arrived on the set. The actors, the lights, and the dolly tracks were all in place.

That day, Mu Deyuan happened to be the designated camera operator. "Hurry up and get into position," said Xie Fei. "Why are you still hanging around?"

However, Mu Deyuan's hands were shaking. He'd been chopping and dragging away the undergrowth all afternoon and had exhausted himself. His hands were weak, and there was no way he could control the camera.

"What's the matter? Are you sick? If there's some reason you can't operate the camera, let someone else do it for now. The sun'll be gone soon."

"No, you can't let someone else shoot! I'm going to do it." Mu Deyuan gritted his teeth, picked up the camera, and began to execute a traveling shot as stipulated. His hands gripped the camera, but they shook a little and his heart pounded. Still, he would not give this opportunity away to someone else. Why had he spent a whole afternoon chopping down saplings if not to try to realize his long-planned setups, and realize them as well as he could?

Hearing the soft whirr of the camera as it turns is the sweetest and most

Sacrificed Youth, directed by Zhang Nuanxin. Photo from the 1985–1986 volume of *China Screen.*

exciting time for any cinematographer. Qiyue, Little Brother Xiao, and Xi'nan performed their roles perfectly. The scenes went well, everything felt right, and all went smoothly. However, even now, if you know to watch for it, when the film is projected you can see there are a few tremors. "I couldn't control my hands," Mu Deyuan recalls wistfully. "They were shaking. But I wouldn't hand over the camera to anyone else, and I went on shooting."

Mu Deyuan stayed on at the Beijing Film Academy after graduation to teach in the Cinematography Department. In 1985 he shouldered the camera for the woman director Zhang Nuanxin and shot *Sacrificed Youth,* a film about educated youths in Yunnan Province. After that, he shot *Slipping into the Golden Triangle* (1988), and in 1989 he started directing in his own right, making *Lonely Ghost in a Dark Mansion* (1989), *No Choice* (1991), *Massacre* (1990), *The Chinese* (1992), and *A Policeman's Honor* (1994).

Professor Xie gave extensive assistance on the shoot for *Our Fields.*

Sometimes when he was not satisfied with the students' shot lists he would produce his own to save time, but this excited opposition and objections from some students. Because this was a graduation work, they felt he should respect their ideas and goals so that they could show their real directing and cinematography abilities. This caused frequent struggles and even deadlocks between teacher and students on the set.[9]

For example, Cinematography Department student Gu Changwei planned a shot for the scene where the members of the reclamation team gather before the two fresh graves to mourn their comrades-in-arms. It involved placing the camera in the center, making a 360 degree pan, and then slowly zooming into a close shot of the male lead, Xi'nan, to illustrate his overwhelming sense of loss. Gu stressed that this drawn out and continuous shot would help to build up a heavy atmosphere. However, Xie Fei felt that there was no need for such a song and dance. The scene could be divided into two shots: a pan around the mourners first and then a straight cut to a close-up of the main actor. A tug of war broke out. Gu Changwei, normally quiet and retiring, even timid, suddenly became extremely stubborn. He gripped the camera tight, holding it close to his body, and said, "This scene's been assigned to me. I've put my plan forward and I'm confident it'll add a lot to the story. If you won't let me shoot it that way, I won't let you shoot it, either. No one will get to shoot it."

This deadlock could not go on. The supervising teacher from the Cinematography Department, Bao Xiaoran, came over to discuss the matter with Xie Fei. "Let him shoot it his way. After all, it is the student's own assignment."

"Very well," said Xie Fei. "We'll do it both ways. We'll shoot it according to Gu Changwei's plan first. Then we'll do it the other way as a back-up." Maybe Xie Fei was such a perfectionist because he had become so immersed in the production that he had forgotten he was a supervisor. Or maybe it was because he was used to dealing with problems in a confident and direct fashion. Whatever the reason, the determination on both sides to defend their artistic positions without giving an inch was very striking.

The production team was in the Great Northern Wasteland for six weeks. Although the living conditions were very rough indeed, the shoot went smoothly and everyone was delighted with the quality of the black-and-white footage. The students felt they could now relax and they said to themselves, "Wait till we get back to Beijing and compare our film with *The Yard,* then we'll see who comes out on top."

■

The short film *The Target* was similar in subject matter to *Our Fields* but different in approach. It was adapted from the short story "The Final Destination for This Train," which is about an educated youth called Chen Xin.[10] After working in the countryside for ten years, he finally returns to the city and is reunited with his family. However, on his return he faces very overcrowded living conditions, which puts a heavy strain on his relationships. His elder brother is married with children and also looks after his old mother together with his younger brother, who is grown up now. They are all packed into their original tiny home. As the one returning, the extra wheel and an outsider, Chen Xin feels awkward. Moreover, because she is worried that he will want a room, his sister-in-law suggests that the family split up and go their own ways. His younger brother feels that his livelihood is threatened by Chen Xin's return; he is in line to take his mother's job on her retirement, but now he will have to give way to his older brother. After ten years of being down in the countryside, everyone is used to his absence. As he travels to and from work, or goes for a stroll along the streets, he suddenly feels that the city is much smaller than he remembers from his youth and that the streets seem much narrower. The pedestrians jostle each other and the passengers on the buses are crammed in so tightly they can barely breathe. The countryside is so vast, so spacious—he felt happy and free there. Actually, life is tough in the countryside—people are poor and the work is much more tiring. But the countryside is open and life is less stressful, and amongst all the hard grind, there is happiness and fulfillment. Amidst the ups and downs of family life, Chen Xin develops doubts about his decision to return to the city. Is the final destination for this train really the last stop in the journey of life? After having made so much effort to return to the city, has the target really been worthwhile?

This short story was adapted into the short film *The Target* by Bai Hong and Li Shaoxu. The city was changed from Shanghai to Beijing, and Chen Xin's destination in the countryside was changed to the Inner Mongolian grasslands. The dawn clouds and dusk light on the grasslands, the herds of cattle, and cooking on the campfire provided magnificent shooting opportunities. The filmmakers felt inspired. The contrast with the cramped living conditions and trivia of daily life in the city, where every little thing had to be haggled over and there were constant tempests in a teacup, was absolutely clear. To the scriptwriters, Beijing and the grasslands were in perfect contrast. And because the film was to be in color, the rich and diverse scenery promised good results.

Our Fields and *The Target* reflected the personal experiences of the class of 1982 in a highly concentrated manner. Although the films were directed by only a few students—Pan Yuanliang, Pan Hua, Bai Hong, and several others—in fact they condensed the common history and feelings of the great majority. Chen Kaige has said repeatedly that, "the experience of the Cultural Revolution was the most important experience in my life. My whole life's creative work is being spent in the expression of this experience." In 1984, he was recommended to Guangxi Film Studio and went there to make a film. The original script he submitted to the studio heads, *Let's Call It Hope Valley,* was about educated youths. At the time, it was not approved for production, and he was told to shoot *Yellow Earth* instead. But then he poured all of his energy into adapting Ah Cheng's novel *King of the Children,* which is further evidence of his obsession with the educated youth theme. In this light, *Our Fields* and *The Target* are very important in understanding the origins of Fifth Generation cinema.

Of course, there are obvious traces of immaturity, roughness, and imitation in both the production values and techniques of these two films. For example, the design and visual style of *Our Fields* is reminiscent of Soviet cinema. Also, in both works the treatment of the educated youth phenomenon tends to be highly emotional. Nevertheless, these two short films express very strongly the typical tragic predicament, fatalism, and overwhelming sense of helplessness experienced by educated youths. They cannot be compared to the later television dramas *Wasted Years* and *There Is a Blizzard Tonight,* the novel *Bloody Dusk,* or the reportage piece *Dreams of China's Educated Youth.* However, *Our Fields* and *The Target* were produced several years earlier. In fact, they could be said to be the earliest cinematic attempts to represent the lives of the educated youths, and because they were also part of the Fifth Generation tendency to reflect on history, their historical importance must not be overlooked.

The short film *We Are Still Young,* which Xia Gang was in charge of,

From left: Chen Kaige, Li Shaohong, Xia Gang, and Geng Xiaozhen, photographed in 1980.
Photo courtesy of Geng Xiaozhen.

must also be mentioned. Adapted from a novel of the same name by Ye Zhizhen, it is a love story involving a girl and three male workers in a large steelworks. The story employed an old narrative formula to accommodate a story about 1980s society. The male characters are Pan, who is handsome and smart; Xu Ping, who is big and strong; and Zhang Minzhu, who is ordinary and plain. In the workshop, everyone is talking about a pretty female worker called Min Xing who has just been transferred there. She is slim, virginal, and so beautiful that she can leave a cafeteria full of men gaping in awe. Min Xing is assigned to the three men's team, and apprenticed to them. All three become her suitors, but plain and short Zhang Minzhu clearly has the least hope of winning her.

Pan and Xu Ping, the two smart and handsome guys, are drawing closer to success, and one of them is certain to win her favor soon. Suddenly, however, they hear that before she was transferred, she had fallen in love with a young worker at the radio factory where she was employed before. What is more, they had a relationship that ruined her reputation and forced her to transfer.

Her beautiful, pure, and virtuous image abruptly dissolves, and her possible lack of virginity becomes an insurmountable obstacle. Xu Ping is the first to withdraw, and Pan hesitates, too. As they are struggling with their dilemma, trying to overcome their initial disappointment, they find that hurt and wounded Min Xing has already turned to Zhang Minzhu's plain but sturdy shoulder to cry on, and that in the process they have become a devoted couple.

The focus on moral dilemmas and patriarchal thinking in this story signaled a new turn; it was a very fresh theme in the early 1980s. It gently satirized the rigidity of male attitudes and critiqued the outmoded ideas of the two conventional heroes. Moreover, because Xia Gang insisted on selecting a complete novice in the film world to play Min Xing, her shyness, absence of affectation, and lack of confidence made her perfect for the part.

This short film was shot in color on location at the imposing Capital Iron and Steel Works. Powerful images of the towering modern blast furnaces and fiery molten steel being poured provided an excellent contrast to the characters' depression, helplessness, and sense of their own insignificance. When work began on this film, Xia Gang, Chen Kaige, Geng Xiaozhen, and Wang Zhihong shared script and direction. Then Chen Kaige was assigned to be assistant director on *My Brother the Yes-man,* and *We Are Still Young* was completed by the team under Xia Gang's leadership. The kind of poignant laughter provoked by this film is evident in the films he was making ten years later. Xia Gang is steady and genial, and his relative lack of ambition and relaxed attitude separate him from his driven and competitive Fifth Generation peers. He is like the rock that emerges steady and firm when the storm waves subside and retreat. Allowing such artists to mature slowly but steadily according to their individual characters and temperaments may well be a necessary precondition for the development of a rich and varied art scene.

■

Of course, classroom exercises are only exercises. No matter how strongly these graduation works displayed their makers' talent and vitality, they cannot be discussed in the same breath as their later feature films. Nonetheless, looking back at the productions of the Fifth Generation directors during their training at the Academy, there are two especially noteworthy points to make.

First, in addition to the events of the Cultural Revolution, the experiences of the educated youths sent up into the mountains and down to the countryside formed a spiritual burden and sad theme shared by all members of that generation. Like other writers and filmmakers in the early part of the post-Mao era, the students had to pour it all out. What was different from these other artists was that the Fifth Generation put even more emphasis on the direct and emotional display of the experiences of the educated youths. Their early film exercises are far from perfect, and even display the immaturity and roughness of complete beginners, but they also show potential. Although the first widely recognized Fifth Generation films were *One and Eight* and *Yellow Earth,* the short films they made in 1981 and 1982 constitute an overture to that kind of historical reflection.

Second, long before Chen Kaige and Zhang Yimou took center stage, Tian Zhuangzhuang's creative vitality and film style had already been systematically demonstrated during his college days, and he was the center of attention among his peers. His eye for subject matter, his on-location style, and his preference for contemporary themes and psychological analysis might well have lit the way for the Fifth Generation film style. However, events took a completely unexpected turn. Zhang Yimou's role as cinematographer determined the visual design and narrative structures of the earliest Fifth Generation films. An emphasis on visual language marked the films directed by Zhang Junzhao and Chen Kaige, *One and Eight* and *Yellow Earth,* and because the films were widely acknowledged, the legend of the Fifth Generation cinema and its style somehow took a new direction.

This turn of events not only changed the destinies of these important artists but also set the direction of this innovative Chinese cinema movement. A turbulent branch current took over from what had been a calm main stream, becoming more and more rich and full until it soon became a surging river. History is full of such unexpected twists and turns.

Graduation photograph for the cinematography class of 1982. Front row (faculty): first from left, Department Chair Wei Zhang; fifth, president of the Academy and director Cheng Yin; sixth, Directing Department Professor Zhang Ke. Second row: first on right, Gu Chang-wei; sixth, Deng Wei; seventh, Zhang Huijun. Third row: second from left, Zhang Yimou; fourth from right, Hou Yong. Photo courtesy of Hou Yong.

CHAPTER 4

GRADUATION

■

Fifth Generation Cinema emerged in 1983 at Guangxi Film Studio. A new studio in an outlying region, production had begun there only recently. There was no battalion of highly credentialed directors hogging the spotlight, so the young people had an opportunity to demonstrate their abilities. Even more important, the young filmmakers were well matched, which enabled a distinct visual style and implicit philosophy to blossom quickly. These were the trademarks that finally gained recognition for the Fifth Generation. Other students in the class of 1982 also shot their debut films around 1983, but they were not recognized as the initiators of a new film movement. It was only the appearance of *One and Eight* and *Yellow Earth* that triggered agreement that a new sort of cinema had appeared in China. So how did this new cinema come into existence?

The origin of this important phenomenon lies in the assignment of Zhang Junzhao, Zhang Yimou, Xiao Feng, and He Qun to Guangxi. Their collaboration was decisive.

One director, two cinematographers, and a production designer—the only component missing was a sound designer. Originally there was a sound designer, one as outstanding as the others. But he refused the assignment and did not go to Guangxi. However, aside from sound, all the important creative roles in the profession were covered. Who made this careful combination of people? Who arranged it all? Was it a deliberate plan? Nobody really knows and opinions differ.

The graduates sent to Guangxi are convinced it happened because the Academy's "third world" accepted their lot and allowed themselves to be sent into exile. Later successes were put down to their own talent and hard work. If other people had been sent there, they may well have never seen the light of day again. But the department heads at the Academy knew there is never an ideal way to assign work to graduates; if it had not been one person who had to go there, then it would have had to be another. Sending a good group to Guangxi really did create an opportunity, and they really were hoping that they might make a name for themselves quickly. There might have been grievances, but there was nothing to be done about it and the plan went ahead.[1]

Many years have passed since all this happened, so why bother to go over it again? It is not just a matter of who was assigned where and whether they went or not; the results of the work assignment led directly to the creative energy behind *One and Eight*, and this is why the story needs to be told.

The process of assigning work placements to graduates began in April 1982. It was a task requiring careful deliberation, and it continued until the end of the semester in late July.

It was a consistent national policy to try to return graduates to the cities where their families lived. In the case of the film industry, if there were no studio in the student's hometown, then every effort would be made to arrange a position in the nearest studio.

Still, regardless of whether or not they were from Beijing, everyone wanted to stay there. The regulations said that, if necessary, the most outstanding graduates in each profession could be given special permission to stay in Beijing. In practice, however, only one in a hundred outsiders ever obtained Beijing residence permits—in other words, almost none. This made the class of 1978's "three worlds" theory of family backgrounds more plausible than ever.

For the most part the facts speak for themselves. Tian Zhuangzhuang was assigned to Beijing Film Studio and Chen Kaige to the Children's Film Studio. Although Xia Gang returned to the municipal town planning company at first, he was soon reporting to Beijing Film Studio. Pan Yuanliang and Geng Xiaozhen were assigned to China News Agency and China Television Drama Production Center, respectively. Naturally, Hu Mei returned to take up a post in the army's August First Film Studio. For those whose families were in Beijing, everything proceeded as it was supposed to, as though it was a golden rule. However, even for those who were placed in Beijing, there were tremendous differences in the standards of the units they went to. And were none of the classmates assigned work outside Beijing as good as or even better than those who stayed? However, the work assignment policy had been implemented consistently for thirty years. The slogan, "The Party calls for sincere obedience—heroes volunteer to go anywhere" appeared on banners strung across the halls of every university each July. Willingness to accept one's work assignment had long been a basic sign of good character.

For the Academy's "ordinary citizens" the question was how to make a good choice among the studios outside Beijing. Inner Mongolia Film Studio and Tianshan Film Studio in Xinjiang Province were not available to graduates, because special minority nationality classes had already been set up to cater to their needs. Emei Film Studio in Sichuan Province and Guangxi Film Studio were the most dreaded possibilities, and of the two Guangxi was especially feared. Therefore, when it came time to fill in the forms saying where they wanted to go, a common strategy was to put down Xiaoxiang Film Studio in Hunan or else Xi'an Film Studio as a first choice.

Wu Ziniu and Liu Miaomiao were assigned to Xiaoxiang Film Studio.

Guangxi Film Studio sent one of its leaders especially to Beijing, and to the Academy in particular, to request a complete set of creative personnel. They could take ten people or even more. The studio had only recently been established and lacked filmmakers. If the young people went there they would have earlier opportunities to make films by themselves, and thereby more rapidly be able to establish control. This situation would be very different from that in older studios like Beijing, Shanghai, and Changchun. There the graduates would have to endure being an assistant director without any hope of showing their own faces for at least eight or ten years. The Film Academy leaders—and especially the veteran teacher and Cinematography Department Party Branch Secretary Wei Zhang, who was from Guangxi himself—agreed to try to meet the request of the Guangxi studio. Since they were going to assign people, they resolved to assign the best possible candidates to Guangxi. They could not proclaim support for a new, remote studio and then send them substandard personnel. That would cause loss of trust and damage Guangxi Film Studio. Therefore, the following assignment list was placed before the leader from Guangxi Film Studio:

Directing Department: Zhang Junzhao
Cinematography Department: Zhang Yimou, Xiao Feng
Production Design Department: He Qun
Sound Department: Tao Jing

The studio leader was overjoyed and happily accepted the proposal.

■

Chen Kaige was very close to He Qun. When he heard the news, he stopped him, advising him not to go on any account and to stay in Beijing. "You've got so many classmates here," Kaige said. "You know someone will look after you."

Tian Zhuangzhuang had just finished shooting *Red Elephant* together with Zhang Yimou, Hou Yong, and Lü Yue. When he heard that Yimou had been assigned to Guangxi, he was very upset and went to report the bad news to his mother. The Children's Film Studio was newly established, it had not filled its staff quota, and it lacked cinematographers. Yu Lan used this argument in her request to the Academy for at least one Cinematography Department graduate.

However, this effort failed.

By then, apart from Tao Jing who categorically refused to go, the other four were already assessing the situation clearly, if sadly. It seemed impossible not to go to Guangxi, so go they would, but as a team. They would stick together through thick and thin. Once they glimpsed an opportunity, they would make the most of it. If they could produce one powerful film it might open some doors for them. On the other hand, if they went their separate ways, they might really be finished. They would stick together as planned and put friendship first. No one would let the others down, and through fire or flood they would tackle the hurdles together.

Zhang Yimou told Tian Zhuangzhuang about their decision, but Tian did not want to accept it. "Don't rush into it," he said. "Think it over again, and think it over carefully. It's never easy to get what you want, and you know how precious a Beijing residence permit is. Getting back here after you've left is harder than getting a ticket into heaven."

Zhang Yimou was silent for a long time, responding in his usual fashion. Then he muttered briefly: "Please thank your mother for me. She's been to a lot of trouble. But I'm still going to go. I've given my word to the guys. If I went back on it, that wouldn't be right."

Zhang Yimou decided to go to Guangxi, and Hou Yong was assigned to Emei Film Studio in Chengdu in Sichuan Province. Tian Zhuangzhuang was crushed. He had worked hard to put together a top-quality film crew. Now he was seeing this crew disperse before his very eyes. It was a bitter pill to swallow.

Zhang Junzhao had been a member of the Communist Party for many years. But when he was assigned to Guangxi, at first he did not know what to do. He went to talk to Party Branch Secretary Zhou Wei. "I'm willing to go to the borderlands," he told him. "My home's in Xinjiang, and that's even more remote. There's a film studio there. If I went to Tianshan Film Studio, wouldn't that fit the bill, too? If not, I could go to Changchun, because my girlfriend's in Dalian. I'm going to marry her as soon as I graduate, so there couldn't be anywhere better than Changchun. Being unable to go to either place and having to go to Guangxi would be unreasonable, both objectively speaking and personally speaking."

"Precisely because you're a Party member, we expect you to take the lead and set a good example," said Zhou Wei. "If you don't go, it'll be hard to mobilize the others. If you go, even though your home is in Xinjiang and your wife is in Dalian, then how can anyone else find an excuse not to?"

Xiao Feng was from Hangzhou, so the closest available studio was either Shanghai or Xiaoxiang. However, both places had already filled their quotas. Xiao Feng is a good painter, a good cinematographer, and an honest guy. There are always people willing to go with the flow and look at the larger picture, and he is just such a person. He is not the heroic sort that fights against the tide to the last. When you are building a grand mansion, you need people like him to do the basic bricklaying. He simply requested permission to go back to Hangzhou to see his parents before going to Guangxi, and so the matter was resolved satisfactorily.

∎

Zhang Junzhao and Xiao Feng traveled to Guangxi by way of Xinjiang and Hangzhou, respectively.

After going to visit his family in Xi'an, Zhang Yimou returned to Beijing. There he joined He Qun and they set off together for Nanning, the capital of Guangxi Province.

They took a night train that left at 11:59 P.M. The platform was empty and windswept. The train slowly started away, and from the carriage window they quietly said goodbye to Xie Xiaojing and Mu Deyuan, who had come to see them off. Mu Deyuan silently passed a melon up to He Qun. Although they all knew that they would see each other again soon, it felt as though they were saying goodbye forever.

As the train wheels ground on in a monotonous and unrelenting manner and the carriage filled with chatter in southern dialects, Zhang Yimou and He Qun gazed at each other in silence.

There is no doubt that the seeds for both the themes and the mood of *One and Eight* were planted as the two exiles exchanged looks on that southbound train. However, a historian would doubtless find this argument absurd and ridiculous, because they did not get the script from the leaders of the Guangxi Film Studio before the spring of 1983, and this journey south to report for duty took place in September of 1982.

One and Eight is about a man whose loyalty is questioned. The victim of great injustice in a perilous situation, he risks his life to prove his innocence. Put simply, this is a film about loyalty and injustice. These themes could be expressed through many stories, and Zhang Yimou and He Qun had had more than a decade's experience of them, over and over without a break for the first half of their lives.

The train rumbled on into the night, and the lights in the sleeping car were turned off, according to the rules. All that was visible was the red tip of He Qun's cigarette. It glowed brighter as he inhaled, illuminating his grotesquely ill-proportioned face. The cigarette smoke wafted by in clouds, obscuring his glare, then letting it appear again.

Time passed as the smoke dispersed.

Zhang Yimou gazed soberly at the fields outside the train window; his past life seemed to float before his eyes. Farewells—how many farewells are there in a lifetime? When his father had been sent as a "counterrevolutionary" to herd sheep in rural southern Shaanxi, Yimou had seen him off. Political discrimination had shadowed him like a ghost from the time he had begun to understand anything, and since childhood his instincts had told him to grit his teeth and say nothing. Observing in silence, he had no childhood at all. Going to work in the countryside—that was another farewell. So was going to the cotton mill in Xianyang. Farewells and more farewells. Being allowed to enroll at the Academy despite the rules had been the only happy farewell in his life—he had grinned like an idiot all the way from Xi'an to Beijing. But ultimately his life seemed to be a vicious circle he could not break. He had graduated and completed his training, and he was fully equipped with all the necessary skills and weapons. All he needed was the battlefield on which to do his duty for his country. But fate was dragging him back to the beginning, and it seemed that everything was starting again from square one. Dark clouds covered the sky once more and he was tragically banished again, looking ahead to what might be a lifetime of obscurity and boredom. He was a hot-blooded warrior at full gallop with his sword drawn, but the generals were white-haired and there was no opportunity to fight for his country.

Zhang Yimou looked back at He Qun, whose eyes were gleaming ferociously.

He wanted to say something comforting, but realized immediately that it would be a waste of breath.

A bitter smile flashed across He Qun's face as he thought, "What a damned joke! I was already living in Beijing without even having to go to the university. But now I've finished studying, and I'm banished thousands of miles away. If I'm not careful, I'll end up in Vietnam!"

He Qun is a good-hearted man, but he has an explosive temper. He is a strange mixture of shyness, modesty, and cynicism. Beneath his chivalrous and impartial mask lies a soft heart. After twenty-odd years of life he had come to understand one thing: you cannot walk among devils unless you put on a fearsomely devilish face yourself. Despite all that, the authorities had seen fit to give him a post in a two-bit southern town!

He Qun was born in 1956. Five years elapsed from when he first set eyes on his father as an infant to the next time when he saw him as a child who truly understood what the word "father" meant. A professor of sculpture in the Central Academy of Art and Design, He Qun's father was sentenced to five years reform through labor because of the Anti-Rightist Movement of 1957. He Qun remembers a skinny, sunburnt man appearing out of nowhere and knocking at the door. When he came in, he hugged

Zhang Junzhao and He Qun at the gate of Guangxi Film Studio. Photo courtesy of He Qun.

He Qun and his younger sister and would not let them go. He carried the two of them down to the little kiosk in the courtyard, bought a bottle of wine for sixty-five Chinese cents, and celebrated this unforgettable reunion together with He Qun's mother. Again in 1967, when the Cultural Revolution came around, the whole family suffered because of his father. They were raided again and again. Rebel factions wearing the red armbands of the Red Guards continually bullied the children. This was when He Qun learned to fight. When beasts wearing the mask of revolution ruthlessly humiliate the vulnerable, a savage growl can strike terror in their hearts. But He Qun paid a predictable price for fighting back with no regard for his own safety. Violent armed struggle and an icy-cold prison cell ended his happy childhood. The sickly and nervous child had disappeared forever, his place taken by a rigid, antisocial, and violent tyrant. He became known far and wide as the "King of Trouble," and even his own kind and affectionate mother despaired for him.

By the end of the Cultural Revolution, He Qun had become a machine repairer at the Sino-Albanian Friendship Commune on the outskirts of Beijing.

He had already studied art under his father's instruction for two years. However, he had to work very hard for the entrance examination to the Academy, improving his general knowledge and practicing his painting and drawing. But this effort took time, and he was not allowed to take leave from the agricultural machinery repair shop. One morning when He Qun walked into work through the main gate of the agricultural machinery repair shop, the iron door hinges snapped because "they were old and in bad shape." One of the doors came down with a crash, pinning He Qun's leg. This constituted a publicly witnessed injury on the job. Because his ankle was hurt it was difficult for him to walk, and he had to rest up while he recovered. This was how He Qun got a chance to conserve his strength and prepare a portfolio for the examinations.

He applied for the Production Design Department in the Academy, but he did not get in.

However, his luck turned, and he was admitted after reexamination. But his four years of college life were dark and depressing times during which the days dragged. This was because, after the recruitment process finished in 1978, the Ministry of Culture received a letter of complaint signed with the name "He Qun." It claimed there had been malpractice in the recruitment procedures for the Production Design Department of the Academy, and that the son of an official in the art world had received special treatment enabling him to gain admission. Although everything was checked and no material evidence against He Qun was found, the incident created a big fuss and calm was not restored for quite a while. The Ministry of Culture ordered a reexamination of the painting examinations for production design candidates, including those of He Qun. After reevaluation by art professors from other colleges, He Qun passed the examination in his proposed major and the Ministry of Culture advised that he should be admitted.

He Qun said repeatedly that he had never written any letter of complaint and handwriting checks also exonerated him. However, he found he had fallen into a vortex: he was the sacrificial lamb in a power struggle. When he arrived at the Zhuxin Village campus, there was an enormous handwritten poster waiting for him. It said he was not welcome.

Dogged by injustice and a sense of inferiority, he felt trapped—as if he were under house arrest for four years. But Zhang Yimou was also admitted against the rules, so they were in the same boat. While they were in Zhuxin Village, they were both very careful to toe the line.

Now, they sat smiling at each other across a compartment in a sleeping car. From their perspective, this outcome was certainly connected to the extremely odd circumstances of their admission four years earlier. "Who else would be consigned to hell?" He Qun thought, as he prepared to bury himself in the red earth of the south for ten years of silence, gathering strength for another fight.

If anyone had told them then that only two years later their films would enter international film festivals, they would certainly have laughed bitterly and told them to stop kidding.

■

However, by falling into a deep ravine of resentment, Zhang Yimou really was jumping to conclusions. Guangxi Film Studio welcomed them very warmly, sending someone to the train station to meet them and giving them each a room of their own. At Beijing or Shanghai Film Studio these actions would have been unthinkable. At the studio, the leaders met them in person and really did give everyone work on a film right away. He Qun did not have to work as assistant, but rather was made a full-fledged production designer. Apart from the fact that the place was remote and the equipment a bit out of date, there was not the slightest reason to complain. They were capable and had the chance to live and work contentedly: what more could Guangxi Film Studio have done for them?

The top director at Guangxi was called Guo Baochang. He had graduated from the Directing Department of the Beijing Film Academy in 1964, and arrived at Guangxi Film Studio by a very circuitous route. But once there, he shot several good films in succession and became a celebrity in Guangxi cultural circles. He was also someone whose word carried a lot of weight with the heads of the studio. They say people from the same school bond naturally. "Don't feel bad," said Guo Baochang. "Relax. As soon as there's an opening, we'll let you guys shoot your own film."

At that time, Guo Baochang was shooting a new film called *Trouble in the Harbor* (1983). Right away, he asked Zhang Junzhao to be his assistant director and He Qun to be his production designer. Zhang Yimou was

From left: He Qun, Zhang Junzhao, Xiao Feng, and Zhang Yimou, while working on *One and Eight*. Photo courtesy of He Qun.

assigned to be assistant cinematographer on Ba Hong's *Under the White Poplar* (1983) and Xiao Feng joined the cinematography team on *The Call of the Cuckoo* (1983). Thus, all four were allotted work much more quickly than their classmates who went to larger studios.

However, assistant work was not their goal. They could not forget that what they really wanted was to work on something major by themselves. Maybe the product would not be earthshaking, but at least it had to have nationwide impact, get the attention of the whole film world, and give them a chance to pour out everything they had bottled up inside themselves.

An important opportunity arrived.

Zhang Junzhao discovered the film script *One and Eight* during Chinese New Year 1983. It had been adapted from Guo Xiaochuan's epic poem, and the screenwriter was Zhang Ziliang from Xi'an. Excited about his find, he told the other three classmates the news. They all felt the script was very strong, bold, and full of masculine vigor. Although there were still a lot of problems with it, those flaws provided a chance for them to revise it thoroughly. They launched a general offensive on all fronts, pressuring and persuading the studio heads to support their request to establish a Youth Film Unit. They agitated to be allowed to make a film by themselves, and to take full responsibility for the results. If they failed, they would accept any punishment. At this point, Guo Baochang was the decisive factor. The head of the studio, Wei Bida, and the vice-head, Zheng Fanping, both trusted him implicitly, and Guo Baochang bravely offered to be an artistic advisor on *One and Eight*. This offer tipped the scales heavily in favor of the young filmmakers, and everything began to look much brighter.

Why was *One and Eight* so attractive to Zhang Junzhao, Zhang Yimou, He Qun, and Xiao Feng? Why did it inspire them so much that they were willing to stake everything on it?

The sad fate of the main character in *One and Eight* echoed their own emotional and mental experiences and gave them an outlet for expression through art. *One and Eight* is about a Communist Party member called Wang Jin who is suspected of collaboration with the enemy during the War of Resistance against Japan. While under investigation, he is imprisoned together with eight bandits and genuine deserters. He cannot talk his way out of the situation, but he stays strong in the face of injustice. On the one hand, Section Head Xu Zhi, who is in charge of eliminating traitors, is unbending in his enforcement of the law. As far as he is concerned, Wang Jin remains a traitor until he has evidence proving his innocence. On the other hand, the bandits who are his fellow prisoners treat him as an outsider, beating him up and insulting him. Under attack from both sides, Wang Jin stands firm. The Japanese mopping-up campaign presses on, and the Chinese Communist soldiers fight as they retreat. At the same time, they still have to escort these dangerous prisoners. On the eve of a violent battle, Section Head Xu Zhi orders the execution of the nine men. Just before he is executed, Wang Jin spits out a declaration of his loyalty: "Heroes hate to die off the battlefield, unable to leave this loathsome world." He tells his comrades he is willing to be executed by hanging so that they can save a bullet for the enemy. The soldiers refuse to believe such a man could be a traitor, and Xu Zhi decides to continue escorting the prisoners while also fighting and retreating. Hopelessly outnumbered in a bloody battle, the Chinese Communist troops suffer terrible losses. Section Head Xu is also seriously wounded. The prisoners break out and, led by Wang Jin, they fight hard to break out of the enemy encirclement. In the end, they escape by the skin of their teeth.

The leaders of Guangxi Film Studio finally made a decision. The script of *One and Eight* would be given to the Academy graduates, to see whether this bunch of youngsters really could cut it. Using a Youth Film Unit to conduct an experiment was also a consequence of the new policy of reform and opening up. If it went well, it would stir up the whole Chinese film industry. If it did not work out, it would mean they had spent some tuition fees and got some experience. "Our little studio has a poor foundation, so we need to be brave and have a go."

However, first the script had to be revised. And it could only be shot after it had passed inspection by the censors. The studio gave them RMB3,000 (approximately US$1500) so they could go north and experience the conditions there, scout for locations, view the north Chinese battlefields where the Japanese mopping-up campaign was resisted, and conduct interviews. They would go deep amongst the people in these historic areas to gather materials, and then finish revising the script.

Zhang Junzhao, Zhang Yimou, Xiao Feng, and He Qun hit the road.

A big change occurred in Chinese film production in 1983. Allowing the Fifth Generation filmmakers to go out and research the script revisions together as a foursome (director, cinematographer, production designer, and sound designer) replaced the system of having the director and screenwriter do it as a two-person team. Furthermore, once the revised screenplay was completed, it no longer had to be treated like scripture to be followed word by word by the crew in the secondary stages of production. The crew no longer blindly implemented the script but engaged fully in creative work in all areas, and the screenwriter could also continue to be involved in the revisions. A child with six mothers was bound to be much stronger than a child with only one. This system began with *One and Eight* and continued on through *Yellow Earth, Big Military Parade,* and *Red Sorghum* until it became an unwritten rule of Fifth Generation filmmaking. Zhang Yimou's later production designer Cao Jiuping and his sound designer Li Lanhua both say he holds script discussions every evening with no prospect of finishing before three or four in the morning. Although by that time none of the others can keep their eyes open, Zhang Yimou is still as fresh as a daisy. They have no idea where he gets his enormous energy. He treats you as if he is trying to squeeze you dry, relentlessly going for the very last drop.

But in 1983, such an approach was a good way to get everyone as actively involved in *One and Eight* as possible. It was also the natural extension of the bond that resulted from four years spent sharing rooms together at Zhuxin Village. It is unlikely that they could have worked this way with other cinematographers and production and sound designers, even if they had wanted to.

What was so different about *One and Eight?* Space, perspective, and sound were all being treated as dramatic elements. Furthermore, these elements could act as the foundation structuring a scene, not just supplementary items in the later realization of a script. This was a film script now, not a literary script, and making the film this way overturned the convention that the director only made explanatory notes on the script, a convention that had been operative in Chinese cinema since the left-wing progressive films of the 1930s. This change was not an attack on their predecessors, however, but rather a natural evolutionary consequence of the growing sense of cinematic specificity—as well as individual identity—in the 1980s.

■

The production team trekked across Hebei, Shaanxi, Gansu, and even Ningxia.

"The Japs never conquered Gansu and Ningxia. You've roamed through more than half of northern China, and even into the Gobi Desert where there's no sign of human life at all. What on earth for?"

This was a fair criticism. If the film went over budget, everyone would be held accountable. But He Qun insisted, "Hebei and Shanxi are completely agrarian now. There are crops and greenery as far as the eye can see. How can we get shots of the scorched earth and ruins after the Japanese 'Three Clean-Ups Policy' during the War of Resistance against Japan? You can't avoid green trees and electricity wires. Who would ever believe these places were a north Chinese battlefield in 1942 during the war? Gansu! Ningxia! It's all bare there, just a vast and wild landscape with almost no sign of life. That's what the 'Three Clean-Ups Policy' area should look like! There mustn't be a spot of green in this film from start to finish!"[2]

These are the origins of the film's scene of devastation when the Japanese army sacks the village, leaving corpses strewn all over the ground. Here, then, the kind of "typical environment" that would have been derived from textual research was being replaced by "artistic imagery" based on atmosphere. As a powerful male voice belts out the anti-Japanese song "In the Taihang Mountains," the shot tilts up from a boundless wasteland into a pale sky, and a weighty national spirit flows out of the earth. Who could continue to fuss about whether this is actually Shanxi or Gansu? Visual aes-

One and Eight. Photo courtesy of He Qun.

thetics are powerful theoretical resources in Fifth Generation cinema, and with the modest seedling that is *One and Eight,* their earliest fruits were appearing.

The arduous process of rewriting the script, using both words and sketches, continued all the way from the countryside of north China back to Guangxi. Xiao Feng created a storyboard that included nearly every camera angle and every stage of every camera movement. Later, He Qun made a very fair comment: "Xiao Feng's effect cannot be underestimated. When it came to the shooting of *One and Eight,* he made at least fifty percent of the contribution."

The script revisions focused chiefly on making Wang Jin more prominent. All available methods were to be used to emphasize this positive main character, to communicate that this Communist Party member endured immense humiliation while carrying out an important mission, and that he was resolute and unyielding. The young filmmakers kept this key task constantly in mind, and it was also a sincere expression of their own feelings. At this point, the pouring out of individual emotions converged naturally with the tribulations of the characters in the script, poised between honor and disgrace amid the larger tragedies of national war.

Another important aim of the revision was to add awesome visual power, so that the film would feel wild, heroic, and stirring. To do this, they selected a distinctive setting composed of tobacco curing kilns, ruined brick kilns, devastated villages, and mountain shrines to communicate dramatic conflict. They took many photographs and drew many illustrations to show where the sets would be constructed as well as the scale of the work needed. They brought all of this material back to Guangxi, where they worked on a detailed shooting script.

However, no matter how much they revised the script, they could not find a dramatic climax to draw the plot to a moving conclusion. Trying to resolve this problem was like running a marathon but not quite making it over the line. Everyone was overcome with anxiety.

They simply could not find a solution. One night He Qun retreated to his room to wash clothes and watch television, where a Yugoslav film called *The Bridge* happened to be on. This film takes place during the Second World War, and tells the story of a team of Yugoslav partisans who are sent on a mission to blow up a big bridge that the German army must cross during a large-scale retreat.

The bridge is high and difficult to access, making their mission very tough. As a small team of the partisans sneaks toward their target, a German garrison force discovers them. To protect the others as they flee, one team member stays back to draw the enemy away. Wounded and out of bullets, he yells to his retreating comrades to throw a hand grenade at him, so that he may die for a cause and not become a prisoner of war.

The sound of the explosion followed by thick clouds of smoke on the screen made He Qun sit up and take notice. It also made a light bulb go off in his head. This was the sort of dramatic climax they would never have come up with by themselves, no matter how they tried. He ran to Zhang Junzhao's room to tell the other three about his big idea.

This is the conclusion of *One and Eight*! Five or six Japanese soldiers surround the character of Yang Qiner, who is a female medic with the unit holding Wang Jin and the bandits. The Japanese have torn off her outer clothing and are about to rape her. The old bandit Smoky's gun goes off. He has used his last bullet to shoot Yang Qiner through the heart, thus preserving her moral integrity as a female soldier.

Some say this form of imitation is an example not to be followed. Others say this scene has completely different moral implications stemming from

One and Eight. Photo from the 1985–1986 volume of *China Screen.*

different national characteristics, so there is no question of plagiarism. No matter what anyone says, the bullet from the old bandit's gun and the shooting of Yang Qiner were radical changes in the way Chinese cinema depicted the War of Resistance against Japan. The magnanimous act of the bandit and the concept of the female soldier falling into enemy hands were both unprecedented, and the visual imagery was new and unfamiliar. These ideas and images rocked the Chinese film world, sparking a real struggle between the film's supporters and its detractors.

Of course, all that was still to come. At this point, although the script revision was now complete, they still had to wait for the censorship decision. Everything hung in the balance. For Zhang Junzhao and the others, the days dragged like years, and it was impossible to guess the outcome.

■

In April 1983, the leaders of the Guangxi Film Studio finally approved the script. Soon afterward, a meeting was held to announce the establishment of the Youth Film Unit assigned to produce *One and Eight,* with Zhang Junzhao as director, Zhang Yimou and Xiao Feng as cinematographers, and He Qun as production designer. Guo Baochang was specially invited to be artistic advisor. Allowing this group to be in charge of their own film less than a year after graduation was truly unprecedented, and the meeting was very solemn. Zhang Junzhao and the others shaved their heads as a sign of their commitment, as though they were staring death in the face. They stood before the entire staff of the studio and read aloud a pledge, vow-

ing that if *One and Eight* failed they would work as assistants for a decade
and never ask to take charge of their own films again. An unwavering order
backed by an oath; everybody in Guangxi Film Studio was waiting now.
It was a very stirring occasion.

> The wind is wailing, cold the River Yi,
> And a hero sets forth, never to return.[3]

When the Youth Film Unit set out, it resembled a daredevil squad setting off on a military mission. Everyone came in a mood of high solemnity to bid them farewell, but when they saw the group they could not
help laughing. Apart from the female medic Yang Qiner, who still had her
two braids, not only the filmmakers but also all the male actors had shaved
heads, which had been oiled and were gleaming darkly. After coming in
as loans from acting troupes all over the country, they had been sent for
a couple of weeks to tan themselves by a reservoir on the outskirts of
Nanning in order to darken the color of their skin. Fierce, rough, and
murderous-looking, all of the actors looked thoroughly disreputable. Seen
from a distance, they looked just like a bunch of bandits—not just the one
and the eight, but the whole company of twenty-plus.

When this bunch arrived at Nanning railway station to catch their train,
they immediately attracted the attention of the railway police. They explained they were making a film for Guangxi Film Studio, and the police
relaxed at once. But when they got to Hebei and had to change trains on
their journey north, they scared the wits out of the public security officers
and the general traveling public, who were convinced they were newly released labor camp prisoners.

Among the actors were Tao Zeru, who was to play the political instructor Wang Jin; Chen Daoming, the section head responsible for the elimination of traitors; Xie Yuan, a traitor; and also Wei Zongwan, Xin Ming,
and Zhao Xiaorui. None of them was famous in 1983, but now nearly all
have become stars. Because many of them really do look very fierce, very
few directors were using them then. But their casting put a new face on
the Eighth Route Army, and its vivid depiction of bandits made *One and
Eight* quite different from all the war movies produced since the 1950s.
Their wretched and vicious appearance was completely different from the
caricatured villains of the past, who were as stereotyped as Chinese opera
masks. Moreover, their courage and patriotism broke completely with the

In *One and Eight,* the production designer He Qun movingly acted the part of a farmer driven mad by the cruelty of war. Photo courtesy of He Qun.

characterization of bandits in previous films, whose depiction was always a formulaic story of collusion with the enemy. As bandits, their malice, meanness, savagery, and violence made people hate them as though they were real bandits. But when their wildness was channeled overnight into determination to fight the enemy and save the nation, then their evident patriotism and willingness to sacrifice their lives revealed their complexity, showing that bandits are human, too.

In addition to tanning themselves under the scorching sun, as soon as they arrived in Guangxi the actors were required to research their characters in depth. When they put on their costumes and were tied together with a coarse rope to walk across the dusty north China plain, they were not simply physically there—each of them had totally assumed his role.

Today, each Fifth Generation director has followed his or her own path. But when they look back from their current separate and individual successes, they all remember fondly the unity and brotherly spirit of mutual support and cooperation during those early filmmaking years. It is a time they can never return to, but it was crucial in the formative days of this artistic movement. It also confirms a general rule concerning film movements: when they are first establishing themselves, young filmmakers have to break through as a group.

"Back then when we were making *One and Eight,* it was really impossible to say whose contribution was bigger and whose was smaller," Xiao Feng remembers wistfully. "Nobody thought about that. We were all just trying our very best. The director, Zhang Junzhao, made the actual revisions to the script. But we came up with lots of brilliant ideas together. Zhang Yimou suggested the scene in which the Japanese army massacres the villagers. Seeing the Ningxia setting, he insisted on a large-scale scene of oppression and discipline. He Qun suggested the scene in which Smoky kills the female medic. But it was all developed and completed through repeated discussions involving several people."

To make over three hundred Eighth Route Army uniforms look old, He Qun got everyone to help. First, the costumes were soaked in water full of washing soda. Then they were beaten with sticks and attacked with metal files before being smeared with mud. Not one of them was allowed to look fake. Producing the setting of the ruined temple was a big job and a complicated one, too. Zhang Junzhao, Zhang Yimou, and Xiao Feng all shoveled earth and water and labored like workmen to make door and window frames. When the artistic advisor, Guo Baochang, who had arrived from Guangxi to supervise production, saw this, he was both moved and angry. "How come I can't see the director?" he shouted. "Where's the director?"

"I'm here, aren't I?" said Zhang Junzhao, walking over, his face splattered with mud.

"Who told you to become a bricklayer?" asked Guo. "Come away from there and stand by the camera. Why aren't your set builders working on this? Why are they letting the director do it himself?"

In actuality, this was unfair to the set construction team. The great majority of scenes on *One and Eight* were done this way, without any concern for status or strict division of labor. If Zhang Yimou were shooting, then Xiao Feng would certainly be helping out. And when Xiao Feng was shooting the long and slow tracking shot across the corpses strewn about after the Japanese massacre—a shot that involved more than two hundred "corpses" lying among the ruins—Zhang Yimou divided the scene up into four parts. Then, so that Xiao Feng could complete this complicated task in one take, Zhang Yimou, the director, the production designer, and the assistant director each assumed responsibility for a section and ensured that

From left: He Qun, Zhang Yimou, Xiao Feng, and Zhang Junzhao, on the set of *One and Eight*. Photo courtesy of He Qun.

none of the actors playing corpses made the slightest movement. They all worked as one.

A major reason for the future success of *One and Eight* was its unique and emphatic visual style, based on the asymmetrical and unbalanced composition of the shots and the shooting of color stock as though it were black and white. It was Zhang Yimou and Xiao Feng who came up with these ideas and worked them through.

The first scene filmed was the one in which the bandits surround political instructor Wang Jin and attack him in the brick kiln in Yi County in Hebei Province. When the first rushes came back, the opinion in the studio was that they were too flat and lacked drama, and that the actors' performances lacked subtlety.

"A bunch of guys fighting—how many dramatic twists and turns can there be in that?" said Zhang Yimou to Xiao Feng. "Even if the actors were divinely inspired, what difference would it make? *One and Eight* is a man's film. There aren't any particularly subtle feelings in it. We must push on with a bold and exaggerated look. Every shot must be from a striking and unusual angle, so that the film is different from everyone else's in every way from start to finish. That way, perhaps it might get recognized as something new. Otherwise, there's a real risk this film will fail." So, that is how they shot the film.

Zhang emphasized that it was not just a matter of every angle being arresting. As far as possible, they also had to avoid placing the actors in the center of the shots. Instead, they were to be on one side of the shot or the other, with scenery obscuring them in order to avoid any subtle expressions of feeling. This was very risky. If it was not done well, it might alienate the audience altogether. But once the decision had been made, they stuck to it. Come what may, they certainly would not shoot the usual way.

The studio leaders were very dissatisfied when they saw the second set of rushes. What on earth were they up to with those weird compositions? And everything was so dark! Did they know how to shoot at all? They did not even put the actors in the center of the frame. What on earth would it all look like when it was edited together? They must be told to do it properly at once, or else they should stop. But fortunately, Guo Baochang defended them to the studio heads again and again, and so they were allowed to continue. He said, "You're looking at a new trend. It's natural for young people to want to experiment. The film isn't finished yet, and in fact this is just the beginning, so isn't it a bit early to be getting upset? They won't be shooting all the remaining scenes like this. I'll go and tell them how you feel."

When Guo Baochang arrived on location, he sought out Zhang Junzhao and the other three, closed the door, and gave them a good talking to. "I defended you in front of the studio heads, but if you go on filming like this, I won't be able to accept it, either. And when the shit hits the fan, I'll be finished, too. Why don't you pull your horns in a bit? You've got to pay more attention to the content. Otherwise, if it doesn't turn out well, I think it could be dangerous."

"There's something to what Guo Baochang says," Zhang Junzhao felt. "We'd better think it over."

However, once Guo Baochang left the room and they were on their own, Zhang Yimou said they must go on taking risks. Retreat amounted to abandoning the effort they had made up to now. Xiao Feng and He Qun were in complete agreement. There was no other option now. They would just have to shoot it this way, making it even more extreme and exaggerated. Having a stark, simple, and unusual look was essential if they wanted to make a successful ambush, and if that was what they were going to do, they should do it thoroughly. Unless they were extreme, no one would pick up on what they were doing.

However, the actors were also against this extreme style because it placed them on the edge of the frame, sometimes even with their faces half in and half out. "We might be ugly and unknown," they said, "but we won't be turned into living props. We've either got our backs to the camera or we're only half in the frame, or we're tiny specks caught between heaven and earth in an extreme long shot so you can't see our faces at all. If you shot megastars like Zhao Dan and Shi Hui that way, even their great talent would be lost to view."

Zhang Yimou's expression hardened and the lines at the edge of his mouth grew grimmer. "We have to shoot it this way through to the end now. If we change halfway through, it'll turn out badly for sure. We must go for the extreme, the most extreme. At the moment it's not bold enough, not extreme enough. We must emphasize the visuals even more. That's the only way the style will become noticeable. I can understand how the actors feel, so let's be frank with them and try to persuade them."

An ordinary-looking audio tape, but one treated as a treasure, was put into a tape player in front of the whole cast and crew for everyone to listen to. It was a recording of one of Professor Zhou Chuanji's classes at the Academy. The topic was the composition of offscreen space and how to deal with the articulation of sound and space. It combined foreign theory with Professor Zhou's own research of many years to produce a fresh perspective. He made the important point that, in the case of the film frame, on-screen and offscreen were linked together to produce a whole. In order to suggest off-screen space, one may compose a single frame incompletely, with only half the character's body in the frame, to imply the connection between the on- and off-screen space. After everything is articulated in the editing process, the result is a more complete and integrated scene.

"So there you are—theory and modern filmmaking techniques. Are you still afraid we're making a mess?"

The actors and most of the crew were completely baffled by what they were hearing. But everyone kept quiet, or at least they kept their opinions to themselves. In general, they thought that whatever it meant, they had never shot a film like this before.

The whole production crew of *One and Eight* on location in Ningxia. Photo courtesy of He Qun.

The actress Lu Xiaoyan resolutely supported the director and the cine-matographers in all of their artistic experiments. A young and innocent student from the Shanghai Academy of Drama, she stood up and spoke out for this way of shooting the film. "We can't say if it's a success or a failure until it's finished and we have the final product in front of us," she said.

She was quite right. Even if it were a failure, it should be an absolute fail-ure, an honorable failure, a failure they had earned. They could not retreat in a half-baked fashion. Even failures can be done properly or botched.

The *One and Eight* filmmakers pushed on bravely and persistently with the style they had already established. The compositions were stark, flat, and full of contrast. In fact, He Qun's sets had already been designed using the most succinct lines to reinforce this effect. The cinematographers Zhang Yimou and Xiao Feng redoubled their efforts to produce highly styl-ized shots. The exposure was either reduced to the point where it was not only colorless but also dark or adjusted so that it was like an etching, with sharp contrasts. The look was all strong forms, shapes, and lines. As they moved from Yi County in Hebei Province to the wastelands of Ningxia, everything was filmed in a bold and integrated way to express an over-whelming feeling of desolation and solemnity. With every scene, they grew increasingly bold and more proficient. As the work mounted up, the penny dropped and the cast and crew finally began to understand what sort of film this was.

Zhang Yimou's distinctive personality and uncompromising spirit are manifested in the quiet persistence with which he shot *One and Eight*. His extraordinary will and his artistic sense were the product of the extreme difficulties he faced in his first thirty years, and his profound reflections on society and history now were synthesized into an artistic language that was being revealed as a result of a rare chance event.

Today, the media has competed to exaggerate the legend of Zhang Yi-mou. His films, the man himself, and even his relationship with the female superstar Gong Li have all become raw material for the production of com-modified cultural sensations. But when we look back to the battler who stepped onto the stage from behind the heavy curtain of history, we do not need to exaggerate to understand him. We can see that he is an ordinary human being, born of other human beings, made of flesh and blood, and reasoning like the rest of us.

Although Zhang Yimou has definite artistic and cinematic talent, his indomitable will may be even more important in accounting for his career successes and the course of his life. The extreme oppression resulting from his father's political history and his unhappy childhood made him a man who gritted his teeth and accepted his fate, not expecting luck to come his way or holding out big hopes. He matured early as a teenager and gradually grew up with an attitude as cold as steel. He took for granted all kinds of humiliations and tribulations. Even his dreams were harsh and stifling, not fantasies or revelations of enlightenment. The gods had sent him down among men and doomed him to labor day and night, to sweat profusely and endlessly, as in the scene in *Old Well* where he carries that enormous square tablet on his back up and down hill.

Although Zhang Yimou was only a cinematographer on *One and Eight,* his stubborn nature and distinctive visual language are plainly visible in the style and the inner meaning of the film. The flat and simple images, the unusual perspectives and clear lines, the reduction of human beings to tiny specks on enormous expanses of land, the preference for still shots and making time stand still—these are all his signature traits. And these elements do not so much reveal a cinematographic style as project his outlook on life; vast is the sky, boundless are the wilds, and human life is as paltry as a leaf floating on an ocean. Maybe the most important thing Zhang Yimou could do as a cinematographer was emphasize his visual language, but by persisting in the thorough realization of this style he also emphasized his will, which was even stronger than his artistic talent. This trait enabled him to endure one difficulty after another in his future career as a director, and it created a freewheeling hero in a legend about art.

With *Red Sorghum,* people saw what seemed to be a high-spirited and talented storyteller. But in fact, from *Ju Dou* to *Raise the Red Lantern* to *The Story of Qiu Ju* and all the way to *To Live,* which film was not burdened with difficulties? Which one did not face innumerable obstacles? Which one did not have to push forward step by step? Which one was not born struggling through all kinds of difficulties? In the minds of the public Zhang Yimou is a victor, hoisting awards high in front of red velvet curtains and shining in the light of endless camera flashes. But looking more coolly from another angle, he is also always the villager carrying that enormous square stone tablet, clambering alone along that rocky precipice in Old Well Village. Perseverance, perseverance, and more perseverance; maybe only Zhang Yi-

One and Eight. Facing the camera is Zhao Xiaorui, who plays the bandit "Eyebrows." Photo from 1985–1986 volume of *China Screen*.

mou himself knows that sort of lonely burden and the profoundly bitter taste of human life.

If you think about it carefully, as he blazed his ever more glorious trail, Zhang Yimou's persistence, coolness, refusal to compromise, and willingness to take risks went far beyond his artistry and skill alone; or perhaps the former traits ensured the maximum development and display of the latter ones. China and the Chinese social and political system produced both Zhang Yimou's unique historical experiences and also this uniquely determined artist. Zhang Yimou used his tremendous drive, fueled by his social experiences, to ensure that his art would shine throughout China. That is the real truth behind the myth of Zhang Yimou.

■

One and Eight was finally completed. A thought-provoking implication found in the conclusion of the film is that the spirit of freedom always runs alongside doctrine and discipline. In their ending, the filmmakers also broke the longstanding rule in Chinese war films that all freedom fighters and Robin Hood-like outlaws who develop political consciousness must be drawn into the ranks of the revolutionary forces. This not only fulfils their political lives but also constitutes the great turning point of their lives in a general sense. However, this was not so in *One and Eight*. The bandit "Eyebrows" carries the severely wounded Section Head Xu Zhi on his back and helps the slightly wounded political instructor Wang Jin as they walk toward the Eighth Route Army encampment. Suddenly, he lets the wounded men go, kneels on one knee, and, supporting himself with his gun, bids the political instructor Wang Jin farewell: "In the language of the bandits, let me call you elder brother. I respect your commitment. You're a real man," he says. "But I cannot accept the discipline of your army. Let me return to my own path."

A vast and empty landscape with only a few tiny human beings—all that can be seen on the far horizon is the figure of Eyebrows and, at a distance, Wang Jin and Xu Zhi heading off in the opposite direction. This scene goes beyond doctrine and discipline: the characters had the same willingness to sacrifice themselves for their country, but they had different souls and different dreams. Thus the language of Chinese war movies, fixed for over thirty years, dissolved in this vast landscape with the resounding clash of these souls.

■

After the screening of the rough cut in a Guangxi Film Studio projection room, there was silence. In the face of this strange newborn, no one knew what to say.

Zhang Yimou frowned in the murky light. "Will it be okay?" he asked Xiao Feng, who sat next to him.

"You're asking me? I don't know, either."

■

In November 1983, *One and Eight* was sent to Beijing for inspection by the censors.

Zhang Junzhao and the other three main filmmakers used the opportunity to borrow a projection room at Beijing Film Studio and invite their friends, teachers, and former classmates to see the film. Their classmates arrived in a rush, and the little screening room was packed. Some sat in extra chairs placed in the side aisles, and others sat on the carpet in front of the screen.

The minute the lights went on after the screening finished, applauding classmates rushed up and crowded the filmmakers. With tears in their eyes, they hugged Zhang Junzhao, Zhang Yimou, Xiao Feng, and He Qun. Cheering, shaking hands, and embracing each other, they celebrated this maiden work. The teachers also came up one by one and offered their congratulations. The old director Chen Huaikai, the cinematographer Nie

Jing, the critic Zhong Dianfei, and others were all delighted. "Although you guys have never been to war, you've made a film that's really moved me," said Zhong Dianfei. "And I'm a veteran of the War of Resistance against Japan."

Zhang Yimou later recalled: "I've won many awards at international film festivals since then, and I've attended many grander and more glorious events than that one. But if you ask when I was most happy and excited, it was that night when *One and Eight* was projected for the first time. That was the first time I saw a film I had made praised by so many of my teachers and friends, and I was overcome with emotion."

One and Eight was not passed by the censors that year. But the news of the Beijing film world's enthusiastic support for it raced across the whole country. Everyone in the film industry heard about it. They knew it was very bold, displayed cutting-edge talent, and had been made by a group of young people. The entire staff of Guangxi Film Studio was inspired by this recognition, and they felt that putting together a Youth Film Unit had paid off. It was time to build on their success and expand their efforts. On the one hand, they respected the instructions from the Film Bureau for the revision of *One and Eight;* on the other hand, they instructed the same group to begin work on their next film at once.

He Qun took this opportunity to give the studio heads the script of *Let's Call It Hope Valley,* which Chen Kaige had entrusted to him to take back to Guangxi. He also strongly recommended Chen to the studio head Wei Bida and the other leaders. "Among the students from the Academy's Directing Department, he's the best," said He Qun. "He wrote *Let's Call It Hope Valley* himself, so if he came to Guangxi to shoot the film that would make it even better."

However, the studio flatly rejected Chen Kaige's script, feeling that its description of what had happened to the educated youths was too depressing and therefore not suitable for production. But they put out the welcome mat for Chen to come to Guangxi to make a film. They even supplied him with a script by the screenwriter Zhang Ziliang. Adapted from Ke Lan's prose piece *Echoes across the Ravine,* the script was given to the Youth Film Unit for revision.

Who could have guessed that *Echoes across the Ravine* would become *Yellow Earth?* The story is about a member of a cultural troupe in the Eighth Route Army in the northern Shaanxi base area during the War of Resistance against Japan. The character goes down into the countryside to collect folk songs. There, he and a country girl fall in love, and this leads her onto the revolutionary path. Although the script was full of local flavor and folk customs, the story and the characters were cliché, and there was nothing new about it to excite anyone.

Chen Kaige hesitated. Could something original and special be made out of this kind of story? At best, it was a melodrama reminiscent of the sentimental folk song about arranged marriage, *Blue Flower.* But if he turned it down, who else would let him direct his own film so soon? Certainly, Beijing Film Studio would not. Well-known directors like Shui Hua, Cheng Yin, Ling Zifeng, Xie Tieli, and his own father, Chen Huaikai, were all in the driving seat there, with one big picture after another lined up for production. Following the principle of providing access to resources according to seniority, there was not even enough work for the middle-aged directors. If Chen Kaige waited at the Beijing Film Studio for his turn in the regular way, the future looked extremely unpromising.

In that case, he wondered, should he accept *Echoes across the Ravine?* The decision was a difficult one. Chen Kaige returned to Beijing from Guangxi. Bumping into Xia Gang, he asked him in a state of indecision, "Do you think I should take this film on?"

At this point, the leaders of the Guangxi Film Studio suggested that Chen Kaige, Zhang Yimou, He Qun, and a few others should team up and go to northern Shaanxi. There they were to go deep into the countryside, interview all kinds of ordinary people, and complete the revisions to the script. Then they could decide how to go about making it into a film.

■

In January 1984, in extremely cold and dry conditions, Chen Kaige, Zhang Yimou, and He Qun set foot on the loess plateau.

There was nothing unusual about the organization of this research trip to northern Shaanxi. Almost every film crew made such trips in order to familiarize themselves with the local situation, revise the script, and scout for locations. But no one foresaw that for Chen Kaige and the others this trip to the northern Shaanxi plateau would become a pilgrimage into the Chinese national culture of their forebears.

Later, Chen Kaige wrote of this pilgrimage:

Yellow Earth. Photo from the 1985–1986 volume of *China Screen.*

We set off from Xi'an together with the screenwriter Zhang Ziliang and the composer Zhao Jiping on 1 January. Once past Tongchuan, we had entered northern Shaanxi. At twenty degrees below zero, the mountain wilderness was a world sealed with ice. But as we traveled past Mount Qiao near the Yellow Emperor's tomb, we saw an expanse of pale green. It is here that our great national forebear the Xuanyuan Emperor rests in peace.[4] Amidst yellow earth stretching as far as the eye can see, green Mount Qiao seemed almost like a living altar, glowing silently day and night. As a descendant of the Yellow Emperor, every Chinese would feel pride and passion there.

When we arrived at the Luochuan Plateau, it was spectacular. This is a central spot from which one can look up, down, and all around. We gazed for a long time at what we were going to represent—the loess plateau. Northern Shaanxi is all earth and mountains. Its undulations are almost like poetic meter. The earth is thick but not fertile, probably because there is so little rain. But after looking at it for a long time, you feel a kind of heavy warmth. On a winter's day the earth is bare, transmitting an expansive feeling. It seems barren but warm inside. Gradually, we made out an almost bare birch-leaf pear tree perched like a pavilion at the top of a distant slope. Silent and lonely, its outline on the exposed winter wilderness seemed to affirm the existence of life.

From left: Zhang Yimou, Chen Kaige, and He Qun, on location for *Yellow Earth*. Photo courtesy of He Qun.

Northern Shaanxi is peaceful. There are mountains and hillocks, ravines and gullies, and not a sound anywhere. But the scenery is very dramatic and strong. This silent land produced our *xintianyou* folk melodies. Many years ago—there was a high hill, a flock of sheep, and a shepherd. After lingering for a long time, he sang in a high, sonorous voice that could be heard for miles around. Once the song was over, all returned to silence. Standing on that hilltop made me think of many things, including how the earliest adventures of the nation were linked to this grand and majestic natural environment, and how its earliest culture was born out of this silence.[5]

In Yan'an, each member of the group personally experienced the historic atmosphere and viewed the surviving cultural artifacts of the revolutionary base area. From there they traveled on to Qingjian, Suide, Mizhi, and Yulin. In the poor and remote mountain country of Ansai, they saw folk paintings and papercuts in the county cultural center. The intensely colored pictures and intricate window decorations were the handiwork of farming men and women. The paintings depicted plowing the fields, sowing the crops, fetching water, and spinning thread. There were babies for the Qingming festival to honor the dead and old men for the Guyu festival marking the rainy season, along with beaming young women, green tigers, purple sheep, and red magpies. Chattering and laughing rural spectators jostled with the filmmakers at the folk exhibition, enjoying the holiday entertainment that had been handed down over thousands of years.

In the county cultural center, they heard the folk singer He Yutang's penetrating and husky-voiced folk songs. His bold, wild, bittersweet, yet naively joyous singing communicated the feelings of many generations and eras running through it. He said nothing. When he finished singing, he simply left. Later, he appeared in *Yellow Earth* as the villager who sings for his liquor at the wedding feast.

After passing through Mizhi and Yulin, the group eventually reached Jia County by the Yellow River.

> Whenever the Yellow River is mentioned, people think of its tumbling, roaring majesty. But when we stood by the Yellow River, its calm and peacefulness struck us more deeply. Carving open two clifflike banks of stone, it flows confidently and freely, displaying its bold and free form as it quietly flows on. Seen from high up and far away between the hills and mountains, it does not seem to be moving at all and appears to have congealed and set. But it is precisely this quality that shows it is a great river. By its side is the land that has been dry for so long, empty and barren. It made us think of countless thousands of years of historical misfortune.
>
> Every one of our few days in Jia County, we walked for miles through the countryside. And every day we would see an old man with rickets hobbling along the frozen river cliffs to draw water from the Yellow River, then silently walk off.[6]

These passages are from Chen Kaige, Zhang Yimou, and He Qun's *Notes on Collecting Folk Songs in Northern Shaanxi*. There they record their genuine responses at that time and communicate a sense of pride and fulfillment on returning to their cultural mother. As a result of these feelings, *Yellow Earth* is different from the short films of their student days and it is also different from *One and Eight*. Their month-long trip through the mountains

Yellow Earth. Photo from the 1985–1986 volume of *China Screen.*

and across the rivers was a cultural journey that opened up a wide territory before them—one of human trouble and suffering in the face of national vicissitudes and the vastness of history. At the time the journey seemed less significant, but experience made them appreciate it more later, and *Yellow Earth* is a revelation of their true feelings, a deeply sincere eulogy to the land, to their mother. The film emits a kind of pure aroma from start to finish, and it is absolutely devoid of the cosmetic beauty that comes with artifice and decoration.[7]

■

In 1984 just before Chinese New Year, Chen Kaige returned to Beijing with a rich store of emotions and a host of material. He closed his door and buried himself in script revisions. Soon, the original melodramatic form of the script disappeared and was replaced with symbolic cinematic poetry. Although many details remained to be hammered out, according to my interview with him, Chen Kaige's aim was clear. He wanted a grand peasant theater, and he would use the collective rituals of northern Shaanxi's rural weddings and rain ceremonies to show the folk customs and way of life in a grand manner. Into this national lifestyle he would insert the characters of Cuiqiao, her father, and her little brother, and he would describe the family's fate.

However, the scroll that Chen had unrolled still lacked one or two key highlights, and it also needed a ringing tone that would express a kind of masculine beauty and rough spirit. Although Chen himself usually preferred grand and mighty beauty, he racked his brains to no avail. He lacked the concrete reference points to come up with something that would meet his own high demands.

At this critical juncture, Zhang Yimou appeared, unannounced, at his side. He had intended to go back to Xi'an to celebrate the New Year according to the Chinese custom with his parents and wife, whom he had left soon after their marriage. But he had cut short his vacation and rushed to Beijing. For Zhang Yimou to be with him at this moment was undoubtedly what he needed and the happiest thing possible.

Zhang had brought a surprise with him. In a Xi'an Television New Year program he had seen the waist-drum dance from Ansai. Several hundred plain and vigorous farmers, wearing black cotton padded jackets and pants and white "sheep stomach"–like towels on their heads, brandished their drumsticks on the loess slope, where they shook the heavens. This was the true spirit of Shaanxi farm folk! Gesticulating madly, in a vigorous manner Zhang described the scene that had fired him up.

Chen Kaige controlled his excitement and focused on Zhang's enthusiastic and inspiring words. To himself, he thought, "The light of success is already beginning to dawn over this film called *Yellow Earth.*"

■

When Chen Kaige and Zhang Yimou joined forces, the birth of Fifth Generation cinema was ordained. And from the first day they worked together, their separation was also preordained. This in turn led to the expansion, fragmentation, and further development of Fifth Generation cinema.

Chen and Zhang have come to represent the Fifth Generation because they both have been deeply nourished by Chinese culture. Their mutual friendship and understanding is clearly reflected in the ideas behind *Yellow Earth,* and the ideas are a revelation of both men's sincere feelings and cultural perspective. In what follows, Chen and Zhang's own production notes for *Yellow Earth* give us the most immediate and direct understanding of the film.

Chen Kaige writes:

We saw the Yellow River at Jia County. . . . It is vast, grand, solemn, and expansive, flowing calmly across the interior of Asia. Its evident freedom and serenity made us think about our national character, full of power but also flowing in that heavy and silent way. However, the riverbanks are vast, the mountains boundless, and the lands parched. The Yellow River flows on unconcerned. It cannot save the vast wilderness that has moved aside to make way for it. This made us think of our long and desolate history. . . .

I have made the flowing of the Yellow River a model for the structure of the film, and given a very large proportion of the film over to images of the river waters seen from a distance. As far as structure is concerned, I think that our film should be rich and varied, with a free and almost indulgent attitude, communicating its message expansively. As far as the individual elements are concerned, they, on the other hand, should be gentle and calm. You can make fire from wood and water can penetrate stone. The film should be unruffled like the surface of the water when there is no wind blowing and there are only the tiniest of waves. Therefore, the dominant will be the sound of the waist drums echoing through the heavens and the pitiful sounds of prayers for rain, and the minor structure will be deep talks in the night or soft singing by the river.

We have already swept away all the elements of the original script that undermined this general structure. We will not describe the confrontation with the dark forces in society or the conflict between father and daughter directly. Nor will we directly express the changes that the characters undergo in response to external forces or expose the immediate motivations for character actions. We hope the film will seem restrained, fitting the characteristics of the times. We also hope the relationships between the characters will be appropriate to our national character.

The essence of the style of this film can be summed up in one word: "concealment."

"The greatest music has the rarest sound. The greatest image has no form."[8] The image summing up the style of the film is "The Yellow River seen from a distance."[9]

Zhang Yimou's cinematographer's notes complement the overall structure established by Chen Kaige, but also have their own voice. He writes:

Front row, first from left, director Chen Kaige; back row, second from the left, cinematographer Zhang Yimou, on location for *Yellow Earth*. Photo courtesy of He Qun.

This area is the land where the ancestor of the Chinese people, the Xuanyuan Emperor, ploughed, planted, and fought military campaigns. It is the cradle of the nation. Making a film here requires deep reflection.

We want to express how vast and stark the sky is, how dense the land is, how the river flows on and on, and how the national spirit struggles constantly to grow stronger. We want to express how roars of power have been produced out of primitive barbarism, and how stirring songs have emerged from the barren yellow earth. We want to express the fate and feelings of the people—bright yearning and seeking amidst love, hate, valor, frailty, ignorance, and virtue.

It is always easier to talk about doing something than to do it.

"Aim high or you'll fall below the average—aim for the average, and you'll certainly fail."

In fact, we only had a very limited palette to work with: the earth, the cave homes, the Yellow River, and the four characters.

"A three-inch vertical brush stroke can represent a height of a thousand feet, and a horizontal brush stroke of a few feet can represent a distance of many miles."[10]

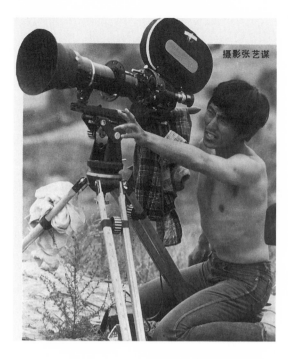

Zhang Yimou shoots
Yellow Earth. From the
1985–1986 volume of
China Screen.

Style:

It is the sonorous and melodic *xintianyou* folk songs carrying far and wide. It is the ravines, which look like they are chopped into the landscape with an axe or a sword. It is the stomping of feet while playing the waist drum. It is the Yellow River, quietly flowing like a sigh.

"Profound, deep, dense." That is the simplest way to put it.

Avoid the delicate but pursue the intense; avoid the complex and go for the pure.

Chuang Tzu said, "When carving and polishing are done, then return to plainness."[11]

Composition:

The composition aims at being "compressed and solid."

"Profound thinkers tend to be expansive, but those whose talents are well practiced know how to cut away excess."[12] In composing the frame, we will insist on excluding all but the most essential things and emphasize a general weightiness.

What is different from *One and Eight* is that we aren't going for powerful shocks but for quiet tranquility.

Movement:

In order to create a profound and dense feeling, we will avoid movement as far as possible.

Film is an art of movement, but movement is not necessarily the only cinematographic technique. "Many layers of mountains give an impression of depth, and even though painted water is still it gives the impression of movement."[13]

In fact, our thinking about our future film has benefited not a little from Lao Tzu's saying, "The greatest square has no corners. The greatest vessel is the last completed. The greatest music has the rarest sound. The greatest image has no form."[14]

If *Yellow Earth* were a grand edifice, the two extracts above would seem like two clear architects' blueprints. Their thinking closely resembles the finished film in all matters great and small, abstract and concrete. In these writings we can see the cultural sources of the two collaborators' rapport and their congenial cooperation. Shared accomplishments in classical Chinese culture enabled Zhang and Chen to experience tacit agreement and profound contentment while working together on *Yellow Earth*. Chen Kaige's free-spirited poetic voice and philosophical profundity found expression in Zhang Yimou's cinematography, the form of which was only decided after Zhang had grasped the inner essence of the subject matter. Without Zhang Yimou's penetrating cultural vision, even the most technically skilled cinematographer could only skim the surface and never see the soul of the Yellow River and the loess plateau. Together, their work expressed what the label "Fifth Generation" meant in a more concentrated and concrete way.

However, Chen and Zhang did not complete *Yellow Earth* alone. The creative designs of the outstanding production designer He Qun were realized in sets that were in no way lacking. The high-quality contributions and cooperation from all concerned were necessary to guarantee the success of

The crew of *Yellow Earth* worked very closely together. Front row, from right: Zhang Yi-mou, Chen Kaige, He Qun, and the folklore consultant, Zhong Ling. Back row, from right: Xue Bai, who played Cuiqiao, and Wang Xueqi, who played Gu Qing. Photo courtesy of He Qun.

Yellow Earth, including the gifted composer Zhao Jiping's music, the sound design, and the editing.

But to understand the evolution of Fifth Generation cinema, we must focus on the character of Chen and Zhang's thinking and its transformations, because their close union crystallized Fifth Generation aesthetic thought into something rich and expansive.

As a filmmaker, Chen Kaige is naturally given to deep reflection. He is profoundly interested in the conditions of human existence and the character of national history, and he is at home with metaphysical and highly abstract thought. He was nurtured by Chinese classical poetry and painting, and he favors a rarefied and subtle style. Poetic feelings and Confucian models make his films full of dense cultural atmosphere and deep political thought. In the late eighties, his philosophy and his cinematic fables became the symbol of China's cutting-edge cinema and the concrete form of early Fifth Generation cinema.

Zhang Yimou, however, is different. Although he was also influenced by Chinese traditional literature, by nature he gravitates toward classical Chinese storytelling. In his visual language system, he prefers a direct and straightforward style and the passionate and bold colors of folk art. Zhang Yimou wants to show a liberated life. He likes pouring powerful dramatic conflicts and movement into popular, straightforward, and noncerebral narratives. In a flow of tumbling and intense images, he depicts life's constraints, displays vital revolts, and denounces the crushing of oppressed lives. When later he moved beyond the avant-garde period of Fifth Generation cinema, Zhang Yimou developed a complete model of popular cinema for a new generation of Chinese.

My remarks here summarize the changes that occurred later in the decade of the Fifth Generation; these outcomes were completely unforeseeable at the time of the making of *Yellow Earth*. However, during the *Yellow Earth* period the unique arrangements of fate brought together the most ideal combination of Fifth Generation members, the freshest experiences, the purest creative motivations, and the most sincere creative friendships. *Yellow Earth* was the newborn baby of historical analysis, and the film was embraced by all 153 members of the class of 1982.

Shooting began on 18 April 1984 and finished on 30 June of the same year.

The birth of *Yellow Earth* made it clear that a new page had been turned in the history of Chinese cinema.

■

In June 1993, Chen Kaige's *Farewell, My Concubine* shared the Palme d'Or at the 46th Cannes International Film Festival. Afterward, Chen Kaige spoke frankly to reporters:

> Many Chinese and foreign reporters ask me which film I feel is my best. I always think of *Yellow Earth* first. It may not be my most mature or most perfectly crafted film, but it is my most sincere and most imaginative work. Back then, we were all new graduates. Now that we have become famous, we may be concerned about more things, our thoughts may be more profound, and the topics we are making films about may

Director Chen Kaige in the early 1990s. Photo courtesy of Chen Kaige.

be bigger. But psychologically, we must completely rid ourselves of the mentality of celebrity, because harboring such an attitude hinders the production of genuinely significant and good films. When we had just graduated from the Academy, we were filled with ambition! All of us had a powerful and urgent desire to create an artistic golden age. Now we must ask ourselves if we still have that drive. Back then, when we had just arrived in the film world, we were really fresh. Do we still have youthful faces, or are we already past our prime? [15]

In China and overseas, many people ask me why the members of the class of 1982 are called the "Fifth Generation," and whether a focus on generations is a suitable way of investigating film history or examining a director's place in the larger collective.

Li Zehou touches on these issues in the prologue to his book *On the History of Modern Chinese Thought*. I include it here for your consideration.

By focusing on generations, we attend to the way in which people's shared social experiences during their early adulthood, from seventeen to twenty-five years of age, assume a historical character in their behavioral habits, thought patterns, emotional attitudes, ideas, values, and moral standards. When they indulge themselves and sigh about "my day" or "our days," these are in fact manifest traces of the way history moves forward in waves. The detailed study of these issues enables a deeper and clearer understanding of the mission of an era and a generation; their moral concerns and their real effects on the future; conflicts due to the generation gap; the distinction between social age, physiological age, and psychological age; and the differences and connections between different generations. The human world is characterized by the supercession of the old by the new. The future becomes the present and the past, and the present and the past combine both the withering and the continuity of generations.[16]

Examining the development of modern Chinese thought from this perspective, Li Zehou divides the last hundred years of Chinese intellectuals into the Xinhai Revolution generation, the May Fourth generation, the Great Revolution generation, the 1938 generation, the Liberation generation, and the Red Guard generation. According to these divisions, he carries out in-depth analysis and argument, on the basis of which he discusses modern Chinese political thought and the relationship between rupture and continuity in the development of personalities and ideals.

From Li Zehou's work it can be seen that, from a certain perspective, it is useful to apply the concept of generations to investigate Chinese film history. The First Generation consists of Zheng Zhengqiu, Zhang Shichuan, and so on. The Second Generation is comprised of Xia Yan, Yang Hansheng, Sun Yu, Cai Chusheng, Wu Yonggang, Fei Mu, and others active in the thirties and forties. The Third Generation is from the fifties and sixties, and includes Shui Hua, Cheng Yin, Zheng Junli, and Xie Jin. The Fourth Generation was delayed for ten years because of the Cultural Revolution and hence appeared in the early 1980s. It includes Wu Yigong, Xie Fei, Zheng Dongtian, Teng Wenji, Zhang Nuanxin, and others. Following close on their heels in the mid-eighties was Chen Kaige, Zhang Yimou, Tian Zhuangzhuang, Wu Ziniu, and the others constituting the Fifth Generation.

Just as Li Zehou pointed out, division into generations not only indicates physiological age but also defines cultural characteristics and social consciousness. Distinguishing the Fifth Generation marks a clear difference—in terms of political thinking, cultural consciousness, and film aesthetics—between them and their predecessors, while allowing for individual differences in artistic pursuits and styles.

On the basis of this conception, in this book I have examined the social history of the Fifth Generation; the sources of their cultural consciousness and their film language; their college days; the budding of their creative consciousness; their move out into society; and the appearance of their first works. By using extensive interviews and historical data and laying particular emphasis on each individual's own character and psychology, I have argued for the appearance of an artistic and creative collectivity and the formation of that specific concept in film culture. In pursuing this intention, I have sought out the source of a film movement. And this bubbling spring later swelled into a rich and diverse main current of Chinese cinema known all over the world as Fifth Generation film.

Continuing to toil on domestic soil or struggling in foreign studios and experiencing the changes of life that come with middle age, the Fifth Generation recollects the rapid passing of the years with sighs. But in their hearts there still exists a treasured space where they harbor a vital and exciting old dream—oh, those unforgettable times in Zhuxin Village!

The cinematography class of 1982 holds up the Academy nameplate in their informal graduation photo. Front row: first from left, Zhang Yimou; second, Zhang Huijun; second from right, Deng Wei; third, Hou Yong. Behind Hou Yong, at left, is Gu Changwei. Photo courtesy of Hou Yong.

POSTSCRIPT

■

Nearly two decades have passed since the first Fifth Generation films, *One and Eight* and *Yellow Earth,* were made in 1983 and 1984. During this time, Fifth Generation cinema has undergone enormous changes both as an art movement and in terms of individual filmmakers' styles.

When discussing film movements from different places and times, we always use the stylistics and aesthetics of their classic periods to determine their characteristics and assess their contributions to film art. For example, Italian neorealism reigned as an artistic movement for about seven years after World War II, from 1945 to 1952. Visconti, De Sica, and Zavattini continued to make films after that, but they cannot be seen as neorealist. The French New Wave is a similar case in point. From this perspective, we can say that the classic period of Fifth Generation cinema lasted from 1983 to 1989. It was during this time that Fifth Generation cinema's political rebelliousness, cultural marginality, and artistic innovation were most pronounced, and its antitraditional cinematic style and composition were particularly evident. Therefore, I believe this was both the initial creative period of Fifth Generation cinema and the period that defines it as an art movement.

Shooting *Horse Thief.* Director Tian Zhuangzhuang is on the right. Photo from the 1985–1986 volume of *China Screen.*

The evolution of Fifth Generation cinema may be roughly divided into three periods.

1983 to 1989: Representative works are Zhang Junzhao's *One and Eight* (1983); Chen Kaige's *Yellow Earth* (1984), *Big Military Parade* (1985), and *King of the Children* (1987); Tian Zhuangzhuang's *On the Hunting Ground* (1984), and *Horse Thief* (1986); Huang Jianxin's *Black Cannon Incident* (1985); Zhang Yimou's *Red Sorghum* (1987); and Wu Ziniu's *Evening Bell* (1988). This was the initial creative period of Fifth Generation cinema, and these films can be called classic Fifth Generation films.

1990 to 1994: Representative works are Zhang Yimou's *Ju Dou* (1990), *Raise the Red Lantern* (1991), *The Story of Qiu Ju* (1992), and *To Live* (1994); Chen Kaige's *Life on a String* (1991) and *Farewell, My Concubine* (1993); Tian Zhuangzhuang's *Blue Kite* (1992); Li Shaohong's *Bloody Morning* (1992), and *A Man at Forty* (1993); He Qun's *Country Teachers* (1993); and Huang Jianxin's *Stand Up, Don't Bend Over* (1992) and *Back to Back, Face to Face* (1993). This is Fifth Generation cinema's period of development and transformation.

1995 on: Representative works are Zhang Yimou's *Shanghai Triad* (1995), *Keep Cool* (1997), and *Not One Less* (1998); Chen Kaige's *Temptress Moon* (1995) and *The Emperor and the Assassin* (1998); Wu Ziniu's *Nanjing 1937* (1995); and Li Shaohong's *Blush* (1995). This can be called the period in which Fifth Generation cinema dispersed. Along with an overall decrease in production, there has been increasingly less evidence of shared artistic characteristics.

■

Over the past decade, numerous Chinese and non-Chinese writings have offered cultural critique and historical reflection about Fifth Generation cinema. In the 1990s, there was strong interest in the use of postcolonial critical methods to assess the Fifth Generation.[1] The most outstanding examples of this work were done by Wang Yichuan and Zhang Yiwu. In *The End of the Zhang Yimou Myth: Cultural and Aesthetic Perspectives on Zhang Yimou's Cinema,* Wang Yichuan systematically analyzes the development of Zhang Yimou's films. He points out that the search for cultural roots and the expression of primal patricidal emotions combine to form the cultural and spiritual core of Zhang Yimou's work. Wang also notes that an important characteristic of Zhang's discursive strategy is the construction of a contextual model consisting of a three-way exchange between the contemporary self, the traditional father, and the Western other. Within this model, the narrative tactics of "striving for difference" and "entertaining the guest" give Zhang Yimou's films an exotic atmosphere and make them Oriental spectacles for Westerners.[2]

In "Zhang Yimou in the Global Postcolonial Context," Zhang Yiwu provides an even more trenchant critique. He argues that Zhang Yimou's films offer up the "other" for consumption by the people of the First World, allowing them to gaze in wonder at a dazzling, strange, and barbarous "Orient," an exotic society and people from the realms of fantasy. He points out that Zhang Yimou's films, like those of most Fifth Generation directors, are fond of fabricated and fanciful "folklore" from the mysterious Orient. It may be said that other Fifth Generation directors construct folklore as an oppressive force confronting the individual in order to express frustration and anxiety about the absence of the individual subject. In Zhang Yimou's films, folklore is not only negative and passive but also a sign of the essential Orient and the basis of the commodified exoticism of the story.

Therefore, Zhang Yiwu asserts, Zhang Yimou's films are ahistorical spatialized myths: "The spatialized 'China' in Zhang Yimou's films is a case of postmodernity manifesting itself in the Third World." He further claims that not only are *Ju Dou* and *Raise the Red Lantern* Oriental spectacles, but even *The Story of Qiu Ju* is deemed full of "emotive fabrications and falsifications about the contemporary circumstances of Chinese people."[3]

All in all, both critics position Zhang's films as cultural commodities in a global postcolonial context, and claim that they have been produced with a postcolonial veneer, using the capital and discursive methods of the First World. These are film texts in which the Third World distorts its own history to provide an "other" for the Western world to consume, and contorted rewritings of an oppressed "hidden history."

■

Postcolonial theory is a valuable aid in both the analysis of contemporary cultural phenomena and the cultural conflicts and discursive relationships between the First World and the Third World in the era of globalization. Therefore, it provides a useful cultural perspective in the discussions on Fifth Generation cinema. However, contemporary world culture is not only characterized by the ever-larger role of transnational capitalism in global culture. Ours is also a polyvocal age in which multiple cultures coexist and develop alongside each other, and no culture's traditions and values should be treated lightly. Indeed, it is from this very position that Third World cultures have finally been able to write their own national histories on the basis of their own linguistic and cultural characteristics. In the process, they have uncovered repressed hidden histories, expressed their own "popular memories," and established the right of different cultures to exist.

From this cultural perspective, has China's Fifth Generation cinema expressed the popular desires of a particular period? Has it related episodes from a forgotten and repressed hidden history? Has it developed the film style of national cinema? Has it revealed an existential value in Oriental culture? I believe the answer to all these questions is "yes."

First, the history of Fifth Generation cinema is divided into different periods. The first period was the initial creative stage, in which the representative works *One and Eight* and *Yellow Earth* reflected on and rewrote Chinese history. This surely can be seen as the uncovering of repressed hidden history. The cinematic representation of war and history diverges markedly from the political discourse of the mainstream, constituting popular rather than party political art. The sharp conflicts between people and nature and culture and the collective in Chen Kaige's *Yellow Earth, Big Military Parade,* and *King of the Children* stem from deep reflection about the social chaos of the Cultural Revolution. The strong affirmation of human consciousness, vitality, and freedom in *Red Sorghum* certainly constituted a revolt and a blow against the repression of human nature in Chinese society over the last half-century and against the Confucian shackles of feudal society's long history. This affirmation of human value and subjectivity is expressed repeatedly in early Fifth Generation films. This is a true reflection of its context, of the reforms, and of the opening up of Chinese society that occurred in the eighties, along with the promotion of subjectivity and individual autonomy. The idea of auteur psychology can also be used to explain this. The filmmakers of the Fifth Generation had emerged from the dark tunnel of the decade of chaos and returned from the countryside, in the north and the south, eager to release their pent-up and overpowering feelings of oppression. These factors constituted the national discursive environment and original creative motivations for early Fifth Generation cinema.

As far as the international context is concerned, early Fifth Generation cinema was only in the stage of "being discovered" and "being recognized." Even *Red Sorghum* was made entirely with Chinese money, let alone earlier films such as *One and Eight* and *Yellow Earth.* They are all 100 percent Chinese productions. So how can anyone talk about them in terms of foreign control? Of course, Western acceptance and approval are not dependent on them putting up the budget or being pandered to by Third World filmmakers. The West has its own standards of discursive legitimation. Furthermore, is it not the case that overemphasizing Western critical responses, and even thinking that "novelty seeking" and "searching for difference" are the yardsticks for Western evaluation of Asian and Chinese cinema, shows bias and an inferiority complex?

The second phase of Fifth Generation cinema, that of development and transformation, is seen as the heyday of the commercialization and international control of Fifth Generation film. Here, the critics focus on *Ju Dou, Raise the Red Lantern, Farewell, My Concubine,* and other such films.

When considering the 1990–1994 period of development and transfor-

Professor Ni Zhen and director Tian Zhuangzhuang in Japan while part of a Chinese film delegation. Photo courtesy of the author.

mation, as well as emphasizing the international situation, one must also research the national situation. An important political incident took place in China in 1989. It has had a powerful impact on political life in China in the nineties and marks a watershed between the eighties and nineties in literature and the arts in China. From the latter half of 1989 and throughout the 1990s, Chinese cinema has been under strict control. This was especially true between 1990 and 1993. Under these circumstances at home, Fifth Generation filmmakers found themselves in an extraordinarily difficult creative environment. *Ju Dou* and *Raise the Red Lantern* were banned and only finally released together after *The Story of Qiu Ju* had been affirmed by mainstream opinion and released. *Blue Kite* has never been released. Although the censors passed *Farewell, My Concubine*, its distribution was limited to a short run in a few theaters.

Any film criticism blind to the local political context can easily push a certain perspective and method to the extreme point where it loses touch with the actual situation and disregards the determinations on the production of the cinematic texts. It is particularly important to note that *To Live*, *Blue Kite*, and *Farewell, My Concubine* are all very concrete representations of contemporary Chinese history. Their protagonists all travel the difficult road from Old China to New China. These are exemplary historical narratives and cinematic representations of a "temporalized" China; they definitely are not "spatialized displays" in which period is unclear. In particular, the lead character in *Blue Kite* takes a difficult journey that extends in time from the fifties all the way to the beginning of the Cultural Revolution. This period includes the immense storm of the 1957 Anti-Rightist Movement, the agrarian famine visited on ordinary people as a result of the Great Leap Forward in 1958, the destruction of human nature caused by the ultra-leftist line, and the political disaster of the tempest that was the Cultural Revolution. However, the cinematic narrative of *Blue Kite* is calm, gentle, and unperturbed. This should be seen as a writing of banished and forgotten "popular memories." It is certainly not a pandering and fawning concoction of Oriental exotica. Therefore, what must be emphasized is that during its second phase, between 1990 and 1994, operating under extremely difficult creative conditions, Fifth Generation cinema produced films that got close to contemporary political history and expressed the fate of ordinary Chinese people in real circumstances. They are profound diachronic descriptions and artistic expressions of the circumstances of individual Chinese people. In this particular political situation, Fifth Generation cinema changed in terms of the distance from which its narratives are recounted (from near to far) and their angle (from high to level), and this provides much food for thought. What Zhang Yimou undertakes in *To Live* and *The Story of Qiu Ju* is precisely a rigorous inquiry into the circumstances of life in China's small towns and rural villages. It is not a "spatialized myth" distant from Chinese reality.

It is worth noting that at no stage in its history has Fifth Generation cinema ever been positively endorsed in China. In terms of both cultural position and film style, it has always been marginalized and never recognized as a legitimate discourse or admitted to mainstream culture. At the same time, its international status is also in a marginal Third World cultural position in relation to Eurocentrism. A few directors winning awards at international film festivals does not change this in the least.

Finally, I must point out the contribution of Fifth Generation cinema's stylistic innovations to the formal language of Chinese cinema. Early Fifth Generation cinema has a fondness for the loess plateau of China's West and dramatic wilderness stories that pit humanity against nature. This constitutes the classic visual repertoire of Fifth Generation cinema, and it can be

Professor Zheng Guoen (in the Mao jacket) and the cinematography class of 1982 welcome Japanese filmmakers Yamamoto Satsuo (wearing hat) and Yamada Yoji (in white jacket) to the Beijing Film Academy. First row: third from left, Zhang Ming. Back row: first from right, Xiao Feng; second, Zhi Lei; third, Zhao Fei; fourth, Hou Yong; fifth, Lü Yue. Standing at the very back is Gu Changwei. Photo courtesy of Hou Yong.

traced back most immediately to the "roots-seeking" nativism of 1980s culture. However, it should also be traced back to the long years that Fifth Generation filmmakers spent in rural and border areas. Their ambivalence toward the land and primordial nature, and their determination to express it, created a special visual style in Chinese cinema. In relatively many long shots the landscape is vast and the horizon wide, dissolving the boundary between the characters and nature, and making them as one. Images of the majestic and desolate area around the Hetao bend of the Yellow River in Ningxia and Inner Mongolia and the North Shaanxi Plateau construct a kind of rough masculine beauty that conveys a feeling of solemnity, full of historical significance. This rough aesthetic style stands in sharp contrast to classical Chinese national style, which has always given preference to the Southern reaches of the Yangtze River with its little bridges and flowing waters as a setting. The Fifth Generation's heroic legends of desolate plateaus are more reminiscent of the robust natural beauty found in the moral tales of the Japanese cinema of Kurosawa Akira, Shindo Kaneto, and Imamura Shohei, indicating a shared avenue of aesthetic exploration within Eastern cinema. In the international cinematic framework, they were both clearly distinguishable from European and American cinema and in a mutually beneficial relationship with them.

The scope of this book is limited to the origins of Fifth Generation cinema and its maiden works. Therefore, it is far from being a complete history of Fifth Generation cinema. However, I feel that recognition of this film movement's germination, birth, and development can benefit from tracing and researching the formative years of its representative members and the origins of their artistic thought. With the passing of time and the increased understanding of historical materials, I regret the gaps in the book and feel they are worth filling. However, excessive amendment would destroy the unity of the book and its original features. If there is an opportunity to write another book that narrates the complete development of the Fifth Generation, I will make detailed additions!

CHARACTER LIST FOR CHINESE NAMES

■

This list contains all Chinese personal names found in the main text in their romanized form, along with the Chinese simplified character form of the name as it appears in the original manuscript. The list is set up word-by-word in alphabetical order according to the letters of the first syllable of the family name, which appears before the given name. If there is no family name, the first syllable of the given name is used.

Ah Cheng	阿城	Cai Chusheng	蔡楚生
Ah Ping	阿平	Cao Jiuping	曹久平
Ai Weiwei	艾未未	Cao Yu	曹禺
		Cao Zuobin	曹作宾
Bai	白	Chen Daoming	陈道明
Bai Hong	白宏	Chen Hao	陈昊
Bao Pao	包炮	Chen Huaikai	陈怀恺
Bao Xiaoran	鲍肖然	Chen Kaige	陈凯歌
Bei Dao	北岛	Chen Misha	陈咪沙
Beisheng	北生	Chen Wenjing	陈文静

Chen Xin	陈信	Huang Shuqin	黄蜀芹
Cheng Yin	成荫	Huang Xiang	黄翔
Chuang Tzu (see Zhuangzi)		Huang Zhen	黄镇
Cui Wei	崔嵬	Huo Qubing	霍去病
Cui Xiaoqin	崔小芹		
Cuiqiao	翠巧	Jiang Haiyang	江海洋
		Jiang Qing	江青
Deng Wei	邓伟	Jiang Shixiong	江世雄
Deng Xian	邓贤	Jiang Yunhui	江韵辉
Deng Xiaoping	邓小平	Jin Shan	金山
Ding Yinnan	丁荫楠	Jin Tao	金韬
Fang Shu	方舒	Ke Lan	柯蓝
Fanny (Fanyi)	繁漪	Kejian	克俭
Fei Mu	费穆	Kong Xiangzhu	孔祥竺
Feng	冯		
Feng Xiaoning	冯小宁	Lao She	老舍
		Lao Tzu (Laozi)	老子
Geng Xiaozhen	耿小震	Lei Han	雷汉
Gong Li	巩俐	Li Dazhao	李大钊
Gu Changwei	顾长卫	Li Lanhua	李岚华
Gu Cheng	顾城	Li Ling	李羚
Gu Qing	顾青	Li Po (Li Bai)	李白
Guan Hanqing	关汉卿	Li Shaohong	李少红
Guo Baochang	郭宝昌	Li Shaoxu	梨少旭
Guo Xiaochuan	郭小川	Li Yalin	李亚林
		Li Zehou	李泽厚
Hai Mo	海默	Lin Biao	林彪
Han Xiaolei	韩小磊	Lin Daqing	林大庆
Han Yu	韩愈	Lin Hongtong	林洪桐
He Qun	何群	Ling Zifeng	凌子风
He Yutang	贺玉堂	Liu	刘
Hong Changqing	洪常青	Liu Miaomiao	刘苗苗
Hou Yong	侯咏	Liu Zongyuan	柳宗元
Hu Mei	胡玫	Lu	鲁
Huang Jianxin	黄建新	Lu Xiaoyan	卢小燕
Huang Rui	黄锐	Lu Xun	鲁迅

Lü Yue	吕乐	Situ Zhaodun	司徒兆敦
Luo Zhongli	罗中立	Sun Li	孙立
		Sun Yu	孙瑜
Ma Desheng	马德生	Sun Yuezhi	孙月植
Ma Jing	马静		
Mao Zedong	毛泽东	Tao Jing	陶经
Meng Qingpeng	孟庆鹏	Tao Zeru	陶泽如
Min Xing	闵星	Teng Wenji	腾文骥
Mu Deyuan	穆德远	Tian Fang	田方
		Tian Han	田汉
Ni Zhen	倪震	Tian Jinfu	田金夫
Nie Jing	聂晶	Tian Zhuangzhuang	田庄庄
Ning Ying	宁瀛	Tiezi	铁子
Ningyu	凝玉		
		Wang Anyi	王安忆
Pan	潘	Wang Cheng	王成
Pan Hua	潘华	Wang Fang	王芳
Pan Yuanliang	潘渊亮	Wang Haowei	王好为
Peng Xiaolian	彭小莲	Wang Jian	王坚
Po	破	Wang Jin	王金
		Wang Junzheng	王君正
Qiyue	七月	Wang Keping	王克平
Qin Wei	秦威	Wang Li	王力
Qu Leilei	曲磊磊	Wang Liping	王立平
Qulin	曲林	Wang Meng	王蒙
		Wang Shuo	王朔
Ruan Lingyu	阮玲玉	Wang Suihan	汪岁寒
		Wang Wenqing	王文清
Sangsang	桑桑	Wang Xiaolie	王小列
Shan Dongbing	单东炳	Wang Xinyu	王心语
Shen Danping	沈丹萍	Wang Xue	王雪
Shi	始	Wang Xueqi	王学圻
Shi Hui	石挥	Wang Yichuan	王一川
Shi Tiesheng	史铁生	Wang Yongge	王永歌
Shu Ting	舒婷	Wang Yuzhang	王玉璋
Shui Hua	水华	Wang Zhihong	王志红
Si Feng	四凤	Wang Ziyin	王子音

Wei Bida	韦必达	Yin Li	尹力
Wei Zhang	韦彰	Yu Lan	于篮
Wei Zongwan	魏宗万		
Wen Lun	文伦	Zeng Nianping	曾念平
Wu Guoying	吴国英	Zhang Chao	张潮
Wu Yigong	吴贻弓	Zhang Fengyi	张丰毅
Wu Yinxian	吴印咸	Zhang Huijun	张会军
Wu Yonggang	吴永刚	Zhang Jianya	张建亚
Wu Zetian	吴则天	Zhang Junjian	张军剑
Wu Ziniu	吴子牛	Zhang Junzhao	张军钊
		Zhang Ke	张客
Xi'nan	希南	Zhang Min	张泯
Xia Gang	夏钢	Zhang Minzhu	张民主
Xia Yan	夏衍	Zhang Nuanxin	张暖忻
Xiangzi	祥子	Zhang Qi	张其
Xiao	肖	Zhang Shichuan	张石川
Xiao Feng	肖风	Zhang Tiesheng	张铁生
Xie Fei	谢飞	Zhang Xianliang	张贤亮
Xie Jin	谢晋	Zhang Yifu	张益福
Xie Tieli	谢铁骊	Zhang Yimou	张艺谋
Xie Xiaojing	谢小晶	Zhang Yiwu	张颐武
Xie Yuan	谢园	Zhang Zhiqiang	张志强
Xin Ming	辛明	Zhang Zhixin	张志新
Xin Qiji	辛弃疾	Zhang Ziliang	张子良
Xu Chi	徐迟	Zhao	赵
Xu Guming	徐谷明	Zhao Dan	赵丹
Xu Ping	徐平	Zhao Fei	赵非
Xu Tongjun	许同均	Zhao Fengxi	赵凤玺
Xu Zhi	许志	Zhao Jiping	赵季平
Xuanyuan	轩辕	Zhao Jinzuo	赵劲作
Xue Bai	薛白	Zhao Xiaorui	赵小锐
Xue Zijiang	薛子江	Zhao Yong	赵雍
		Zheng Dongtian	郑洞天
Yang Hansheng	阳翰笙	Zheng Fanping	郑凡平
Yang Qiner	杨芹儿	Zheng Guoen	郑国恩
Ye Xin	叶辛	Zheng Junli	郑君里
Ye Zhizhen	叶之臻	Zheng Ming	郑鸣

Zheng Zhengqiu	郑正秋	Zhou Ping	周萍
Zhi Lei	智磊	Zhou Puyuan	周朴园
Zhong Dianfei	钟惦棐	Zhou Wei	周伟
Zhong Jingzhi	钟敬之	Zhu De	朱德
Zhong Ling	钟灵	Zhu Lin	朱琳
Zhou Chuanji	周传基	Zhuangzi	庄子
Zhou Enlai	周恩来		

CHINESE FILM TITLE LIST

■

This list contains all the Chinese films mentioned in the main text, along with their original titles. Wherever possible, we have tried to use the English-language export title, which is why some titles are quite different from their Chinese originals.

After Separation	大撒把
The Apprentice Lawyer	见习律师
Apricot Blossoms in March	杏花三月天
Army Nurse	女儿楼
As You Like It	如意
At the Beach	海滩
Back to Back, Face to Face	背靠背，脸对脸
Ballad of the Yellow River	黄河谣
Be There or Be Square	不见不散
Big Military Parade	大阅兵
Big Mill	大磨坊
Black Cannon Incident	黑炮事件

Black Snow	本命年
Bloody Morning	血色清晨
Blue Flower	蓝色的花
Blue Kite	蓝风筝
Blush	红粉
Border Town	边城
The Bride	出嫁女
The Call of the Cuckoo	杜鹃声声
Chen Huansheng Comes to Town	陈焕生上城
Chief Eunuch Li Lianying	大太监李莲英
The Chinese	中国人
Come on, China	加油，中国队
Conned	上一当
The Cool Clear Stream	清亮的小溪
The Corner Forgotten by Love	被爱情遗忘的角落
Country Teachers	凤凰琴
The Dove Tree	鸽子树
The Drive to Win	沙鸥
Dr. Sun Yat-sen	孙中山
The Emperor and the Assassin	荆轲刺秦王
Evening Bell	晚钟
Family Feud	家丑
Farewell, My Concubine	霸王别姬
Far from War	远离战争的年代
For Fun	找乐
The Goddess	神女
The Great Start	伟大的起点
Heaven's Blood	天出血
The Herdsman	牧马人
Heroic Sons and Daughters	英雄儿女
Horse Thief	盗马贼

I Love You No Matter What	爱你没商量
The Imp	霹雳贝贝
Innocent Babbler	杂嘴子
In Praise of Longjiang	龙江颂
In the Heat of the Sun	阳光灿烂的日子
In Their Prime	他们正年轻
Ju Dou	菊豆
Keep Cool	有话好好说
King of the Children	孩子王
The Last Clue	世界疑案的最后线索
The Last Day of Winter	最后一个冬日
The Last Shot	最后一个镜头
The Legend of Tianyun Mountain	天云山传奇
Life on a String	遍走遍唱
The Lin Family Shop	林家铺子
Little Soldier Zhang Ga	小兵张嘎
Lonely Ghost in a Dark Mansion	黑楼孤魂
A Man at Forty	四十不惑
Massacre	大毁灭
Me and My Classmates	我和我的同学们
Meridian of War	战争子午线
Mutiny	哗变
My Brother, the Yes-man	应声阿哥
My Memories of Old Beijing	城南旧事
My September	我的九月
Nanjing 1937	南京1937
Neighbors	邻居
New Legends of Old Soldiers	老兵新传
Nobody Applauds	无人喝彩
No Choice	别无选择
Not One Less	一个都不能少

Old Well	老井
One and Eight	一个和八个
On the Beat	民警故事
On the Dock	海港
On the Hunting Ground	猎场扎撒
Our Corner	我们的角落
Our Fields	我们的田野
The Ozone Layer Vanishes	大气层消失
Poem on a Red Leaf	红叶题诗
A Policeman's Honor	刑警荣誉
Prison Car to the West	西行囚车
The Probationary Team Member	候补队员
A Question for the Living	死者对生者的访问
Raise the Red Lantern	大红灯笼高高挂
Red Elephant	红象
The Red Lantern	红灯记
Red River Valley	红河谷
Red Sorghum	红高粱
Regret for the Past	伤逝
Reverberations of Life	生活的颤音
Rickshaw Boy	骆驼祥子
The Romantic Adventures of Mr. Wang	王先生欲火焚身
Royal Heart and Soul	义胆忠魂
Sacrificed Youth	青春祭
Samsara	轮回
San Mao Joins the Army	三毛从军记
Secret Decree	喋血黑谷
September	九月
Shanghai Triad	摇啊摇，摇到外婆桥
The Silver Snake Murders	银蛇谋杀案
Slipping into the Golden Triangle	秘闻金三角
Song Jingshi	宋景诗

Song of the Red Flag	红旗谱
Song of Youth	青春之歌
Spring in a Small Town	小城之春
Stand Up, Don't Bend Over	站直了，别趴下
Story from Yunnan	云南故事
The Story of Qiu Ju	秋菊打官司
Street Angel	马路天使
The Sun Has Ears	太阳有耳
Taking Tiger Mountain by Strategy	智取威虎山
The Target	目标
Teenage Years	十四，五岁
Temptress Moon	风月
Three Women	女人的故事
To Live	活着
A Tried and Tested Warrior	烈火金刚
Troubled Laughter	苦恼人的笑
Trouble in the Harbor	海湾不平静
Troubleshooters	顽主
Under the White Poplar	白杨树下
Unexpected Passion	遭遇激情
An Unfinished Chess Game	一盘没有下完的棋
The Vanished Woman	消失的女人
The Virus, the Gold, Sunday	病毒，金牌，星期天
We Are Still Young	我们还年轻
The Wedding	结婚
Widow Village	寡妇村
Wild Boar Forest	野猪林
Woman, Demon, Human	人*鬼*情
Woman from the Lake of Scented Souls	香魂女
Women Generals of the Yang Family	杨门女将
Xiaohua	小花

The Yard 小院

Yellow Earth 黄土地

Zhou Enlai 周恩来

NOTES

■

All translations are by Chris Berry unless otherwise noted. Undocumented quotations of Fifth Generation filmmakers are from the author's interviews, March through May 1994.

NOTES TO TRANSLATOR'S INTRODUCTION

1 Tony Rayns, "Chinese Vocabulary: An Introduction to *King of the Children* and the New Chinese Cinema," in Chen Kaige and Tony Rayns, King of the Children *and the New Chinese Cinema* (London: Faber and Faber, 1989), 1.

2 Ni Zhen, *Tansuo de Yinmu* (The exploratory screen) (Beijing: Zhongguo Dianying Chubanshe, 1994), and *Gaige yu Zhongguo Dianying (Reform in the Chinese cinema)* (Beijing: Zhongguo Dianying Chubanshe, 1994).

1. ADMISSION

1 The literature in English on experiences of the Chinese Cultural Revolution is large and growing. For a bibliography, see Tony H. Chang, comp., *China during the Cultural Revolution, 1966–1976: A Selected Bibliography of English Language Works* (Westport, Conn.: Greenwood Press, 1999). Personal memoirs from the younger generation include Feng Jicai, *Voices from the Whirlwind: An Oral His-*

tory of the Chinese Cultural Revolution (New York: Pantheon Books, 1991); Gao Yuan, *Born Red: A Chronicle of the Cultural Revolution* (Stanford: Stanford University Press, 1987); Liang Heng and Judith Shapiro, *Son of the Revolution* (London: Chatto and Windus, 1983); and Ma Bo, *Blood Red Sunset: A Memoir of the Chinese Cultural Revolution*, trans. Howard Goldblatt (New York: Viking, 1995). For accounts of its effects on those slightly older, see, for example, Chen Chen, *Come Watch the Sun Go Home* (New York: Marlowe, 1998); Yang Jiang, *A Cadre Life School: Six Chapters*, trans. Geremie Barmé (Hong Kong: Joint Publishing Co., 1982); and Yue Daiyun and Carolyn Wakeman, *To the Storm: The Odyssey of a Revolutionary Chinese Woman* (Berkeley: University of California Press, 1985).

2 Deng Xian, *Zhongguo Zhiqing Meng* (Dreams of China's educated youth), (Beijing: Renmin Wenxue Chubanshe, 1993). For accounts in English of the educated youth movement, see, for example, Luo Zi-ping, *A Generation Lost: China under the Cultural Revolution* (New York: Holt, 1991), and Stanley Rosen, *The Role of Sent-Down Youths in the Chinese Cultural Revolution: The Case of Guangzhou* (Berkeley: Institute of East Asian Studies, University of California, Berkeley, 1981).

3 The best account in English of the development of the Chinese film industry after 1949 is Paul Clark, *Chinese Cinema: Culture and Politics since 1949* (New York: Cambridge University Press, 1987).

4 The Film Technology Department had three majors: film machinery, film processing, and film sound. It ceased operation after the Cultural Revolution broke out in 1966, but when the Beijing Film Academy was restored to full operation in 1978, the Sound Department was formally established and the other two majors were transferred to other schools.

5 Ah Cheng, *The King of Trees*, in *Three Kings*, trans. Bonnie S. McDougall (London: Collins Harvill, 1990), 148; original cited in Chen Kaige, *Shaonian Kaige* (Young Chen Kaige) (Taipei: Yuanliu Chuban Gongsi, 1991), 144.

6 Ah Cheng, *The King of Chess* and *The King of Children*, in *Three Kings*, trans. McDougall; Ye Xin, *Cuotuo Suiyue* (Wasted years) (Beijing: Zhongguo Qingnian Chubanshe, 1982); Ye Xin, *Sishengzi* (Bastard) (Beijing: Zhongguo Wenlian Chubanshe, 1989); Deng Xian, *Zhongguo Zhiqing Meng;* and Deng Xian, *Daoguo zhi Hun* (Soul of the nation) (Beijing: Renmin Wenxue Chubanshe, 1991).

7 Wang Li, *Shici Gelü* (Study of the rules and forms of classical poetry) (Beijing: Zhonghua Shuju, 1977). *A Dream of Red Mansions (Honglou Meng)* is sometimes translated as *Dream of the Red Chamber,* and it also appears in English as Cao Xueqin, *The Story of the Stone: A Chinese Novel,* trans. David Hawkes and John Minford, 5 vols. (Harmondsworth: Penguin, 1973–1986).

8 Han Yu (768–824) and Liu Zongyuan (773–819) were famous Tang dynasty prose writers. Li Po (701–762) is a famous and much-translated Tang dynasty

poet. Xin Qiji (1140–1207) is a southern Song dynasty poet renowned for his patriotism.

9 The discussion on the connection between government and self-cultivation occurs in many places in works attributed to Confucius, but in particular in the text of *The Great Learning (Da Xue)*, section 5. The saying is from *The Works of Mencius,* book 7, part I, chapter 9, section 6.

10 Chen Kaige, "Qinguoren" (Man of the Qin), in *Lun Zhang Yimou* (On Zhang Yimou), ed. Ying Xiong et al. (Beijing: Zhongguo Dianying Chubanshe, 1994), 285.

11 China's Qingming, on which the dead are commemorated, is on 5 April. Premier Zhou Enlai had died earlier in 1976, and his opponents, the Gang of Four, were still in power. Many ordinary citizens gathered in Tiananmen Square on this Qingming, and the result was a political gathering as well as a mass mourning. The event was suppressed by the Gang of Four and declared a "counter-revolutionary incident" until 15 November 1978, when it was declared to have been "revolutionary" after all. During these years, the symbolic importance of Premier Zhou among those hoping for change was enormous.

12 Biographies of Premier Zhou Enlai include Han Suyin, *Eldest Son: Zhou Enlai and the Making of Modern China, 1898–1976* (New York: Hill and Wang, 1994), and Dick Wilson, *Chou: The Story of Zhou En Lai 1898–1976* (London: Hutchinson, 1984).

13 On 29 July 1976, an earthquake registering 7.8 on the Richter scale struck the city of Tangshan, killing over two hundred thousand people. Natural disasters on this scale were perceived in imperial China as signs that dynasties were coming to an end. Ironically, a few months later Chairman Mao died and the Gang of Four was toppled.

14 Shi Xiang, "Zhou Zongli Bangongshi de Dengguang" (The lamp in Premier Zhou's office), in *Zhou Zongli Song* (Eulogies for Premier Zhou) (Tianjin: Tianjin Renmin Chubanshe, 1977), 98; translation from *Chinese Literature,* no. 3 (1977): 38.

15 Li Dazhao (1889–1927) was one of the founders of the Communist Party of China. The Chinese character for *zhao* is somewhat unusual, which explains the teacher's confusion. Later on I mention that Zhang Junzhao was already a member of the Communist Party at this stage in his life, so perhaps it is not so surprising that he would select the name of Li Dazhao in this circumstance.

16 In 1956, in response to the calls issued by the Party and the government during the Hundred Flowers Movement, many people expressed criticisms of society and the government. In 1957, over five hundred thousand individuals were condemned and punished as Rightists, a verdict that was only finally rectified in the late seventies.

17 Tu Fu (Du Fu), "Dreaming of Li Po," in *The Columbia Book of Chinese Poetry,* ed. and trans. Burton Watson (New York: Columbia University Press, 1984), 231.

18 Hong Changqing is the male lead character in the ballet *The Red Detachment of Women*. He is the Party's representative on the detachment. This ballet was made into a model opera by Mao's wife, Jiang Qing. Therefore, after 1966, everybody in literature and the arts had to study and perform it.

19 When he wrote these lines, the poet Du Fu had been separated from his family in Loyang by seven years of rebellion; Du Fu, "On Hearing Imperial Forces Have Recovered the Northeast," in *Du Fu's Laments from the South*, ed. David R. McCraw (Honolulu: University of Hawai'i Press, 1992), 153.

20 Cen Shan, "Song of White Snow in Farewell to Secretary Wu Going Back to the Capital," trans. Xu Yuan-zhong, in *300 Tang Poems: A New Translation*, ed. Xu Yuan-zhong, Loh Bei-yei, and Wu Juntao (Hong Kong: The Commercial Press, 1996), 210.

21 Cen Shan, "Song of Running-Horse River in Farewell to General Feng on His Western Expedition," trans. Xu Yuan-zhong, in *300 Tang Poems*, ed. Xu, Loh, and Wu, 205.

22 Zhang Xianliang, "Body and Soul," trans. Philip F. C. Williams, in *Prize-Winning Stories from China, 1980–1981*, ed. Ke Yunlu, Zhang Xianliang, et al. (Beijing: Foreign Languages Press, 1985), 58–92, originally published as *Ling Yu Rou* (Tianjin: Baihua Wenyi Chubanshe, 1981); Zhang Xianliang, *Mimosa* (Beijing: Panda Books, 1985), originally published as *Luhuashu* (Beijing: Shiyue Wenyi Chubanshe, 1984); Zhang Xianliang, *Half of Man Is Woman*, trans. Martha Avery (London: Viking, 1988), originally published as *Nanren de Yiban Shi Nüren* (Beijing: Zhongguo Wenlian Chuban Gongsi, 1985).

23 The Huangpu Military Academy was established by the Guomindang (KMT Nationalist Party) in Guangzhou (Canton) in 1924, and was closely associated with both Sun Yat-sen and Chiang Kai-shek. Many high officers in the KMT armed forces graduated from the military academy, and so it was regarded with particular dislike by the Communist Party.

24 This saying is drawn from volume 1, book 2, chapter 4 of *The Analects* by Confucius. The complete saying is: "At fifteen I set my mind upon wisdom. At thirty I stood firm. At forty I was free from doubts. At fifty I understood the laws of Heaven. At sixty my ear was docile. At seventy I could follow the desires of my heart without transgressing the right." William Edward Soothill, *The Analects of Confucius* (New York: Paragon Book Reprint Corporation, 1968), 149–51.

2. NOSES TO THE GRINDSTONE

1 Named after the left-wing author Lu Xun, the academy was a comprehensive arts school established and run in the revolutionary base area of Yan'an between 1938 and 1945. On Jiang Qing, see Ross Terrill, *Madame Mao, the White-Boned Demon: A Biography of Madame Mao Zedong* (Stanford: Stanford University Press, 1999).

2 On 7 May 1966, Mao issued a directive that led to the establishment of rural

"cadre schools," where intellectuals and other suspect individuals were sent for "reeducation" during the Cultural Revolution.

3 The title of the policy comes from Hua Guofeng, Mao Zedong's short-lived successor before Deng Xiaoping's ascent to power. Hua Guofeng declared that everyone should "resolutely defend whatever policies Chairman Mao has formulated, and unswervingly adhere to whatever instructions Chairman Mao has issued."

4 The Gang of Four had declared the 1976 mourning of Premier Zhou Enlai in Tiananmen Square "counterrevolutionary," and they used the occasion to fire Deng Xiaoping from various posts he had been restored to only the year before.

5 Accounts of the political and social changes that followed Mao's death in 1976 include Richard Baum, *Chinese Politics in the Age of Deng Xiaoping* (Princeton: Princeton University Press, 1994); Fox Butterfield, *Alive in the Bitter Sea* (London: Hodder and Stoughton, 1982); Roger Garside, *Coming Alive: China after Mao* (New York: Mentor, 1981); and Harry Harding, *China's Second Revolution: Reform after Mao* (Washington, D.C.: Brookings Institution, 1987).

6 Ts'ao Yu (Cao Yu), *Thunderstorm*, trans. Wang Tso-liang and A. C. Barnes (Beijing: Foreign Languages Press, 1978); Ts'ao Yu (Cao Yu), *Sunrise: A Play in Four Acts*, trans. A. C. Barnes (Beijing: Foreign Languages Press, 1978); Cao Yu, *The Peking Man*, trans. Leslie Nai-Kwai Lo (New York: Columbia University Press, 1986); Lao She, *Rickshaw*, trans. Jean M. James (Honolulu: University of Hawai'i Press, 1979); Lao She, *Teahouse*, trans. John Howard-Gibbon (Beijing: Foreign Languages Press, 1984); Tian Han, "Mingyou zhi Si" (The death of a famous opera performer), in *Zhongguo Xin Wenxue Daxi, 1927–1937: Xijuji Yi* (Anthology of modern Chinese literature, 1927–1937: Volume 15, drama– part 1) (Shanghai: Shanghai Yishu Chubanshe, 1985), 100–131. For background, see Colin Mackerras, *Chinese Theatre in Modern Times: From 1840 to the Present Day* (London: Thames and Hudson, 1975).

7 Lao She, "Black Li and White Li," in *Blades of Grass: The Stories of Lao She*, trans. William A. Lyell and Sarah Wei-Ming Chen (Honolulu: University of Hawai'i Press, 2000); Lao She, *Crescent Moon and Other Stories* (Beijing: Panda Books, 1985); Lao She, *Dragon Beard Ditch: A Play in Three Acts* (Beijing: Foreign Languages Press, 1956); Lao She, *Beneath the Red Flag*, trans. Don J. Cohn (Beijing: Panda Books, 1982). See also George Kao, ed., *Two Writers and the Cultural Revolution: Lao She and Chen Jo-hsi* (Hong Kong: Chinese University Press, 1980); David Der-wei Wang, *Fictional Realism in Twentieth-Century China: Mao Dun, Lao She, Shen Congwen* (New York: Columbia University Press, 1992); and Britt Towery, *Lao She: China's Master Storyteller* (Waco, Tex.: Tao Foundation, 1999).

8 For more information on Soviet montage theory, see Richard Taylor, *The Politics of the Soviet Cinema, 1917–1929* (New York: Cambridge University Press, 1979).

9 Film Archive of China and the Editorial Department of New World Press, *Joris*

Ivens and China (Beijing: New World Press, 1983); Rosalind Delmar, *Joris Ivens: 50 Years of Film-Making* (London: British Film Institute, 1979).

10   Launched in the cities after World War I, the May Fourth Movement advocated the adoption of Western science and democracy as fundamental to national salvation. When the Treaty of Versailles after World War I granted Chinese territory to Japan as a reward for having fought with the Allies, Chinese students held demonstrations on 4 May 1919, which explains the name of the movement.

11   Originally spoken by Mao, this saying was taken up again in 1978 and became closely associated with Deng Xiaoping and his "pragmatic" reforms.

12   The trial was held between 20 November 1980 and 25 January 1981. All the defendants were found guilty. On the trial, see Chi Hsin, *The Case of the Gang of Four — With First Translation of Teng Hsiao-ping's "Three Poisonous Weeds"* (Hong Kong: Cosmos Books, 1977).

13   The title is a mathematical term. Hsu Chih (Xu Chi), "The Goldbach Conjecture," trans. Huang Yinghao, *Chinese Literature*, no. 11 (1978): 78–85. David S. G. Goodman gives an excellent account of the Democracy Movement of the late seventies in *Beijing Street Voices: The Poetry and Politics of China's Democracy Movement* (London: Marion Boyars, 1981).

14   Located in central Beijing, Democracy Wall was used by citizens participating in the Democracy Movement of the late seventies to post handwritten flyers and articles.

15   This poem by Bei Dao was written during the Qingming demonstrations in Tiananmen Square in April 1976 protesting the Gang of Four. It was published and circulated more widely in 1978. These lines follow on from those given in the main text on page 87. Bei Dao, "The Answer," trans. Bonnie S. McDougall, in *Seeds of Fire: Chinese Voices of Conscience,* ed. Geremie Barmé and John Minford (Hong Kong: Far Eastern Economic Review, 1986), 286.

16   Zhang Zhixin was a Communist Party member who made the mistake of expressing some doubts about current policy and events. She was arrested in 1969 and humiliated, tortured, and eventually executed in 1975. In 1979, her case was made public as part of Deng Xiaoping's ongoing struggle with the left wing of the party, some of whose leaders could be held indirectly responsible for Zhang's fate. A relatively full account of the Zhang Zhixin story is given in Garside, *Coming Alive,* 278–85. Jonathan Chaves analyzes Zhang Zhixin's post–Cultural Revolution transformation in "A Devout Prayer for the Passion of Chang Chih-Hsin," *Modern Chinese Literature Newsletter* 6, no. 1 (1980): 8–25.

17   Lu Xinhua, "The Scar," trans. Wang Mingjie, in *Prize-Winning Stories from China 1978–1979,* ed. Liu Xinwu et al. (Beijing: Foreign Languages Press, 1981), 108–22, originally published as "Shanghen," in *Zhongguo Xin Shiqi Wenxue Jingpin Daxi* (An anthology of outstanding literature from China's new era) (Beijing: Zhongguo Wenxue Chubanshe, 1993), 150–61; Cong Weixi, "Daqiang Xia de Hong Yulan" (Hong Yulan under the Wall), in *Xin Shiqi Zhongpian Xiaoshuo Mingzuo Congshu: Cong Weixi Ji* (Collections of famous medium-length

short stories from the new era: Cong Weixi anthology) (Fuzhou: Haixia Wenyi Chubanshe, 1986); Lu Yanzhou, *Tianyun Shan Chuanqi* (The legend of Tianyun Mountain) (Tianjin: Baihua Wenyi Chubanshe, 1980).

18 Wang Meng, "The Eyes of Night," trans. Wang Mingjie, in *The Butterfly and Other Stories* (Beijing: Panda Books, 1983), 102–12, originally published as "Ye de Yan," in Wang Meng, *Ye de Yan ji Qita Xiaoshuo Ji* (The eyes of night and other short stories) (Guangzhou: Guangzhou Huacheng Chubanshe, 1981); Wang Meng, "Voices of Spring," trans. Bonnie S. McDougall, in *The Butterfly and Other Stories,* 138–54, originally published as "Chun zhi Sheng" in *Ye de Yan ji Qita Xiaoshuo Ji;* Wang Meng, "A Dream of the Sea," trans. Denis C. Mair, in *Selected Works of Wang Meng; Volume 1: The Strain of Meeting* (Beijing: Foreign Languages Press, 1989), 289–303, originally published as "Hai de Meng," in *Ye de Yan ji Qita Xiaoshuo Ji;* Wang Meng, "Kite Streamers," trans. Lü Binghong, in *The Butterfly and Other Stories,* 155–85, originally published as "Fengzheng Piaodai" in *Ye de Yan ji Qita Xiaoshuo Ji;* Wang Meng, "Shen de Hu" (Deep lake), in *Shen de Hu Zhongduanpian Xiaoshuo Ji* (Deep lake anthology of short stories) (Guangzhou: Huacheng Chubanshe, 1982); Wang Meng "Xin de Guang" (Light of the heart), in *Shen de Hu Zhongduanpian Xiaoshuo Ji;* Wang Meng, "Bolshevik Salute," trans. Wendy Larson (Seattle: University of Washington Press, 1990), originally published as "Bu Li" in *Ye de Yan ji Qita Xiaoshuo Ji;* Wang Meng, "The Butterfly," trans. Gladys Yang, in *The Butterfly and Other Stories,* 35–101, originally published as "Hudie" in *Ye de Yan ji Qita Xiaoshuo Ji.* Other important collections of post-Mao literature include Jeffrey C. Kinkley, ed., *After Mao: Chinese Literature and Society, 1978–1981* (Cambridge: Harvard University Press, 1985), and Helen F. Siu and Zelda Stern, eds., *Mao's Harvest: Voices from China's New Generation* (New York: Oxford University Press, 1983). For analysis of Wang Meng's writing of this period, see Philip Williams, "Stylistic Variety in a PRC Writer: Wang Meng's Fiction of the 1979–1980 Cultural Thaw," *Australian Journal of Chinese Affairs,* no. 11 (1984): 59–80.

19 Wang Meng, "The Eyes of Night," 102–3.

20 Wang Shuo, "Wanzhu," (Masters of Mischief) *Shouhuo,* no. 6 (1987): 24–56. On the "modernist" culture of the 1980s, see Jing Wang, *High Culture Fever: Politics, Aesthetics, and Ideology in Deng's China* (Berkeley: University of California Press, 1996), and Zhang Xudong, *China's Modernism in the Era of Reforms* (Durham: Duke University Press, 1997).

21 Bei Dao, "The Answer," 286.

22 Gu Cheng, "When I Blink," trans. Donald Finkel with Chang Sheng-Tai, in *A Splintered Mirror: Chinese Poetry from the Democracy Movement,* trans. Donald Finkel (San Francisco: North Point Press, 1991), 53. See also Seàn Golden and Chu Chiayu, eds., *Selected Poems by Gu Cheng* (Hong Kong: Renditions Press, 1991).

23 Shu Ting, "A Boat with Two Masts," in *Selected Poems* (Hong Kong: Renditions Press, 1994), 19.

24 The "Stars" art exhibition opened earlier in the fall in the China Art Gallery but was quickly closed down. For further details and an extensive discussion of the contemporary art scene, see Robin Munro, "Unofficial Art in China," *Index on Censorship* 11, no. 6 (1982): 36–39.

25 An exhibition of the works of this German socialist artist was held in Beijing in 1979. She has been famous in China since the 1930s.

26 Zhang Nuanxin and Li Tuo, "The Modernization of Film Language," trans. Hou Jianping, in *Chinese Film Theory: A Guide to the New Era,* ed. George S. Semsel, Xia Hong, and Hou Jianping (New York: Praeger, 1990), 10–20. Originally published in *Dianying Yishu,* no. 3 (1979): n.p.

27 On Stalin and the Soviet cinema, see Richard Taylor and Derek Spring, ed., *Stalinism and Soviet Cinema* (New York: Routledge, 1993).

28 *The Goddess* starred Ruan Lingyu (widely considered the greatest female star of the times) and was about a woman who turned to prostitution to pay her son's school fees. *Spring in a Small Town* is a psychological film about the relationships between a woman and two men. Praised by some as one of the most subtle Chinese films ever made, it was and remains controversial because it does not engage in the national and political issues of the day, which led some critics to condemn it as indulgent. On *The Goddess,* see William Rothman, "*The Goddess:* Reflections on Melodrama East and West," in *Melodrama and Asian Cinema,* ed. Wimal Dissanayake (Cambridge: Cambridge University Press, 1993), 59–72, and Zhang Yingjin, "Prostitution and Urban Imagination: Negotiating the Public and the Private in Chinese Films of the 1930s," in *Cinema and Urban Culture in Shanghai, 1922–1943,* ed. Zhang Yingjin (Stanford: Stanford University Press, 1999), 160–80. Unfortunately, I am not aware of any significant work in English on *Spring in a Small Town.* For a less positive evaluation of *Song of Youth,* see Jay Leyda, *Dianying: An Account of Films and the Film Audience in China* (Boston: MIT Press, 1972), 246–47.

29 On the model operas, see Paul Clark, *Chinese Cinema: Culture and Politics since 1949* (New York: Cambridge University Press, 1987), 133–37.

30 In the mid-eighties, Wu made a film called *The Dove Tree* for Xiaoxiang Film Studio, which was about China's late-seventies border war with Vietnam. It was banned because its protests against the brutality of war were considered unpatriotic. Both *Ballad of a Soldier* (1959) and *The Forty-First* (1956) are war films by the Soviet director Grigorai Chukraj made during the "thaw" period.

31 *Lovers' Symphony* is a Soviet film from the late seventies.

32 On the films of the early 1980s, see the piece by one of the directors, Zheng Dongtian, titled "Only Seven Years: Thoughts on the Explorations of Middle-Aged and Young Directors (1979–1986)," trans. Hou Jianping, in *Chinese Film Theory: A Guide to the New Era,* ed. George S. Semsel, Xia Hong, and Hou Jianping (New York: Praeger, 1990), 85–96.

3. FIRST STEPS

1 Shi Tiesheng, *Wo de Yaoyuan de Qingpingwan* (My far-away Qingpingwan) (Beijing: Shiyue Wenyi Chubanshe, 1985).

2 Shi Tiesheng, *Ming Ruo Qin Xian* (Life on a string) (Jiangsu: Jiangsu Wenyi Chubanshe, 1994).

3 Shi Tiesheng's "Women de Jialuo" (Our corner) can be found in *My Far-Away Qingpingwan*, 33–54.

4 Jin Shan (1911–1982) acted in the classic *Midnight Song* (1937) and directed such films as *Along the Sungari River* (1946) and *Storm* (1959).

5 The famous veteran director Ling Zifeng's films include *Sons and Daughters of China* (1948) and *Rickshaw Boy* (1981).

6 Wang Anyi, "Life in a Small Courtyard," trans. Hu Zhihui, *Chinese Literature*, no. 7 (1981): 64–84.

7 Sergei Eisenstein, *The Film Sense*, ed. and trans. Jay Leyda (London: Faber and Faber, 1948); Lev Kuleshov, *The Four Fundamentals of Film Direction* (Moscow: Goskinofotoizdat, 1941), translated and published by Beijing's China Film Press in 1961 as *Dianying Daoyan Jishu;* Daniaier Alihong (Daniel Arijon), *Dianying Yuyan de Yufa*, trans. Zhou Chuanji (Beijing: Zhongguo Dianying Chubanshe, 1981), originally published as *Grammar of the Film Language* (New York: Hastings House, 1976).

8 Discussion of the depiction of minority nationalities in *On the Hunting Ground* and *Horse Thief* can be found in Chris Berry, "Race (*Minzu*): Chinese Film and the Politics of Nationalism," *Cinema Journal* 31, no. 2 (1992): 45–58; Dru C. Gladney, "Tian Zhuangzhuang, the Fifth Generation, and Minorities Film in China," *Public Culture*, no. 8 (1995): 161–75; and Zhang Yingjin, "From 'Minority Film' to 'Minority Discourse': Questions of Nationhood and Ethnicity in Chinese Cinema," *Cinema Journal* 36, no. 3 (1997): 73–90.

9 For Xie Fei's views, see his "My View of the Concept of Film," trans. Hou Jianping, in *Chinese Film Theory: A Guide to the New Era*, ed. George S. Semsel, Xia Hong, and Hou Jianping (New York: Praeger, 1990), 76–84.

10 Wang Anyi, "The Final Destination for This Train," in *Shanghai Literature* 1981, no. 10 (1981), 4–18.

4. GRADUATION

1 At this time there was no open job market in China. Everyone was guaranteed employment, but the employment was assigned to them on the completion of their education.

2 The "Three Clean-Ups Policy" was named for the three elements that comprised it—killing, burning, and looting.

3 Sima Qian, *Shiji Xuan* (Selections from the great historian's records) (Hong Kong: Jintai Tushu Gongsi, 1967), 797–98.

4   This legendary figure is widely acknowledged as China's first monarch.

5   Chen Kaige, "Qianli Zou Shanbei: Pinqiong he Xiwang de Shouji" (A thousand miles through northern Shaanxi: Notes on poverty and hope), *Dianying Yishu*, no. 4 (1986): 29.

6   Ibid., 31.

7   The script for *Yellow Earth* is available in Bonnie S. McDougall, *The Yellow Earth: A Film by Chen Kaige* (Hong Kong: Chinese University Press, 1991). Major critical writing in English on the film includes Rey Chow, "Silent is the Ancient Plain: Music, Filmmaking, and the Conception of Reform in China's New Cinema," *Discourse* 12, no. 2 (1990): 82–109; Mary Ann Farquhar, "The 'Hidden' Gender in *Yellow Earth*," *Screen* 33, no. 2 (1992): 154–64; and Esther C. M. Yau, "*Yellow Earth*: Western Analysis and a Non-Western Text," in *Perspectives on Chinese Cinema*, ed. Chris Berry (London: British Film Institute, 1991), 62–79.

8   Lao Tzu, *Dao Te Ching: The Book of the Way and Its Virtue*, trans. J. J. Duyvendak (London: John Murray, 1954), 97.

9   Chen Kaige, "Huang Tudi Daoyan Chanshu" (Director's notes for *Yellow Earth*), *Beijing Dianying Xueyuan Xuebao*, no. 1 (1985): 110–15.

10 Zong Bing, *Lun Hua Shanshui* (Landscape painting) (Beijing: Beijing Daxue Chubanshe, n.d.), 177.

11 Chuang Tzu (Zhuang Zi), "The Mountain Tree," in *The Complete Works of Chuang Tzu*, trans. Burton Watson (New York: Columbia University Press, 1968), 213.

12 Liu Xie, *Wenxin Diaolong Zezhu* (Selections from "The literary mind and the carving of dragons"), ed. Zhao Chongyi (Nanning: Lijiang Chubanshe, 1982), 284. Available in English as Liu Hsieh (Liu Xie), *The Literary Mind and the Carving of Dragons*, trans. Vincent Shih (New York: Columbia University Press, 1959).

13 Da Zhongguang, "The Painting Basket," in *Zhonghua Meishu Congshu* (Anthology on Chinese painting), ed. Huang Binhong and Deng Shi (Nanjing: Jiangsu Guji Chubanshe, 1997), 9.

14 Zhang Yimou, "Huang Tudi Sheying Chanshu," (Cinematographer's notes for *Yellow Earth*), *Beijing Dianying Xueyuan Xuebao*, no. 1 (1985): 116–19.

15 Cited in *Wenhui Dianying Shibao*, June 1986.

16 Li Zehou, *Zhongguo Xiandai Sixiangshi Lun* (On the history of Chinese modern thought) (Beijing: Dongfang Chubanshe, 1987).

POSTSCRIPT

1   On the use of postcolonial theory in Chinese film scholarship, see Ben Xu, "*Farewell, My Concubine* and Its Nativist Critics," *Quarterly Review of Film and Video* 16, no. 2 (1997): 155–70.

2   Wang Yichuan, *Zhang Yimou Shenhua de Zhongjie: Shenmei yu Wenhua Shiye*

zhong de Zhang Yimou Dianying (The end of the Zhang Yimou myth: Cultural and aesthetic perspectives on Zhang Yimou's cinema) (Zhengzhou: Henan Renmin Chubanshe, 1998).

3 Zhang Yiwu, "Quanqiu Houzhimin Huajing zhong de Zhang Yimou" (Zhang Yimou in the global postcolonial context) in *Lun Zhang Yimou* (On Zhang Yimou), ed. Ying Xiong et al. (Beijing: Zhongguo Dianying Chubanshe, 1994), 54–68.

INDEX

■

Ni Zhen is Professor at the Beijing Film Academy.
He is the author of *The Exploratory Screen* (1994) and *Reform in the Chinese Cinema* (1994), and his major film scripts are *Raise the Red Lantern* (Silver Lion and Venice International Film Festival, 1991) and *Blush* (Silver Bear and Berlin International Film Festival, 1994).

■

Library of Congress Cataloging-in-Publication Data
Ni Zhen.
Memoirs from the Beijing Film Academy: the genesis
of China's fifth generation / by Ni Zhen ; translated
by Chris Berry.
p. cm. — (Asia-Pacific)
Original title in Chinese not available.
Includes index.
ISBN 0-8223-2956-5 (alk. paper)
ISBN 0-8223-2970-0 (pbk. : alk. paper)
1. Motion pictures—China.   2. Motion picture producers and
directors—China—Biography.   3. Beijing dianying xueyuan—
History.   I. Title.   II. Series.
PN1993.5.C4 N52 2002
791.43′0233′092251—dc21   2002005107